CONCEPTS AND TOOLS IN PRACTICE

Multicultural Law Enforcement:
Strategies for Peacekeeping
in a Diverse Society

CONCEPTS AND TOOLS IN PRACTICE

A Study Guide to Accompany

Multicultural Law Enforcement: Strategies for Peacekeeping in a Diverse Society

Third Edition

Herbert Z. Wong

Robert M. Shusta

Pearson Education
Upper Saddle River, New Jersey 07458

Executive Editor: Frank Mortimer, Jr.
Associate Editor: Sarah Holle
Managing Editor: Mary Carnis
Production Management: Naomi Sysak
Production Editor: Naomi Sysak
Production Liaison: Brian Hyland
Director of Manufacturing and Production: Bruce Johnson
Manufacturing Buyer: Cathleen Petersen
Design Director: Cheryl Asherman
Printer/Binder: Bindrite Graphics
Cover Design: Denise Brown

Pearson Prentice Hall™ is a trademark of Pearson Education, Inc.
Pearson® is a registered trademark of Pearson plc
Prentice Hall® is a registered trademark of Pearson Education, Inc.

Pearson Education LTD   Pearson Education Australia PTY, Limited
Pearson Education Singapore, Pte. Ltd   Pearson Education North Asia Ltd
Pearson Education, Canada, Ltd   Pearson Educaçion de Mexico, S.A. de C.V.
Pearson Education–Japan   Pearson Education Malaysia, Pte. Ltd

10 9 8 7 6 5 4 3 2 1

ISBN 0-13-114052-3

CONTENTS

Introduction   vii

PART 1: Impact of Cultural Diversity on Law Enforcement   1

    Chapter 1: Multicultural Communities: Challenges
          for Law Enforcement   3

    Chapter 2: The Changing Law Enforcement Agency:
          A Microcosm of Society   16

    Chapter 3: Multicultural Representation in Law Enforcement:
          Recruitment, Retention, and Promotion   27

    Chapter 4: Cross-Cultural Communications
          for Law Enforcement   39

PART 2: Cultural Specifics for Law Enforcement   53

    Chapter 5: Law Enforcement Contact with Asian/Pacific
          Americans   55

    Chapter 6: Law Enforcement Contact with African
          Americans   68

    Chapter 7: Law Enforcement Contact with Latino/Hispanic
          Americans   82

    Chapter 8: Law Enforcement Contact with Arab Americans
          and Other Middle Eastern Groups   96

    Chapter 9: Law Enforcement Contact with Native Americans   111

**PART 3: Multicultural Law Enforcement Elements in Terrorism
   and Homeland Security   125**

    Chapter 10: Multicultural Law Enforcement and Terrorism:
           Overview, Response Strategies, and Multijurisdictional
           Actions   127

    Chapter 11: Multicultural Law Enforcement
           and Homeland Security   138

PART 4: Response Strategies for Crimes Motivated by Hate/Bias and Racial Profiling   151

Chapter 12: Hate/Bias Crimes: Victims, Laws, Investigations, and Prosecutions   153

Chapter 13: Hate/Bias Crimes: Reporting, Monitoring, and Response Strategies   163

Chapter 14: Racial Profiling   174

PART 5: Cultural Effectiveness for Peace Officers   187

Chapter 15: Peace Officer Image and Cultural Sensitivity   189

Chapter 16: Emerging Strategies, Roles, and Technology for Peace Officers in Multicultural Law Enforcement   199

Appendix A: Self-Assessment of Communication Skills in Law Enforcement   211

Appendix B: Impact of Diversity on Law Enforcement Behaviors and Practices Survey   215

Appendix C: Multicultural Community and Law Enforcement Workforce Survey   223

Appendix D: Practice Question Answers   231

INTRODUCTION

From a diverse team of writers whose expertise spans law enforcement and cross-cultural relations, *Multicultural Law Enforcement: Strategies for Peacekeeping in a Diverse Society* (Third Edition) is written to address the most current issues facing police today. It provides comprehensive coverage of sensitive topics and issues related to diversity and multiculturalism which are critical to law enforcement in the twenty-first century. The t ex tbook contains insightful as well as practical information and guidelines on how law enforcement professionals can work effectively with diverse cultural groups, both inside their organizations as well as within the c o mmunity. The focus is upon the cross-cultural and racial contacts that police officers and civilian employees have with citizens, co-workers, v i ctims, and suspects from diverse backgrounds. The textbook contains information on racial profiling, hate crimes, community-based policing, undocumented immigrants and immigrant women, urban dynamics, and gays and lesbians in law enforcement.

This Study Guide provides those who are using the textbook, *Multicultural Law Enforcement: Strategies for Peacekeeping in a Diverse Society*, Third Edition, with an opportunity to more thoroughly engage the materials presented. Preparation for classroom lectures, in-class group exercises, class discussions, homework assignments, additional self-study activities, and of course examinations will be facilitated through the use of this companion Study Guide.

There are several types of study materials included in this Study Guide that may be used in various ways:

1. Beginning each chapter, the Overview provides a summary of the important key issues and themes in the chapter. The Overview also provides the background and context needed to understand the chapter's materials relative to the larger topic of multicultural law enforcement.

2. The Learning Objectives for both the chapter in the textbook and in the Study Guide are presented in the Rationale for the Focus on the Key Concepts and Tools. This section describes what you should expect to learn from the use of the textbook and the Study Guide. If you refer to these objectives, you will find the major points provided within each chapter. Each chapter also has an Introduction which provides information on the basic contents of the chapter.

3. The Key Concepts for each chapter are provided as an Outline of Key Presentation Points. These outlines should be used for your study preparation to ensure that no key points are missed from within the chapters.

4. The True or False, Multiple Choice, Fill-in-the-Blanks, and Discussion questions are specifically provided for you to use to test your knowledge of the material after thoroughly reading the chapters. The answers to the True or False, Multiple Choice, and Fill-in-the-Blanks questions are on the last pages of the Study Guide. However, do not be too quick to glance at the answers. Complete the questions, check your answers, and then go to the textbook and look up the information for the questions that you missed. Self-tests in a small discussion group or study group are effective approaches for using these questions, as well.

5. In each chapter of this Study Guide, there will be a boxed section providing a case in which we ask, "What are your thoughts and what would you do?" We have also provided a set of Critical Thinking Questions following each situation that may be applicable to the specific case, as well as to other cases involving multicultural law enforcement issues. Please feel free to apply these critical thinking questions to any exercise or situation in the textbook (or any other text or real-life situation).

6. In the Tools and Skills in Practice section, we have provided some techniques that you may use and skills that could be developed in order to understand and to be more knowledgeable about the impact of diversity on law enforcement in multicultural communities. Some of the tools provided within these sections could be used in conjunction with class projects, term papers, and classroom exercises.

7. In the chapters' Self-Study Activities sections, the activities provided will assist you in answering some of the self-study questions at the end of each chapter in the textbook. The Self-Study Activities will allow you to prepare for group discussions both in the classroom and with your peers.

8. In the Appendices of the Study Guide are copies of the questionnaire tools highlighted within the textbook. The questionnaire tools provided within the Study Guide are formatted so that they can be easily copied and used in self-study, classroom, small group, and community projects and activities.

We wish you the best in your study of multicultural law enforcement and the strategies important for peacekeeping in a diverse society. We hope that this Study Guide assists you in your academic and professional career endeavors.

Herbert Z. Wong, Ph.D.
Robert M. Shusta, Captain Ret., M.P.A.
Multicultural Law Enforcement:
Strategies for Peacekeeping in a Diverse Society, Third Edition

CONCEPTS AND TOOLS IN PRACTICE

Multicultural Law Enforcement: Strategies for Peacekeeping in a Diverse Society

Part 1

IMPACT OF CULTURAL DIVERSITY ON LAW ENFORCEMENT

Part 1 of Multicultural Law Enforcement introduces readers to the implications of a multicultural society for law enforcement, both within and outside the police agency. Chapter 1 discusses aspects of the changing population and presents views on diversity. Chapter 2 discusses demographic changes that are taking place within law enforcement agencies, as well as reactions to diversity in the law enforcement workplace and responses to it. Chapter 3 discusses challenges in recruitment, retention, and promotion of police personnel from various racial, ethnic, and cultural backgrounds. Chapter 4 provides practical information highlighting the dynamics of cross-cultural communication in law enforcement.

Chapter 1

Multicultural Communities: Challenges for Law Enforcement

OVERVIEW

Dramatic changes in the ethnic and racial makeup of the population have created new challenges at all levels of police work. Willingness to gain cultural information about the new communities that law enforcement officers serve will ultimately benefit them in their interactions with people of different backgrounds. Officers' knowledge of cultural differences, coupled with an ability to demonstrate respect for those differences, can result in an increased rapport and more effective communication with people from various ethnic and racial backgrounds. As a result of the negative cultural experiences that community members may bring to their relationships with the police, trust within many ethnic communities has to be earned. Members of the law enforcement profession have to examine their words, behaviors, and actions to evaluate whether they are conveying professionalism and a respect for all people, regardless of their race, culture, religion, or ethnic background. Law enforcement agencies must be free of all expressions of prejudice on the part of their officers and civilian employees. Finally, law enforcement agencies, in partnership and collaboration with communities, are likely to experience decreased crime rates and increased trust and cooperation with citizens of all backgrounds.

RATIONALE FOR THE FOCUS
ON THE KEY CONCEPTS AND TOOLS

Officers and practitioners involved in multicultural law enforcement need to be able to:

1. Describe key challenges for law enforcement related to the increasing multicultural population in the U.S.

2. Discuss the differences between references to a "melting pot" versus a "mosaic" society, and provide a historical overview of the context in which these terms have evolved

3

3. Describe demographic trends in the U.S. related to immigration from the early 1900s to the present

4. Make the connection between strong community policing and improved police–minority group relations

INTRODUCTION

Chapter 1 discusses law enforcement challenges related to the growing multicultural population in the United States. It begins with the need for an increased understanding of the diverse populations with which law enforcement officials interact. The discussion of our mosaic society incorporates a brief historical perspective on immigration. Mini case studies illustrate the points of contact between a person's culture and a particular crime or offense. Practical reasons are presented regarding the importance of officers' understanding of the cultural backgrounds of the groups they commonly encounter. Highlights are provided on the nature of prejudice and how it interferes with effective police work, but can be overcome through the professional behavior of law enforcement officers. Community-based policing is presented, along with its implications for positive relations and contact with diverse immigrant and ethnic communities. The chapter ends with tips for improving law enforcement in multicultural communities.

KEY CONCEPTS

Outline of Key Presentation Points

1. Introduction: Quote by the Director of the Census, 1998–2001
2. Some Important Definitions for Law Enforcement
3. USA to UN on the Elimination of Racial Discrimination
4. Melting Pot and Mosaic Differentiation
5. Reactions to Multicultural Population and to Diversity
6. Recommendations for Protecting the Civil Rights of Diverse Communities
7. Overlap of Race, Culture, and Ethnicity
8. Population Trends
9. Immigrants, Undocumented Immigrants, and Foreign Born in the U.S.
10. Immigrant Women: Victims of Domestic Violence
11. Interplay between the Police and the Culture
12. Prejudice in Law Enforcement
13. Community Policing

PRACTICE QUESTIONS

True or False

_F_ 1. The United States, compared to virtually all other nations, has experienced very limited growth in its multicultural population.

_T_ 2. Today, law enforcement is under a powerful microscope in terms of how citizens are treated.

_F_ 3. History has always supported the metaphor of the melting pot in America, especially with regard to the first and s e cond generations of most groups of newcomers.

_T_ 4. By 2050, the non-Hispanic white population will be the slowest-growing racial group in America.

_F_ 5. "Marriage by capture" is a tradition considered to be an acceptable form of eloping by the Hmongs from Southeast Asia. This provides an excellent example of how sensitivity to cultural issues among law enforcement could allow this to be seen as a legally acceptable form of marriage by Hmongs in the United States.

_T_ 6. The Instructor's question asked of police officers participating in a cultural diversity program, "Raise your hand if you are a racist," was used to facilitate positive discussion among fellow officers.

_T_ 7. According to research, people who tend to mistreat or oppress others because of their prejudices often were m i streated themselves.

_F_ 8. An officer or civilian employee who does nothing in the presence of racist or other discriminatory behavior by his or her peers is showing legal job performance and proper respect for the Code of Silence among police officers.

_T_ 9. According to the 2000 Bureau of Justice Statistics Report, "Two-thirds of all local police departments and 62 percent of sheriffs' offices had full-time sworn personnel engaged in community policing activities."

_T_ 10. Community policing enables the placing of officers in closer proximity to members of the community and thereby improves police knowledge of the area in which they work.

Multiple Choice

1. A lack of knowledge of cultural differences by law enforcement officers can result in:
    a. Violation of individual rights of citizens
    b. Officer safety
    c. Increased officer risk issues
    d. All of the above

2. The authors suggest that America's multicultural society might best be described as a:
    a. Homogeneous society
    b. Melting pot
    c. Mosaic or tapestry
    d. None of the above

3. Typical criticisms of immigrants, now and historically, include:
    a. "They adapt too quickly to American society"
    b. "They don't learn our language"
    c. "Their customs and behavior are valued too strongly by outsiders"
    d. "They blend too quickly into mainstream culture"

4. In March 2002, the U.S. Census Bureau reported that approximately this many U.S. residents had been born in other countries?
    a. 350,000
    b. 3.5 million
    c. 13.5 million
    d. 32.5 million

5. In the example about a San Francisco Bay Area Samoan community barbecue which included a fair amount of drinking resulting in fights, the authors suggested in responding to neighbors' complaints that the police should:
    a. Come in with a show of force and the fighting would cool down quickly
    b. Overlook the neighbors' complaints and do nothing
    c. Locate the leader, or the "chief," of this group and let that person help solve the problem
    d. Hold a community meeting of the neighbors, Samoan party goers, and police representatives

6. Prejudice is a judgment or opinion formed before facts are known, usually involving:

    a. Favorable impressions about unknown groups of people

    b. Unfavorable thoughts and ideas by police officers of other police officers very similar to themselves

    c. Negative or unfavorable thoughts about groups of people

    d. Neutral thoughts and impressions about criminals and other negative elements of society

7. Contemporary community-based policing is described as:

    a. An effective problem-solving approach

    b. An approach that enables officers to work with civilians outside the conventional channels by meeting with community groups and learning of their concerns

    c. A method that allows community members to understand the "culture" of law enforcement and to help them grasp the reasons for which officers make the decisions they do

    d. All of the above

8. Community-based policing is one of several terms that police agencies across the nation use to refer to working partnerships with communities. Another commonly used term is:

    a. Community Opportunistic Policing (COP)

    b. Problem-Oriented Policing (POP)

    c. Police Active Involvement/Deployment (PAID)

    d. Community Officers-Deputies Enforcement (CODE)

9. As a result of implementing community-oriented policing since 1995, Deputy Chief Ondra Berry of Reno indicated that drive-by shootings:

    a. Went down from an average of 140 shots fired calls a month to an average of 20 calls per month

    b. Increased slightly; however, overall gang activities went down

    c. Decreased slightly with overall gang activities going underground

    d. Went up from an average of 50 shots fired calls a month to an average of 178 calls per month

10. The Police Executive Research Forum (PERF) outlined five different perspectives on community policing within agencies throughout the U.S. Which of the following was *not* one of the five perspectives identified?

    a. Community revitalization perspective: Focusing on preventing deterioration of neighborhoods by having police pay closer attention to fear-inducing characteristics of neighborhoods

    b. Problem-solving perspective: Maintaining that the most critical element of community policing is the problem-solving efforts in which the police and community (residents, other g overnment agencies, and private bu s inesses) participate

    c. Economic-incentive perspectives: Attempting, via community policing, to have officers and law enforcement departments save monies in the funding levels of police services to minority communities

    d. Customer perspective: Developing proactive mechanisms for determining the needs of the public relative to police functions; the approach uses routine surveys of citizen and advisory groups to accomplish this goal

Fill-in-the-Blanks

1. A multicultural community is simply one that is comprised of many different ethnic and _racial_ groups.

2. Through increased awareness, knowledge, and skills, law enforcement as a profession can increase its "cultural _competence_."

3. Law enforcement officials need to be aware of the overlap between race and ethnicity and that many individuals consider themselves to be _multiracial_

4. Officers must be aware of "_racial_ flash points" that are created when immigrants move into economically depressed areas with large and diverse populations.

5. Many immigrants _fear_ the police because in their native countries police engaged in arbitrary acts of brutality in support of repressive governments (e.g., in Central America).

6. _Cultural_ is defined as beliefs, values, patterns of thinking, behavior, and everyday customs that have been passed on from generation to generation.

7. In law enforcement, the expression of prejudice as bias discrimination and racism is _illegal_ and can have tragic consequences.

8. Stereotyping is a _shorthand_ way of thinking about people who are different.

9. Community-based policing represents a more _democratic_ style of policing. It allows for openness and dialogue.

10. Members of the law enforcement profession have to examine their words, behaviors, and actions to evaluate whether they are conveying professionalism and _respect_ to all people.

Discussion

1. Discuss how a diverse society makes any law enforcement officer or manager's job more difficult. For example, how do issues such as racial tensions within diverse cultural and multi-ethnic populations complicate police procedures and encounters with citizens?

2. Discuss whether you agree or disagree with the explanations provided by Jang and colleagues (1995) for the high rate of domestic violence experienced by immigrant women. What are your thoughts about the implications that these higher rates of domestic violence experienced by immigrant women pose for law enforcement?

3. Discuss how prejudice is acquired during "normal" socialization. Provide examples of how police officers could exhibit the kind of prejudice that results when a person belongs to a group that holds negative views of another specific group(s) (e.g., southern whites and blacks, Arabs and Jews, Chinese and Japanese, Puerto Ricans and Mexicans).

4. Discuss how Reno, Nevada's police–community partnership in creating the Gang Alternative Partnership Center might have instituted practices that could be applicable to a local community in your area. Provide some examples of activities that might be implemented in your Gang Alternative Partnership Center.

5. Give two or three examples of how you might use the "Eight Tips for Improving Law Enforcement in Multicultural Communities" in training police officers to be more sensitive to cultural issues in minority communities.

INTRODUCTION TO CASE STUDIES

In each chapter of this Study Guide, there will be a boxed section providing a case in which we ask, "What are your thoughts and what would you do?". We have also provided a set of "critical thinking questions" following each situation that may be applicable to the specific case, as well as to any other case involving a multicultural law enforcement issue. Please feel free to apply these critical thinking questions to any exercise or situation in this text (or any other text or real-life situation). Here are the questions that we ask you to apply to each situation:

1. *What are the facts (observable, verifiable, testable, and confirmable)?* Central to the resolution and solving of a problem is the ability to obtain the "facts" of the matter. Here we ask you to determine if the facts can be "proven" to be true:

    a. Observable: that is, one or more people should be able to see the same thing and come to the same conclusion with regard to these facts (for example, a red car and a blue car were involved in a head-on collision);

    b. Verifiable: that is, one can determine if something is factual by asking an independent or expert source to verify the correctness of the conclusions drawn about the facts gathered (for example, the skid marks indicate that the blue car was speeding, lost c o ntrol, crossed the double line, and crashed into the red car);

    c. Testable: that is, one can pose a question with respect to the incident that can be answered in a way in which the facts can be revealed using a measurement tool or science-based test (for example, for the question of whether alcohol was involved, both drivers passed their breathalyzer tests, and alcohol was ruled out as a contributing factor);

    d. Confirmable: that is, two or more people can independently provide testimony of similar facts on the event or situation (for example, three eye-witnesses saw the blue car, driven by a teenage driver going about 45–50 mph in a 25 mph residential zone, side-swipe a parked car, lose control, and crash head on into the red car in the opposite lane).

    "Facts" which do not meet the observable, testable, verifiable, and confirmable criteria may not be "facts"—instead they may be assumptions, opinions, or reactions.

2. *What are the assumptions?* Often we believe something to be true without having any proof of our beliefs. These would be our assumptions (for example, we may say that the teenage driver in the blue car was "careless" or "reckless" or "inexperienced" based upon our beliefs about what we had seen. However, we would not have any "proof" of our beliefs or actual "facts" about our assumptions made.

3. *What are the possible stereotypes?* In working with multicultural and diverse communities and groups of people there are always myths and stereotypes made about these groups or communities. One needs to examine if any of these myths and stereotypes might be affecting the specifics of the event or situation. For example, in our car crash example, what are the myths and stereotypes of

teenage drivers, of drivers who exceed the speed limit, of young people and responsibility, etc. Might one have assumptions or come to some conclusion based upon these myths and stereotypes?

4. *What would be your personal "reactions" or "opinions" with respect to this situation?* As a result of the varied experiences that law enforcement and criminal justice personnel may bring to the multicultural communities, one's own "personal" reactions and opinions about an event may be important (and may sway one's actions on the matter). As such, one critical area for clarity, understanding, and review of possible negative as well as positive influences is one's own "personal" set of reactions and opinions on the matter.

5. *What would be the possible reactions or "opinions" to this situation by the "other parties who are involved"?* As a result of the varied experiences that others in multicultural communities (oftentimes outside of law enforcement) may have with respect to a particular situation, the "other party who is involved" may have "reactions" and "opinions" about an event that may be important to understand from a law enforcement perspective.

6. *Would someone from the community of the "other parties who are involved" see something different or have a different opinion? What would they see differently and how would the opinion be different (if applicable)?* Not only are the perspectives important for the "other party who is involved" but also for the "community" of which the "other party" may be a member. Such community perspectives provide understanding, awareness, and sensitivity to the matter from a multicultural group perspective.

7. *From a law enforcement perspective, what would be your "professional" reactions to this situation?* One can have both a "professional" reaction and point-of-view and one's own "personal" perspective. In law enforcement, as in any area involving professional conduct, it would be important to see both (for self-understanding and for professional effectiveness).

8. *What actions would you take in this situation?* Briefly describe the actions you would take in the case study or situation at hand, and provide a brief explanation as to the reason you took that action.

9. *If you had to explain your actions to the community of the "other parties who are involved," other observers, and your superiors in front of the news media, what would you say?* Oftentimes, the action taken may not be clear or there might be conflict among different groups regarding the actions taken. Being able to explain one's actions clearly, as well as in a way that will satisfy the multicultural community, the public, the department, and one's superiors, is a key component of successful multicultural law enforcement practice. Oftentimes, the actions taken may be ethically, legally, and professionally correct;

WHAT ARE YOUR THOUGHTS AND WHAT WOULD YOU DO?

A call comes over dispatch that a security guard at a shopping mall in a predominantly white neighborhood has seen four Hispanic males. The security guard reports that they are gang members because they are all wearing matching leather jackets and red ball caps. He reports that they have just opened and closed their car trunk and are now entering the mall. The security guard notifies the merchants, some of whom immediately begin closing their stores. You are the officer in the vicinity of the mall who responds to the call just as the juveniles are leaving the mall and are heading toward their car. In the meantime, several merchants continue to be anxious about the "gang members" and close their stores. What are your thoughts and what would you do?

Critical Thinking Questions

1. What are the facts (observable, verifiable, testable, and confirmable)?
2. What are the assumptions?
3. What are the possible stereotypes?
4. What would be your *personal* reactions to this situation?
5. What would be the possible *juveniles'* reactions to this situation?
6. Would someone from the Latino/Hispanic American community see something different? What would they see differently (if applicable)?
7. What would be your *professional* reactions to this situation?
8. What actions would you take in this situation?
9. If you had to explain your actions to the Latino/Hispanic American community, the store owners, and your superiors in front of the news media, what would you say?

---

however, the explanation of the actions taken may cause conflict because of a lack of awareness and/or sensitivity to the multiple parties who are involved. Our critical thinking questions allow us to look at the different possible perspectives and arrive at responses which might be more productive and effective in multicultural law enforcement situations.

TOOLS AND SKILLS IN PRACTICE

Provided below are some tools that one could use and skills that one could develop to understand and be more knowledgeable about the impact of diversity on law enforcement in multicultural communities.

1. *Obtaining Demographic Data on Multicultural Communities—* Law enforcement officers need to be able to obtain demographic information and background data on the multicultural communities that they serve. There are several ways to obtain this information:

a. City, County, Region, and/or State Websites: Go to the websites for the municipalities that you are interested in knowing more about and use search terms like "population," "race," and "diversity."

b. Use the U.S. Census Website and Reports: Go to http://www.census.gov and search for information about the specific populations that are of interest to you.

c. Use Search Engines: Use search engines like "Google" or "Yahoo" and enter the search term "population" and the name of your city, county, region, and/or state.

d. Ask for References from your Local or College Librarian: The head librarian in your city or at a college campus would be able to direct you to the sources of demographic data on file or in reports.

2. *Identifying Cultural Groups and Community Leaders*—Knowing the key cultural groups in one's service area and the community leaders within these groups is critical toward understanding the multicultural resources of your area. Two ways to obtain this information are:

a. Use the On-line Information from the Key Newspapers of Your Area: Search on an ongoing basis the on-line news sources of your local area for the cultural groups that you are interested in researching. Keep a journal of the groups that emerge, as well as the members, leaders, and/or representatives named in the news articles.

b. Search "LexisNexis Academic" On-line in Your College Library: Search the news sources for your local area for the prior year using the search terms of the group and the name of your city or area of interest. Keep a journal of your findings.

3. *Scanning for Police and Diverse Community Issues*—For your city or area of interest, go to the on-line reports for the: (a) "Police Commission," (b) "Public Safety Commission" and/or (c) "Emergency Services Commission." Scan the minutes of the meetings for law enforcement and other public safety issues identified. Note any recurring issues or trends involving different multicultural communities. If on-line services are not available in your area, go the Town Hall or City Hall and read the past minutes of the above-noted Commissions for the last six months to one year—the minutes of the Police Commission and other meetings are usually open to the public.

4. *Developing Community Partnerships*—Once you begin to get a sense of the different groups in your community and the key leaders of those groups, it would be important to get information on the kinds of services these communities may need by accessing information

through the different resource guides. Go on-line or in person to obtain some of the community resource guides available in your local area. Depending upon the diversity of your community, some of these resources might focus on ethnic or racial groups, children, elderly, people with disabilities, and so forth. Review these resource guides to identify the needs of these groups, and make a list of the needs. Brainstorm some ways that the local law enforcement agencies might be able to form community partnerships with these community-based agencies to address the needs that you have identified through the review of the materials and guides.

5. *Issues in Improving Law Enforcement in Multicultural Communities*—Begin building a file in your computer or on 3 × 5 index cards (or in a "blank book" journal). On a daily basis, as you observe your work, the news, or any other sources, note interactions between law enforcement and aspects of the multicultural community that are going well and those that could have gone better. For those interactions that have gone well, identify the key elements and/or aspects that made it go well. For those interactions that could have gone better, brainstorm about ways that the situation could have been improved. What could have been done differently to attain a more positive outcome? In a short amount of time, your file will contain many useful ideas for improving law enforcement services in multicultural communities.

SELF-STUDY ACTIVITIES

Your Perspectives about Diversity

It is important for those in the criminal justice and public safety professions to understand their personal perspectives about community and workplace diversity. To do this, we suggest the following self-study exercise. Brainstorm two lists for yourself: (a) list all of the positive contributions of community and workplace diversity that might apply to your current and future work in law enforcement as you see it, and (b) list all of the negative barriers, obstacles, and elements to your current and/or future public s e r vice work resulting from community and workplace diversity. Review your lists, and determine where you might stand: Are you (a) tolerating diversity (but hoping it will go away), (b) accepting and wanting to utilize the resources resulting from diversity, and/or (c) embracing diversity and wanting to leverage this resource as much as possible?

Race, Culture, and Ethnicity as Helping or Complicating Law Enforcement

In the 1988 study entitled Policing Multi-Ethnic Neighborhoods, Alpert and Dunham say that ethnicity complicates every police procedure. Do race, culture, and ethnicity complicate police procedures and interactions? To answer this question, we suggest the following self-study exercise. Brainstorm two lists for yourself: (a) list all of the positive aspects in which race, culture and ethnicity may help and facilitate law enforcement efforts (e.g., cultural value for respecting authority), and (b) list all of the negative aspects in which race, culture, and ethnicity may hinder or be a barrier to law enforcement efforts (e.g., past negative experiences with law enforcement). Review your lists, and explain how you see race, culture, and ethnicity may or may not complicate police procedures.

Dealing with Illegal Immigrants

How do the police departments in your local area deal with illegal and undocumented immigrants? One way to answer this question is to review in one or more of your local newspapers the section on "Police Actions" taken for a six-month period. Do you see any mentioning of the lack of identification papers with regard to immigration status, etc.? List all cases in which such mentioning was made. What were the actions taken by the police on those cases? What policy do you think is guiding the police in your local area regarding undocumented immigrants? Do you think that officers are instructed not to inquire as to immigrant status unless a crime has been committed? How do you think police officers should deal with illegal immigrants in your local area?

Chapter 2

The Changing Law Enforcement Agency: A Microcosm of Society

OVERVIEW

Officers who traditionally worked in a predominantly white male work-force must learn to work with increasing numbers of women, gays and l e sbians, blacks, Hispanics, Asians, and others within our diverse society. In this chapter we have suggested that to be effective in this new environment, officers must have a working knowledge of conflict resolution techniques to reduce racial and ethnic problems.

The chapter focused on concerns and issues of members of under-re p re sented ethnically and racially diverse groups, as well as women and gays and lesbians in law enforcement. The importance of support and mentoring programs for women and diverse groups was stressed. Such programs help them make transitions into organizations, cope with stress, and meet their workplace challenges more effectively.

In the chapter we provided suggestions for law enforcement executives whose jurisdictions are pluralistic and whose workforces are diverse. Law enforcement leaders must be committed to setting an organizational tone that does not permit bigoted or discriminatory acts, and they must act swiftly against those who violate these policies. They must monitor and deal quickly with complaints both within their workforce and from the p u blic they serve.

RATIONALE FOR THE FOCUS ON THE KEY CONCEPTS AND TOOLS

Officers and practitioners involved in multicultural law enforcement need to be able to:

1. Identify how the ethnic, racial, gender, and lifestyle composition of law enforcement agencies is changing in the United States

2. Understand the terms lesbian, gay, bisexual, and transgender

3. Discuss recommendations on methods for defusing conflicts within the law enforcement organization related to gender, lifestyle, race, and ethnicity

4. Explain the role of the chief executive in providing a workplace environment which is comfortable for all employees and one which is sensitive to those from diverse backgrounds

5. Understand that officers must have knowledge of conflict resolution techniques in order to reduce racial and ethnic problems in their communities

INTRODUCTION

The ethnic, racial, gender, and lifestyle composition of law enforcement agencies is changing in the United States. Chapter 2 addresses the increasingly pluralistic workforce and provides examples of racism and cultural insensitivity within the law enforcement agency. Suggestions are provided for defusing racially and culturally rooted conflicts and for addressing issues related to women, gay men, and lesbians in law enforcement. The chapter ends with recommendations for all employees who work within a diverse workforce and particularly emphasizes the role of the chief executive.

KEY CONCEPTS

Outline of Key Presentation Points

1. Population Statistics for the U.S.
2. Population Statistics for the Instructor's State and Local Areas
3. Ethnicity and Race in America
4. Ethnicity and Race in the Instructor's State and Local Areas
5. The Dimensions of Diversity (from Marilyn Loden's *Implementing Diversity*)
   a. Primary dimensions
   b. Secondary dimensions
6. Law Enforcement Environment Is Changing
7. The Changing Workforce
8. Ethnic and Racial Issues within the Law Enforcement Workforce
9. Alameda Police Department's Posted Mortal Sins
10. Police Fraternal Organizations
11. Assignment Based on Officers' Dimensions of Diversity
12. Women in Law Enforcement
13. The EEO Act Prohibits Employment Discrimination
14. Women Employed as Police Officers
15. Gender Issues in Law Enforcement
16. Gay Men and Lesbians in Law Enforcement
17. The Chief Executive

PRACTICE QUESTIONS

True or False

_____ T   1. According to the Bureau of Justice Statistics Report (October 2002), the percentage of change in minority representation between 1990 and 2000 among local police officers and sheriffs' offices had increased.

_____ T   2. Law enforcement is still predominantly a white male occupation.

_____ T   3. According to David Shipler, the basic framework for combating and defusing racism include setting the tone from the top (command commitment) as a core element.

_____ T   4. Although citizens appreciate having officers of their own color or national origin work their communities, this deployment strategy may result in unfairness.

_____ T   5. The most recent research, according to the National Center for Women and Policing (1999), shows that nationally less than 15% of sworn personnel are female.

_____ F   6. Few of the recent national studies on sexual harassment have examined sexual harassment in police agencies, but those that have done so indicate that the problem is minimal in police departments.

_____ T   7. Women police officers report that the double standard is less common because of the emphasis that law enforcement places on Community-Oriented Policing.

_____ T   8. Research studies have shown that the presence of openly lesbian, gay, bisexual, and transgender personnel has enhanced service and did not negatively impact morale or unit cohesion in integrated police departments.

_____ T   9. Officers whose self-image is based upon their job, perceiving themselves as "John Wayne," are generally the most uncomfortable with the concept of working with gay officers.

_____ T   10. Law enforcement executives are aware that before employees can be asked to value diversity in the community, it must be clear that diversity within the organization is valued.

Multiple Choice

1. According to the authors, the first step in addressing the problem of racism is for police department personnel on all levels to:
   a. Establish strong penalties and rules prohibiting any discussion about racism in the department
   b. Admit that racism exists rather than denying it
   c. Request cooperation and assistance from the Police Officers Associations
   d. Require all officers to sign an Oath of Non-Bias and Non-Racist Conduct

2. The authors recommend that police department command must encourage the use of conflict resolution techniques by:
   a. Officers of all backgrounds as a way of handling issues prior to their becoming flash points
   b. Minority officers who have discrimination and EEO grievances with their departments
   c. Woman officers who have sexual harassment and other grievances with their departments
   d. None of the above

3. Which of the following behaviors is considered a "mortal sin" for the Alameda Police Department?
   a. Sexism, offensive sexual remarks, sexual harassment, sexual discrimination
   b. Disrespectful language about the elderly and ageism remarks
   c. Avoidance and resistance to community-policing approaches
   d. Not attending voluntary diversity training workshops

4. In what year did the International Association of Chiefs of Police pass a resolution supporting the use of policewomen?
   a. 1908
   b. 1922
   c. 1945
   d. 1973

5. The Law Enforcement Management and Administrative Statistics (LEMAS) report, issued by the U.S. Department of Justice in 2001, showed that the overall percentage change of sworn women sheriffs' deputies nationwide for the ten-year period from 1990 to 2000:

   a. Increased from 10.8% to 23.3%
   b. Increased from 8.1% to 10.6%
   c. Stayed about the same within the decade
   d. Decreased from 15.4% to 12.5%

6. In November, 1998, the International Association of Chiefs of Police (IACP) released the results of a study it had commissioned entitled "The Future of Women in Policing." Which of the following was *not* one of the stated topics within of the study?

   a. Attrition and resignation of women officers
   b. Determining whether a glass ceiling exists as a barrier to promotions
   c. Gender discrimination and sexual harassment
   d. Physical training to increase stamina and use of force when necessary

7. Research studies of homosexuals in the military and in law enforcement have included the following behaviors being consistently observed:

   a. Gay soldiers or police officers walked hand in hand in the work setting
   b. Gay and lesbian officers danced together at work-related holiday functions
   c. Bisexual and transgender officers made passes at non-gay colleagues
   d. None of the above

8. As of June, 2003, how many states have passed laws prohibiting discrimination based upon sexual orientation?

   a. 3
   b. 14
   c. 27
   d. 41

9. Executive leadership is crucial to managing a diverse workforce and establishing good minority–community relations for its role in:
    a. Managing organizational change
    b. Developing police–community partnerships (community-based policing)
    c. Providing new leadership models
    d. All of the above

10. Police leaders must institute policies that develop positive attitudes toward a multicultural workplace and community at which earliest point in an officer's career?
    a. At the selection process to include the background interviews, polygraphs, and psychological exams
    b. At police academy training
    c. At field training and community policing assignments
    d. At continuing education and workplace training

Fill-in-the-Blanks

1. As microcosms of their communities, law enforcement agencies _increasingly_ include among their personnel more women, e t hnic and racial minorities, gays and lesbians.

2. In May 2000, the federal government concluded that there was sufficient evidence of _civil rights_ violations within the Los Angeles Police Department (LAPD) to file a so-called pattern and practice discrimination suit.

3. David Shipler, the researcher, recommends that law enforcement combat and defuse racism by using the _U.S. Army_ model developed during a time of extreme racial tension in the early 1970s.

4. Some cities use _cultural affairs_ committees made up of people from diverse groups in the community and the officers who provide these police services, to better ensure responsiveness to the multicultural communities.

5. In 1968, the _Indianapolis_ Police Department made history by assigning the first two female officers to patrol on an equal basis with their male colleagues.

6. Police Department executives must institute a _zero tolerance_ s exual harassment policy and send that message throughout the department.

7. For a nondiscrimination policy to be implemented effectively, m a nagers must provide regular and ongoing _training_ at all levels of their department.

8. In the past, police departments' methods or models of management and organizational behavior were based upon implicit assumptions of a homogeneous, _all white male_ workforce.

9. Researchers Jamieson and O'Mara (1991) indicate that the modern manager must move from the traditional "one-size-fits-all" management style to a _flex management_ model.

10. Today productivity must come from the collaboration of culturally diverse women and men and demands that employees be selected, evaluated, and promoted on the basis of _performance & competency_, regardless of sex, race, religion, or place of origin.

Discussion

1. Discuss how Dr. Sondra Thiederman's approach, which is based on conflict resolution and crisis intervention techniques training that many police and correctional officers receive in their academy t r a i ning, might be applicable to multicultural awareness for police officers' in-service training.

2. Discuss how the passage of the of the Equal Employment Opportunity (EEO) Act played an important role in opening up police department to diverse groups. The EEO Act prohibited employment discrimination on the basis of race, color, religion, sex, or national origin. Selection procedures, criteria, and standards were changed or eliminated and/or made "job related."

3. Sue Jones, Chief of Police of the Healdsburg, California, Police Department, says that the concept of the "brotherhood" still exists, in which women, in order to be accepted, had to "become one of the guys." Discuss how the concept of the "family of law enforcement" might be a better concept than the "brotherhood" when it comes to being inclusive of women and minority officers.

4. Successful training programs on gay, lesbian, and transgender issues have been completed at the San Francisco, Alameda, and Sacramento Police Departments and the Santa Clara Sheriff's Department. Discuss some of the key components that had made these programs successful and how you might implement such training programs in the police department of your local community.

5. Discuss the five key management skills that are required of the modern manager in using the "flex management" model successfully in police departments.

WHAT ARE YOUR THOUGHTS AND WHAT WOULD YOU DO?

A fellow male officer is telling you in the presence of other officers in the men's locker room that he thinks that the new female officer on the shift is a lesbian. He says what she really needs is a man to straighten her out. What are your thoughts and what would you do?

Critical Thinking Questions

1. What are the facts (observable, verifiable, testable, and confirmable)?

2. What are the assumptions?

3. What are the possible stereotypes?

4. What would be your *personal* reactions to this situation?

5. What would be the possible *female officer's* reactions to this situation?

6. Would someone from the Women's Police Officers Association or the gay/lesbian community see something different? What would they see differently (if applicable)?

7. What would be your *professional* reactions to this situation?

8. What actions would you take in this situation?

9. If you had to explain your actions to the Women's Police Officers Association, the gay/lesbian community, and your superiors in front of the news media, what would you say?

TOOLS AND SKILLS IN PRACTICE

1. *Being Aware of the Police Service and Community Recipient Interconnection*—For the city or town of your interest, search through the on-line editions and/or the printed edition of: (a) one or more major newspapers and (b) two or more ethnic/community newspapers for a six-month period. Make a list and summary of the positive news stories of police service with the diverse communities. Make a second list and summary of the negative news stories. Briefly list on a monthly basis the top three to five police/community themes identified.

2. *Identifying Law Enforcement Diversity Workforce Issues*—For your city or town of interest, go the on-line reports (or the actual Minutes of the meetings on file) for the: (a) "Police Commission," (b) "Public Safety Commission," and/or (c) "Emergency Services Commission." Scan the Minutes of the meetings for law enforcement and other public safety "workforce diversity" issues. Note any recurring issues or trends involving different multicultural workforce groups. If on-line services are not available in your area, go the Town Hall

or City Hall and read the past Minutes of the above-noted Commissions for the last six months to one year—the Minutes of the Police Commission and other meetings are usually open to the public.

3. *Reviewing Law Enforcement Agency Workforce Composition*—Go the websites of: (a) the Police Department for your town or city (or to one that is for the nearest large-sized city in your area of i n t e rest), and (b) the Personnel or Human Resources Department of your town or city. Within the two websites, search for and identify the workforce compositions of the law enforcement and criminal justice agencies. Searching terms such as, "women," "minorities," "African American," "workforce percent," "number of women," etc., will usually bring up the information in the website. At a minimum you should get numbers and percentages by gender. Most cities and towns will have information about the workforce composition by race and ethnicity, as well (some may only indicate that a few, e.g., two or three, are "minorities" without further specification). Workforce composition information and tables are often found in the "Annual Reports" to the community for cities and towns.

4. *Understanding Senior Law Enforcement Leadership's Focus on Serving Multicultural Communities*—Go to the website of the Police Department for your town or city (or to one that is for the nearest large-sized city in your area of interest). Within the Police Department's website, search for and identify as many d o cuments and/or articles by senior law enforcement leaders and/or executives (e.g., Chief of Police, Deputy Chiefs, etc.) as possible. Make a list and summary of any content or comments about serving the diverse and multicultural communities of the area. Revi ew your list and summary of comments to determine the emphasis, importance, and attitude of senior law enforcement leadership's focus on service to multicultural communities.

SELF-STUDY ACTIVITIES

Measuring Responsiveness to Diversity

Use the check-list and scoring sheet (in Exhibit 2.3 of the textbook) for the Police Department for your town or city (or for one that is for the nearest large city in your area of interest). Respond to the questions and score your responses. Determine how responsive your police department has been to the diversity of the jurisdiction it serves by comparing your findings to the range of scores. If you were to discuss your findings with the command officer for that city and town, what recommendations would you have for initiatives that his or her department might undertake to address the issues of community diversity?

Defusing Racially and Culturally-Rooted Conflicts

Go to the website for the Peace Officer Standards and Training (POST) for your state. Inquire using search terms such as "diversity training," "diversity awareness," "multicultural," "sensitivity training," "community policing," etc. What types of "diversity" and "multicultural training programs do the police academies in your region provide on defusing racially and culturally-rooted conflicts? What training of this type does your local city or county law enforcement agency provide to officers? Go to the websites for the POST organizations in your surrounding states. What types of diversity and multicultural training are offered there? Make a list of the training p r ograms available and compare this list to what is offered in your state and local law enforcement agencies.

Women in Law Enforcement

Using the findings from your search in the Products and Tools section above for:

1. Item #3, "Reviewing Law Enforcement Agency Workforce Composition," how many women officers are there in your local city or county law enforcement agency? How many of those women are in supervisory or management positions? Are any of the women assigned to nontraditional roles such as special weapons and tactics teams, motorcycle enforcement, bomb units, hostage negotiations, or community relations? Write a brief summary of what you would report if asked about this issue.

2. Item #2, "Identifying Law Enforcement Diversity Workforce Issues," have there been incidents of sexual harassment of women employees? If so, how were the cases resolved? Has the agency you are examining implemented any programs to increase the employment of women, such as flextime, childcare, mentoring, awareness training, or career development? Has the agency been innovative in the recruitment efforts for women applicants? Discuss your findings in a group setting. Write a brief summary of what you would report if asked about this issue.

Diversity in Law Enforcement

Using the findings from your search in the Products and Tools section above for:

1. Item #3, "Reviewing Law Enforcement Agency Workforce Composition," comment on the diversity in your local city or county law enforcement agency. What is the breakdown in your agency's hierarchy? For example, who holds supervisory or management positions? Write a brief summary of what you would report if asked about this issue.

2. Item #2, "Identifying Law Enforcement Diversity Workforce Issues," have there been reported acts of discrimination against people of diverse backgrounds? Has the agency you are examining implemented any programs to increase the employment of minorities? Write a brief summary of what you would report if asked about this issue.

Chapter 3

Multicultural Representation in Law Enforcement: Recruitment, Retention, and Promotion

OVERVIEW

Recruiting, hiring, retaining, and promoting a diverse workforce will remain important issues in law enforcement for a long time. Too many of the issues of equity and diversity have not been resolved in the law enforcement wo r kplace, by the courts, or even in the legislative and executive branches of the U.S. government. The number of people available and qualified for entry-level jobs will continue to decrease; more employers, both public and private, will be vying for the best candidates. This seems to be true regardless of the economic condition of federal, state, or local government.

Hiring and promoting women and minorities for law enforcement careers are achievable goals when agencies use strategies outlined in this chapter. As more and more departments move toward community policing, the need to recruit and retain female and minority officers is becoming critical.

With changes in the hiring, screening, and promotional policies and practices of law enforcement agencies come an unprecedented opportunity to build a future in which differences are valued and respected in our c o mmunities and our workforces. Progressive law enforcement executives must strive to secure the most qualified employees to serve the public. To do so, they must not only be committed to the challenges of affirmative hiring (where legal) but also be capable of educating and selling their workforce on the legitimate reasons, both legal and ethical, for such efforts. Law enforcement agencies, to be competitive in the market for qualified employees, must develop new ways to recruit targeted people or risk losing highly skilled potential employees to other occupations.

Effective strategies and successful programs are presented for implementing changes in the recruitment and promotion of a diverse workforce. Law enforcement will have to use innovative and sophisticated marketing techniques and advertising campaigns to reach the population of desired potential applicants, and must develop fast-track processes for hiring these candidates. A transition is taking place as police continue to move away from the aggressive, male-dominated (and predominantly white) police departments and culture of the past. Most law enforcement observers agree that with the shift to community policing, women can thrive and minorities will stay. Law enforcement agencies must overcome the common perception that policing is a male-oriented profession that requires only physical strength. Departments are looking for people who are community oriented and who have good interpersonal skills and community sensitivity, not just physical strength. Increasing numbers of police departments are finding that women and minority employees bring a diversity of community and interpersonal skills, as well as being able to meet the physical strength qualifications for law enforcement professionals.

Although it contributes to better police–community relations, improvement in protected class representation in law enforcement and other criminal justice professions will not alone resolve misunderstandings. Increased numbers of diverse staff members provide the critical potential for improved dialogue, cooperation, and problem-solving within both the organization and the community the organization serves. Community and law enforcement officials should remember that serving multicultural and multiracial neighborhoods can never be the sole responsibility of workforce members from diverse ethnic and racial groups. In most jurisdictions, their limited numbers make this level of responsibility unrealistic. All staff should be prepared to understand and relate to diverse groups in a professional and sensitive manner, whether the people contacted are perpetrators, victims, or witnesses

RATIONALE FOR THE FOCUS ON THE KEY CONCEPTS AND TOOLS

Officers and practitioners involved in multicultural law enforcement need to be able to:

1. Understand the historical perspective of women and minorities in law enforcement

2. Discuss the ongoing challenges of recruitment trends with respect to women and minorities in law enforcement agencies

3. Explain recruitment difficulties and strategies for recruitment success

4. Understand the importance of retention and promotion of minorities and women in law enforcement careers

5. Identify promotional policies and practices in law enforcement agencies that would demonstrate the valuing of differences in our workplaces and communities

INTRODUCTION

Chapter 3 discusses recruitment trends and the probability that recruitment of women and minorities will be an ongoing challenge for law enforcement agencies. A brief historical perspective of women and minorities in law enforcement is provided, including a profile of their numbers in state, county, and local agencies across the country. We discuss reasons for recruitment difficulties and offer strategies for success. The retention and promotion of minorities and women are addressed in the final section of the chapter.

KEY CONCEPTS

Outline of Key Presentation Points

1. Introduction: Demographic Projections
2. Profile of Federal, Local, and County Personnel
3. Recruitment Crisis in Law Enforcement
4. Recruitment Difficulties
5. Recruitment Strategies
6. Selection Process
7. Examples of Successful Recruiting Programs
8. Equal Employment Opportunity and Affirmative Action
9. Mini-Case Study: What Would You Do?
10. Retention and Promotion of a Diverse Workforce
11. "Glass Ceiling" Issues for Women and Minorities
12. How to Go Through the "Glass Ceiling"
13. Mini-Case Study: What Would You Do?

PRACTICE QUESTIONS

True or False

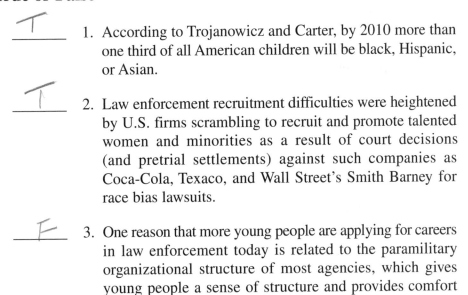

_T___ 1. According to Trojanowicz and Carter, by 2010 more than one third of all American children will be black, Hispanic, or Asian.

_T___ 2. Law enforcement recruitment difficulties were heightened by U.S. firms scrambling to recruit and promote talented women and minorities as a result of court decisions (and pretrial settlements) against such companies as Coca-Cola, Texaco, and Wall Street's Smith Barney for race bias lawsuits.

_F___ 3. One reason that more young people are applying for careers in law enforcement today is related to the paramilitary organizational structure of most agencies, which gives young people a sense of structure and provides comfort resulting from the hierarchical leadership in charge.

_____ 4. The study commissioned by the International Association of Chiefs of Police, completed in 1998, *The Future of Women in Policing: Mandates for Action*, concluded that targeted programs are more likely to attract diversity to law enforcement.

_____ 5. The authors recommend that police executives should publicly delineate to the community the specific hiring and promotion goals of the department through methods which are both formal (e.g., media) and informal (e.g., community-based policing, networking with organizations representing diverse groups).

_____ 6. The San Jose, California, High School Police Academy is a year-long academy program that helps both students and law enforcement agencies by preparing students for careers and giving recruiters a larger pool of candidates.

_____ 7. An agency whose hiring procedures screen for unacceptable biases demonstrates to the community that it seeks police officers who will carry out their duties with fairness, integrity, diligence, and impartiality—officers who will respect the civil rights and dignity of the people they serve and work with.

_____ 8. In 2003, the Supreme Court of the United States ruled that the University of Michigan's Law School admissions policy, which uses race as a factor, was not in violation of the Constitution's 14th Amendment and that race can be considered in the admissions process to the School of Law.

_____ 9. In 1998, the International Association of Chiefs of Police published a comprehensive analysis of women in policing, which involved surveys of 800 police departments, and reported that nearly 10 percent of the departments listed gender bias as the reason that women were not promoted.

_____ 10. The 1998 study by the International Association of Chiefs of Police found that about 60 percent of the women who leave law enforcement occupations do so between their second and fifth year on the job.

Multiple Choice

1. The Christopher Warren Commission report on the Los Angeles Police Department, released soon after the 1992 riots following the first Rodney King trial, cited the problems of racism and bias within the LAPD. The commission recommended:

    a. Improved hiring and promotions processes that would benefit all groups

    b. Greater recruitment and hiring of those from military police and detention center backgrounds who would have more experience in controlling riots and community uprisings

    c. More training for Special Weapons and Tactics (SWAT) police components to prevent riots

    d. All of the above

2. Currently, there is a shortage of applicants for police departments and a struggle for departments to maintain authorized strength. Which of following might be factors contributing to the reduction of the once-substantial law enforcement applicant pool?

    a. The percentage of the population between 16 and 24 years old is shrinking in the labor force

    b. Young people between the ages of 15 and 29 are arrested each year for crimes that disqualify them for police work

    c. During the next decade, white men will account for only one in four new workers

    d. All of the above

3. The Police Executive Research Forum (PERF) created a nationwide task force to address the issue of decreasing numbers of qualified police applicants. The problem most frequently reported was:

    a. Inability to recruit candidates with criminal justice training at the Community College level

    b. Difficulty in recruiting Asians, blacks, Hispanics, and other minorities

    c. Over-abundant candidates who only wanted law enforcement management and executive positions

    d. All of the above

4. Police executives point to Albuquerque as a potential model for other departments regarding recruitment. Between 1995 and 2002, female recruits increased from 8 percent in academy classes to _____ percent.

   a. 11
   b. 22
   c. 33
   d. 44

5. Robert Jones, professor of psychology at Southwest Missouri State University, says that recruiters can get a clear appraisal of applicants in service related jobs, such as law enforcement, by applying the five basic traits of human behavior. The five traits are:

   a. Emotional stability, extroversion versus introversion, openness to experience, agreeableness versus toughness, and conscientiousness
   b. Intelligence, social consciousness, community versus politics, diversity, and decision-making
   c. Self-esteem, "can-do" attitude, equity, fairness, and value orientation
   d. Other-mindedness, empathy, society versus individuality, kindness, and generosity

6. Retention of any employee is usually the result of:

   a. Good work on the part of the employee
   b. Positive environment wherein all employees are treated with dignity and respect
   c. Reasonable opportunities for career development
   d. All of the above

7. Affirmative action and consent decrees:

   a. Have been completely successful in achieving parity in the hiring of women and individuals from ethnically diverse backgrounds in law enforcement
   b. Have been moderately successful in achieving parity in the hiring of women and individuals from ethnically diverse backgrounds in law enforcement
   c. Have had no effect in achieving parity in the hiring of women and individuals from ethnically diverse backgrounds in law enforcement
   d. Have been completely unsuccessful in achieving parity in the hiring of women and individuals from ethnically diverse backgrounds in law enforcement

8. Penny Harrington, a former Portland, Oregon, police chief and past executive director of the National Center for Women and Policing in Los Angeles, said about women in law enforcement:

    a. Things are getting worse
    b. The younger generation is less likely to speak out than did the first group of women
    c. Women who have complained or sued have reported retaliatory verbal abuse, petty reprimands from supervisors and managers, dead-end assignments, and, in some cases, no backup on patrol
    d. All of the above

9. Law enforcement agencies must assess applicants along a range of dimensions. Which of the following is *not* a dimension of assessment:

    a. Racial, ethnic, gender, sexual orientation, and cultural biases
    b. Current and past illegal drug use
    c. Work history, military record, and credit history
    d. Home ownership in urban, inner city, and poverty location

10. According to Vest (2001), some of the ways in which law enforcement agencies can begin to bridge language and generation barriers and to develop trust among the diverse groups that they will serve in the future include which of the following strategies?

    a. Officers must learn about cultural practices, such as ethnic holidays, traditions, and customs
    b. Officers should be encouraged to volunteer for shifts in community agencies serving the immigrant and the elderly populations
    c. Officers should make regular rounds by visiting the local restaurants, churches, mosques, temples, and culture-specific language schools
    d. None of the above

Fill-in-the-Blanks

1. To recruit and retain a representative staff and provide effective services, law enforcement executives must have a clear understanding of their _communities_ and their own workforce.

2. Federal agencies (INS, FBI, U.S. Customs, etc.) employed 88,496 full-time agents as of June 2000, of which __14.4__ percent were women and __30.5__ percent were members of a racial or ethnic minority.

3. The top three tests in which applicants to law enforcement positions fail were the written test, background investigation, and _polygraph_.

4. _Fast Tracking_ is an aggressive recruitment process wherein a preliminary, qualifying check quickly takes place concerning the driving, credit, and criminal history of the applicant before any other screening process occurs.

5. The San Francisco Police Department utilizes _Community leaders_ representing the diversity of the community to be involved in the selection process, including sitting on oral boards for applicants and in all of the hiring processes.

6. A department seeking to hire applicants from diverse groups cannot have _internal_ problems, either real or perceived, related to racism, discrimination, or hostility toward female or homosexual officers.

7. _Role model and mentoring_ programs should be established to give recruits and junior officers the opportunity to receive support and important information from senior officers of the same race, ethnicity, gender, or sexual orientation.

8. Because of the emphasis on _community-oriented policing_, law enforcement recruiters must also seek applicants who demonstrate the mentality and ability to serve others, and not just fight crime.

9. The study by the National Center for Women and Policing (NCWP), published in 2001 by the Bureau of Justice Assistance of the Department of Justice, offers recommendations for greatly increasing the pool of qualified female applicants. The study stressed the importance of developing a _strategic marketing plan_.

10. Authors and advocates for the promotion of women have used the term _glass ceiling_ to describe an unacknowledged barrier that inhibits those officers from reaching ranks above entry level.

Discussion

1. Discuss which of the 10 most frequent causes of the failure to attract and retain high-level minority and female employees (discussed in *Cultural Diversity at Work*, a newsletter addressing multicultural issues) are most pertinent to law enforcement in your local area.

2. Delineate and discuss some of the best practices used by law enforcement agencies to attract and recruit a diverse workforce. Which of these practices do you see employed by the law enforcement agencies in your local area?

3. Provide some examples of some of the "targets" that should be included as part of the advertising campaign in the strategic recruitment plan for a police agency. Discuss how some of the "targets" might be different depending upon the diversity of the local community served by the police agency.

4. Summarize some of the questions and interviewing procedures that could be used to elicit the applicant's own statements about racial issues. How could they be used as well for interviews with references? Who could provide clues about how the applicant feels about and treats members of other racial, ethnic, gender, and sexual-orientation groups? Provide some examples of questions to be included for such interviews.

5. Highlight the services available from the National Center for Women and Policing to assist law enforcement agencies that wish to increase the number of women employees in their workforce. Which of these services might be most applicable to your local law enforcement agencies to help increase their number of women employees?

WHAT ARE YOUR THOUGHTS AND WHAT WOULD YOU DO?

Your department has hired its first Vietnamese, non-sworn, outreach coordinator to combat distrust of police officers by many Southeast Asians and to help overcome the language barriers. The department created this position because the city's Vietnamese population has grown by 500 percent since the last census. A fellow officer is telling you in the presence of other officers in the break area that he thinks the Department should not be hiring people, who might not be qualified as a sworn officer. He thinks that this position is a waste of tax payers' money. What are your thoughts and what would you do?

Critical Thinking Questions

1. What are the facts (observable, verifiable, testable, and confirmable)?
2. What are the assumptions?
3. What are the possible stereotypes?
4. What would be your *personal* reactions to this situation?
5. What would be the possible *Vietnamese, non-sworn, outreach coordinator's* reactions to these remarks?
6. Would someone from the Vietnamese and Asian/Pacific American communities see something different? What would they see differently (if applicable)?
7. What would be your *professional* reactions to this situation?
8. What actions would you take in this situation?
9. If you had to explain your actions to the Vietnamese and Asian/Pacific American communities, the Police Commission, and your superiors in front of the news media, what would you say?

TOOLS AND SKILLS IN PRACTICE

1. *Using Gap Analysis to Understand the Diverse Workforce Challenges*—Knowing the needs and gaps in police and criminal justice services for the ethnic, racial, and cultural groups in one's service area is critical toward understanding the multicultural c h a llenges of your area. Log-on to the on-line information from the key newspapers of your area, as well as any of the "community" news sources in your area. Search these on-line news sources of your local area for the cultural groups and for issues identifying service "gaps" or "needs" for these cultural groups on an ongoing basis. Keep a journal of the groups that emerge, their service gap issues, and the statements from the police or criminal justice a g e ncies for resolution of these service gap issues. Compile your findings from the lists that you developed about the "gaps" that exists for police services in your service area.

2. *Scanning for Effective Recruitment Activities and Efforts*—Two approaches are suggested to obtain information about effective recruitment activities and efforts:

   a. Go online to the Peace Officers Standards and Training (POST) organization for your state (or for a nearby state). Go the their "Reports section," and "research sections" (or the POST "library collections of reports"), and use the search terms such as "recruitment," "women," "minorities," "gays," "lesbians," "retention," "promotion," and "workforce strategies." Read the online summary of reports (and actual reports, if available). Make a list of the recruitment activities and strategies that are highlighted for your area by the POST reports.

   b. Go online to the website http://www.DiversityInc.com and use search terms such as "recruitment," "women," "minorities," "gays," "lesbians," "retention," "promotion," "police recruit-ment," and "workforce strategies." Read the online summary of reports (and actual reports, if available). Make a list of the recruitment activities and strategies that are highlighted based upon the information from a national perspective. From the two lists of recruitment activities gathered, write a brief summary report regarding what would be your recommended set of top six actions for your local area law enforcement recruitment efforts.

3. *Gathering Information on Retention and Promotion Outcomes and Results*—Two approaches are suggested to obtain information about retention and promotion outcomes and results for the law enforcement agencies in your area: Go the websites of: (a) the Police Department for your town or city (or to one that is for the nearest large-sized city in your area of interest), and (b) the Personnel or

Human Resources Department of your own town or city. Within the two websites, search for and identify the retention and promotion information of the law enforcement and criminal justice agencies. Searching terms such as, "women," "minorities," "African American," "retention," "promotion," "termination," "turnover," etc., will usually bring up the information in the website. At minimum you should get numbers and percentages by gender. Most cities and towns will have information about the workforce turnover by race and ethnicity, as well (some may only indicate that a few, e.g., two or three employees, have "retired," or "left their employment" without further specification). Workforce change and turnover information and tables are often found in the "Annual Reports" to the community for cities and towns. If on-line services are not available in your area, go the Town Hall or City Hall and read the past "Annual Reports" for such information. Record in your journal the retention, promotion, and turnover information that you have obtained.

4. *Developing Awareness of Workplace and Agency Culture*— Complete the form provided in Appendix C in this Study Guide ("Multicultural Community and Law Enforcement Workforce Survey") based upon your impressions of the law enforcement agency in your local area. You may also want to get one other person who is not in your class, but who is a resident of your community, to complete the survey form as well. Score the survey responses for both forms. Based upon the scores in the survey forms, make a list of the workplace and agency cultural issues that are positive and another list of issues that are negative. To corroborate your observations, use the on-line information from the key newspapers of your area: Search the on-line news sources of your local area for police workplace and agency issues on an ongoing basis. Keep a journal of the issues that emerged and match them to the issues identified from your survey observations.

SELF-STUDY ACTIVITIES

Institutional Racism in Law Enforcement

Law enforcement agencies typically operate under the pretense that all of their members are of one color and that the uniform or job makes everyone brothers or sisters. Many members of diverse ethnic and racial groups, p a rticularly African Americans, do not agree that they are consistently treated with respect and believe that there is institutional racism in law enforcement. Caucasians clearly dominate the command ranks of law enforcement agencies. For your survey and corroborative efforts using the findings based upon the Products and Tools for Item #4 above ("Developing Awareness of Workplace and Agency Culture"), summarize your findings as to whether subtle forms of institution racism are most prevalent or are there actual conscious efforts on the part of the persons empowered to make decisions. Consider whether tests and promotional processes give unfair advantage to white applicants and whether they d i scriminate against department employees of other races and ethnicities. Do officers from diverse groups discriminate against members of other, different cultures?

Employment of a Diverse Workforce and Police Practices

Using the findings based upon the Products and Tools for (a) Item #1 above ("Using Gap Analysis to Understand the Diverse Workforce Challenges"), and (b) Item #3 ("Gathering Information on Retention and Promotion Outcomes and Results"), summarize your findings as to the status of the employment of a diverse workforce for police practices in your city or county. Is there evidence that significant changes in the ethnic or racial composition of the department alter official police policy? Can the same be said of gay and lesbian employment? Does employment of protected classes have any significant effect on the informal police subculture and, in turn, police performance? Provide examples from your findings to support your conclusions, and write a brief summary report of any recommendations you might make to the leadership of the police department.

Chapter 4

Cross-Cultural Communications for Law Enforcement

OVERVIEW

In cross-cultural communication in law enforcement, officers' own filters and perceptions influence the assessment of each situation and the reactions the officers choose to exhibit. Each officer has unique "blind spots" and emotional "buttons" that may negatively affect the communication.

Officers must keep in mind that rapport building is related to trust for many persons of diverse backgrounds. The more trust that officers earn with members of ethnic communities, the more helpful these group members will be when officers need cooperation and information. To improve communication across cultures, it is essential that people in law enforcement understand the overall style of communication of different groups, including the special challenges facing men and women in the profession, and that they utilize multicultural communication skills.

Two key points are made in this chapter regarding police officer communication:

- Officers have traditionally used styles of communication and language that at one time were considered acceptable, not only within the police agency but with citizens as well. Because of cultural diversity in the population and the accompanying need to respect all individuals, the unspoken rules about what is appropriate have changed dramatically.

- Through communication, officers have tremendous power to influence the behavior and responses of the citizens with whom they contact. This is true of all citizens, regardless of background. A lack of knowledge of the cross-cultural aspects of communication will diminish that power with people whose backgrounds differ from that of the officer.

RATIONALE FOR THE FOCUS ON THE KEY CONCEPTS AND TOOLS

Officers and practitioners involved in multicultural law enforcement need to be able to:

1. Understand the impact of language barriers in everyday situations with citizens and develop skills that demonstrate sensitivity toward speakers of English as a second language

2. Explain typical communication dynamics in cross-cultural and cross-racial encounters

3. Identify verbal and nonverbal communication style differences across cultures

4. Understand the need and identify skills for professional cross-cultural communication in challenging situations

INTRODUCTION

Chapter 4 begins with a discussion of language barriers and their implications for law enforcement, and gives examples of police departments' efforts to work with limited English-speaking populations. Commonly held attitudes about non-native English speakers are explained, along with the challenges involved in second-language acquisition. The section on language barriers and law enforcement ends with a list of tips for communicating in situations in which English is an individual's second language. The chapter provides an overview of specific issues that law enforcement professionals face with regard to communication in a diverse environment. Several common reactions are highlighted regarding the communication with people from different backgrounds, including defensiveness, over-identification, denial of biases, and the creation of "we–they" attitudes. In addition, responses to citizens' accusations of racial profiling as well as communication post 9/11 are discussed. Information is given on the key issues and the skills required for interviewing and gathering data, particularly across cultures. A section covers cross-cultural nonverbal differences, emphasizing areas of contrast of which officers should be aware. The final section presents male–female communication issues, particularly within law enforcement agencies.

KEY CONCEPTS

Outline of Key Presentation Points

1. Language Barriers and Law Enforcement
2. Enhancing Officers' Communication
3. Communication: The Process
4. Communication: When Verbal and Nonverbal Aspects Contradict

5. Proxemics by Dr. Edward T. Hall

6. Proxemics: A Scientific Look at Personal Space

7. Gestures: Four Requirements

8. High- and Low-Context Communications

9. Your Voice and Intelligibility

10. Rate of Speech in the U.S.

11. Building Rapport Using Neuro-Linguistic Programming (NLP)

12. Using Language or Style to Become Just Like One of "Them"

13. Walking on Eggshells

14. "You People," or the "We–They" Elements

15. "You Stopped Me Because I'm Black, or Mexican, etc."

16. Dr. George Thompson's "Verbal Deflectors" or "Verbal Judo"

17. Communication Considerations: Post 9/11

18. Attitudes Toward Non-Limited English Speakers

19. Tips for Communicating When English Is a Second Language

20. Using Translators

21. Male–Female Communications in Law Enforcement

PRACTICE QUESTIONS

True or False

_____ 1. Members of the second and third generations of an immigrant family almost always become fluent in English, while many of the first-generation immigrants (the g r a n dparents and the parents) struggle, sometimes partly learning English and sometimes never learning it at all.

_____ 2. High context people tend to have preferences for harmonious communication and for avoidance of disagreement.

_____ 3. The type of communication approach one uses in Neuro-Linguistic Programming (NLP) is that of "using the o p p osite" nonverbal and verbal behaviors as observed in a witness, victim, or interviewee.

_____ 4. George Thompson, founder and president of the Verbal Judo Institute, Inc., advocates using "nonverbal discriminators" when citizens make such remarks as "You stopped me because I'm . . ."

_T_ 5. George Thompson believes that in some situations, people bring up race and ethnicity to throw the officer off guard.

_T_ 6. The "come here" gesture (beckoning people to come with the palm up) is very insulting in most of Asia and Latin America, according to Levine and Adelman (1992).

_T_ 7. In many cultures, as is true for many ethnic minorities in the United States, greater weight and belief are placed on the visual and nonverbal aspects of communication.

_F_ 8. In general, Latin Americans and Middle Easterners prefer speaking at a greater physical distance apart from each other than do northern Europeans, Asians, or the majority of Americans, who prefer closer distances.

_T_ 9. Women allowed into what has been termed the "brotherhood" in law enforcement have generally had to "become one of the guys" to gain acceptance into an historically male-dominated profession.

_T_ 10. Sexual innuendoes and patronizing terms can contribute to a hostile working environment and can be forms of sexual harassment.

Multiple Choice

1. Several factors affect an immigrant's positive ability to use English at any given moment. Which one of the following, in particular, is of special significance to law enforcement officers?

   a. The person is comfortable with the officer
   b. The person is fearful of the officer
   c. The person is highly anxious in the situation
   d. None of the above

2. Which one of the following characteristics would be exhibited by people or cultural groups who tend toward the high context end of the communication continuum?

   a. Able to say "No" to anyone easily
   b. Able to answer "Yes" and "No" to questions quickly
   c. Tend to avoid conflict
   d. Focus on narrow context in interactions

3. In an attempt to show how tolerant and experienced a person is with members of minority groups, which one of the follow phrases might be used by that person to incorrectly demonstrate his/her tolerance?

     a. Some of my best friends are (name of the group)
     b. I'm not prejudiced toward (name of the group)
     c. I once knew someone who was also (name of the group)
     d. All of the above

4. For the officer, which one of the following is *not* a key issue in any interviewing and data-gathering situation in a multicultural law enforcement situation?

     a. Establishing interpersonal relationships with the parties involved to gain trust and rapport for continual work
     b. Ensuring that those in the multicultural community appreciate and recognize the positive work of the police department
     c. Giving information about the workings of the law enforcement guidelines, resources, and available assistance
     d. Bolstering and supporting the different parties' abilities and skills to solve current and future problems on their own

5. Which of the following gestures might be consider offensive in cross-cultural communications?

     a. The "OK" sign in Brazil
     b. The good luck gesture in Vietnam
     c. Both "a" and "b"
     d. None of the above

6. When in the presence of people from different cultural backgrounds, some find that they have a tendency to work hard not to offend. Which of the following behaviors might be indicative of trying hard not to offend?

     a. Talking loudly and in a demanding tone
     b. Communicating as if one were walking on egg shells
     c. Insisting that one's opinion is the correct opinion
     d. All of the above

7. Cultural and racial put-downs are often attempts to make people feel better about themselves. Which of the following statements is an example of cultural and racial put-downs?

     a. "They are all lazy"
     b. "They are all criminals"
     c. "They are all terrorists"
     d. All of the above

8. Officers accused of racially or ethnically motivated stops truly need to remain professional and not escalate a potential conflict or create a confrontation. Which of the following behaviors are recommended?

    a. Use George Thompson's verbal deflectors

    b. Try to communicate professionalism, both verbally and nonverbally

    c. Strengthen one's own self-control by working on one's own reactions and stress level

    d. All of the above

9. Since 9/11, many Arab Americans, in particular, feel that they are automatic suspects when approached by law enforcement representatives. According to Dr. James Zogby, President of the Arab American Institute Foundation in Washington, D.C., which of the following actions would ensure better interaction between law enforcement officers and members of the Arab American community?

    a. Sit down and engage in dialogue with Arab American community leaders

    b. Inform them of their Miranda rights before asking any questions and talking

    c. Tell them that you are acting on behalf of the FBI, CIA, and Department of Homeland Security

    d. None of the above

10. When interviewing and data gathering in the area of hate incidents and crimes (as well as about threats by means of phone calls or letters targeted at individuals of particular backgrounds), which of the following are ways for the officer to handle possible hysterical or at least highly emotional reactions from other people of the same background?

    a. Provide the community reassurance of law enforcement's response and actions

    b. Respond sensitively to heightened anxiety on the part of group members and do not downplay their fears

    c. Take the time necessary to deal with multiple community members and widespread fears

    d. All of the above

Fill-in-the-Blanks

1. Officers need to be aware of the potential for inadvertent *discrimination* based on a citizen's language background, which could fall under "language and national origin *discrimination*."

2. Every communication act involves a message, a *sender*, and a receiver.

3. Lower context communication tendencies involve preferences for getting right to the point, and behaviors such as _*beating around the bush*_ are seen as negative.

4. One of the key tools in law enforcement is Neuro-Linguistic Programming (NLP), a communication model and a set of techniques for establishing *rapport*.

5. Officers attempting to establish rapport with citizens should not p r etend to have too much familiarity with the language and culture or use words selectively to demonstrate how _*cool*_ they are (e.g., using "señor" with Spanish-speaking people, calling an African American "my man," or referring to a Native American as "chief").

6. Some may say "I'd like to get to know you people better" or "You people have made some amazing contributions"; the usage of "You people" may be another signal of _*prejudice*_ in one's mind.

7. In the area of data-gathering and interviewing, the officer in a m u lticultural law enforcement and peacekeeping situation cannot assume that his or her key _*motivations*_ are the same as those of the other parties involved.

8. Albert Mehrabian of the University of California at Los Angeles described in the well-known book, *Silent Messages,* the general impact among two or three people when a person's verbal and n o n -verbal messages contradict each other. In this scenario, it is almost always _*the obvious body language*_ including facial expressions, that convey an individual's true feeling.

9. To show one's _*boot*_ in many cultures (for example to a Thai or Saudi Arabian) is insulting because the _*boot*_ is considered the dirtiest part of the body.

10. All people unconsciously keep a comfortable distance around themselves when communicating with others, resulting in invisible walls that keep people far enough away; this sub-category of nonverbal communication is called _*proxemics*_.

Discussion

1. Discuss how an officer might communicate with a high-context person for rapport-building and for building trust. Provide several examples of questions the officer might ask and information that the officer might provide about himself/herself. Name several ethnic or cultural groups that might use a high-context style in communications.

2. Discuss approaches that an officer might use for building rapport and trust within a multicultural community. Provide several examples of these approaches used by law enforcement officers within your local community.

3. Discuss the problems an officer might have in using a language style or using language to become just like one of "them." What are the pros and cons when using this approach? What kind of feedback might you give a fellow officer with whom you are working who tends to use a language style or use language to become just like one of "them"?

4. Exhibit 4.5 in this text chapter lists key values or motivators for police officers. Discuss for any given situation how these values may be at odds with what motivates the victim, suspect, or ordinary citizen of any background. Provide several examples of how the key values and motivators for police officers may differ with those of the victim, suspect, or ordinary citizen of a cultural background.

5. Discuss why the "people are people everywhere" argument and "just treat everyone with respect" advice both fall short when one learns that there can be basic differences in the areas of behavior and communication across cultures. Summarize some of the typical ways people attempt to accommodate or react to cultural or racial differences and how they may cover up their discomfort in communication across cultures (as highlighted in this text chapter).

TOOLS AND SKILLS IN PRACTICE

1. *Observing Cross-Cultural Communication*—Go to a public place where you might be certain that you will be able to observe cross-cultural communications without being obvious or intrusive (e.g., Information Desk at the local department of motor vehicles, ethnic/cultural restaurant, student lounge for international students on the college campus, etc.). Observe both "cross-cultural," as well as "similar culture" interpersonal interactions and communications (use your own rules for deciding which interactions would be "cross-cultural" and which one are "similar culture"). Make your observations and record them on 3 × 5 cards along the following eight dimensions:

WHAT ARE YOUR THOUGHTS AND WHAT WOULD YOU DO?

In late 1992, Marge Schott, the 61-year-old owner of the Cincinnati Reds, was accused of making racist remarks over a period of years; she was accused of allegedly calling two Reds outfielders her "million dollar niggers" and admitted to keeping a swastika armband in her desk drawer. She also told The *New York Times* that Hitler was "good" but that he went too far. One of the issues surrounding her racially and culturally insensitive remarks was that her comments were made in front of other people, but that no one said anything to her or objected. Some felt that she should have been confronted. You are in a social gathering and overhear one of your fellow officers making such a racist or derogatory remark similar to that of Mrs. Schott. What are your thoughts and what would you do?

Critical Thinking Questions

1. What are the facts (observable, verifiable, testable, and confirmable)?

2. What are the assumptions?

3. What are the possible stereotypes?

4. What would be your *personal* reactions to this situation?

5. What would be the possible *social gathering attendees'* reactions to this situation?

6. What would someone from the African/American community's reactions be to this situation? What would they see differently (if applicable)?

7. What would be your *professional* reactions to this situation?

8. What actions would you take in this situation?

9. If you had to explain your actions to the African American community, the host of the social gathering, fellow police officers, and your superiors in front of the news media, what would you say?

---

1. Display of emotions and expressions of feelings

2. Communication style: loud or soft

3. Expressions of appreciation; conventions of courtesy (i.e., forms of politeness)

4. Gestures, facial expressions, and body movements

5. Eye contact

6. Touching

7. Interpersonal space (conversational distance)

8. Having an easy time or having a hard time communicating

Summarize your observations by making a list of the things that seem to be present when the parties are having an easy time communicating (for both cross-cultural, as well as for "similar culture" interactions). Make a second list of the things that seem to be present when the parties are having a difficult time communicating (for both cross-cultural, as well as for "similar culture" interactions). What recommendation might you make regarding cross-cultural communications from your observations?

2. *Developing Strategies for Communicating with Non- or Limited-English Speakers*—Begin building a file in your computer or on 3 × 5 index cards (or in a "blank book" journal). On a daily basis, as you observe in your work, in the news, or in any other sources, note any interactions involving people with non- or limited-English speakers: (a) with people in general and (b) with those involving law enforcement personnel. Record aspects of these interactions that appear to be going well and those that could have gone better. For those interactions that have gone well, identify the key elements and/or aspects that made them go well. For those cross-cultural interactions involving people with non- or limited-English speakers that could have gone better, brainstorm about ways in which the situation could have been improved. What could have been done differently to attain a more positive outcome? In a short amount of time, your file will contain many useful ideas for improving cross-cultural interactions and communications with non- or limited-English speakers for law enforcement services in multicultural communities.

3. *Interviewing and Data-Gathering Skills for Diverse Communities*—Once you have information about the different groups in your community and the key leaders of those groups (using the Tools and Skills from Chapter 1), it will be important to get information on the needed services of the identified community groups by going onsite to do some information interviewing. First, go in person to obtain some of the community resource guides available in your local area. Review these resource guides to identify the needs of these groups, and make a list of the needs and services offered. Arrange for brief information-gathering interviews with these agencies regarding their resources and the community needs addressed by their services. Begin building a file in your computer or on 3 × 5 index cards (or in a "blank book" journal). Record aspects of your interviews that appear to be going well and those that could have gone better. For those aspects that have gone well, identify the key elements of your interview that made it go well. For those interview aspects that could have gone better, brainstorm about ways that the situation could have been improved. What could have been done differently to attain a better outcome? In a short amount of time, your file will contain many useful ideas for improving interview approaches and data-gathering methods with multicultural communities. Once you have some degree of comfort level interviewing within multicultural community service

agencies and programs, you may wish to look at other venues like city and county services and agencies, ethnic/cultural businesses in the area, etc.

4. *Using Cultural Awareness and Cultural Diversity Training*—Three approaches are suggested to obtain information about using cultural awareness and cultural diversity training:

a. Go online to the Peace Officers Standards and Training (POST) organization for your state (or for a nearby state). Go to the training courses, and use search terms such as "multicultural training," "sensitivity training," "cultural awareness," "diversity," and "diversity training." Read the online summary of training courses (and actual outlines and curriculum of the courses, if available). Make a list of the cultural awareness and cultural diversity training activities and strategies that are highlighted for your area by the POST in your state.

b. Go online to the website http://www.DiversityInc.com and use search terms such as "multicultural training," "sensitivity training," "cultural awareness," "diversity," and "diversity training." Read the online summary of the training courses and the vendors who offer such courses (and outlines of the courses, if available). Make a list of the cultural awareness and cultural diversity training activities and strategies that are highlighted based upon the information from a national perspective.

c. Go online to the Personnel or Human Resources Department for your city or town (or for a nearby city or town). Go the their training courses offered section, and use the search terms such as "multicultural training," "sensitivity training," "cultural awareness," "diversity," and "diversity training." Read the online summary of training courses (and actual outlines and curriculum of the courses, if available). Make a list of the cultural awareness and cultural diversity training activities and strategies that are highlighted for your area by your city or town. From the three lists of cultural awareness and cultural diversity training activities gathered, write a brief summary report about which cultural awareness and cultural diversity training activities would be useful to you, your community, and the law enforcement agencies in your area.

SELF-STUDY ACTIVITIES

The Origins of Stereotypes

From lists of cultural awareness and cultural diversity training activities gathered as part of the Tools and Skills #4 ("Using Cultural Awareness and Cultural Diversity Training") in this chapter, how many of the training programs dealt with stereotypes in the workplace and in the community? In Chapter 4, we argue that officers need to recognize how their early experiences in life and later adult experiences shape their perceptions and "filters" about people from groups different from their own. From your findings for the Tools and Skills #4 ("Using Cultural Awareness and Cultural Diversity Training") in this chapter, how are stereotypes dealt with in the workplace? What kinds of training emphases are placed upon early experiences and "filters" in cultural awareness training?

Police Officer Interaction with Speakers of Other Languages

The following dialogue illustrates a typical interaction between a police officer and a nonnative speaker of English, in this case a Vietnamese man. Using the strategies and suggestions developed from the Tools and Skills Exercise #2 ("Developing Strategies for Communicating with Non- or Limited-English Speakers") in this section, analyze this interaction by being specific as to how the officer can improve.

Situation:	An officer pulls a car over, gets out of the car, and approaches the driver. The driver, who is Vietnamese, says, in poor English, "What happen? Why you stop me?"
Officer:	I pulled you over because you ran a red light.
Citizen:	(No response)
Officer:	This is a traffic violation. (Receives no feedback.) Do you understand?
Citizen:	(Nodding) Yeah, I understand.
Officer:	I'm going to have to issue you a traffic citation.
Citizen:	(Staring at officer)
Officer:	Where's your driver's license?
Citizen:	License? Just a minute. (Leans over to open glove compartment, but finds nothing. He gets out of car and goes to trunk.)
Officer:	(Irritated and slightly nervous) HEY! (In a loud voice) What's going on here? I asked to see your driver's license. Are you the registered owner of this car?
Citizen:	Yeah. I go get my license.
Officer:	(Speaking much louder) Wait a minute. Don't you understand? Are you not the owner of this car? Do you even have a license?
Citizen:	Wait. (Finds license in trunk and produces it for officer)
Officer:	OK. Would you mind getting back into the car now?
Citizen:	(Does nothing) Yeah, I understand.
Officer:	(Pointing to the front seat) Back into the car!
Citizen:	(Does as told)

Note: The officer could make improvements in at least four areas: (1) choice of words, (2) manner of asking questions, (3) use of idioms (there are at least two or three that could be changed to simple English), and (4) tone and attitude.

Cultural Observations and Discussions

From your findings from the Tools and Skills #1 in this chapter ("Observing Cross-Cultural Communication"), try to find someone from a particular culture with whom you can discuss some of your cultural observations and findings. Discuss your findings along the following topic areas:

1. Display of emotions and expressions of feelings
2. Communication style: loud, soft, direct, indirect
3. Expressions of appreciation; conventions of courtesy (i.e., forms of politeness)
4. Need (or lack thereof) for privacy
5. Gestures, facial expressions, and body movements
6. Eye contact
7. Touching
8. Interpersonal space (conversational distance)
9. Taboo topics in conversation
10. Response to authority

Write a brief report about areas of your observations that you found confirmed and areas that were different from your observations.

Discomfort with Unfamiliar Groups

In your development of the Tools and Skills #3 ("Interviewing and Data-Gathering Skills for Diverse Communities") in this text chapter, were there elements of discomfort and uneasiness during the interviews? How much discomfort, if any, did you experience? If the situation was uncomfortable, did it affect your effectiveness at communication or your professionalism? What were the elements that made your interviews uncomfortable and uneasy for you?

Part 2

CULTURAL SPECIFICS
FOR LAW ENFORCEMENT

Part 2 presents information on Asian/Pacific, African American, Latino/Hispanic, Middle Eastern, and Native American cultural backgrounds with regard to the needs of law enforcement and criminal justice representatives. In these culture-specific chapters, general information is presented on the following areas: historical background, demographics, and diversity within the cultural group. Following the introductory information, we present specific details relevant to law enforcement and criminal justice in the following areas: communication styles (both verbal and nonverbal), group identification terms, offensive labels, stereotypes, and family structure. Each chapter ends with key· concerns for officers related to the particular cultural group, a summary of recommendations for law enforcement officials, and resources for additional information about the cultural group.

Chapter 5

Law Enforcement Contact with Asian/Pacific Americans

OVERVIEW

As a result of the early immigration laws and other discriminatory treatments received by Asian/Pacific Americans in the United States, the experiences of Asian/Pacific Americans with law enforcement officials has been fraught with conflicts, difficulties, and mixed messages. The label Asian Americans/Pacific Islanders encompasses over 40 very diverse ethnic and cultural groups. Law enforcement officials need to be aware that great differences exist between the 40 diverse ethnic groups (e.g., different cultural and language groups) as well as the differences that may result from the individual life experiences of members within any one of the 40 groups (e.g., generational differences). There is tremendous diversity among Asian/Pacific Americans, and one way to understand individuals within these communities is to look at some of the motivating forces that might affect decisions by Asian/Pacific American citizens. A seven-part typology is provided that will assist officers in viewing some of these motivational bases. Although there are many ethnicities, c u ltures, and languages among the 40 or more groups within Asian/Pacific American communities, one way to understand the impact of their immigration and life experiences is by learning the motivational determinants of individuals within different generational and immigrant groups. The self-preferred term for referring to Asian/Pacific Americans varies with contexts, groups, and experiences of the individual. Law enforcement officials need to be aware of terms that are unacceptable and derogatory and the terms that are currently used. Many Asian/Pacific Americans are concerned with their ability to communicate clearly, and this is of particular concern among Asian/Pacific Americans who are immigrants and refugees. Peace officers need to take the time and be aware that bilingual individuals and non-native English speakers want to communicate effectively with them.

Cultural differences in verbal and nonverbal communication often result in misinterpretation of the message and of behaviors. Officers need to be aware of nonverbal aspects of Asian/Pacific Americans in their c o mmunication styles, including eye contact, touch, gestures, and affect (show of emotions). Verbal aspects such as accent, limited vocabulary, and incorrect grammar may give officers the impression that an Asian/Pacific American individual is not understanding what is communicated.

RATIONALE FOR THE FOCUS ON THE KEY CONCEPTS AND TOOLS

Officers and practitioners involved in multicultural law enforcement need to be able to:

1. Summarize the historical background, demographics, and diversity within the Asian/Pacific American community in the United States

2. Discuss the implications of communication styles, group identification terms, myths and stereotypes, and family structure of Asian/Pacific Americans for law enforcement

3. Understand the impact of the extended family and community, gender roles, generational differences, adolescent and youth issues upon law enforcement contact

4. Highlight key law enforcement concerns and skills, resources, and practices for addressing some of these concerns

INTRODUCTION

Chapter 4 provides specific ethnic and cultural information on Asian Americans and Pacific Islanders. The label Asian Americans/Pacific Islanders encompasses over 40 different ethnic and cultural groups. For ease of use, we will use the shortened version Asian/Pacific Americans to refer to members of these ethnic groupings. Demographics and elements of diversity among Asian/Pacific Americans are presented, as well as issues related to ethnic and cultural identity. Aspects of the Asian/Pacific American family are discussed, including myths and stereotypes, assimilation and acculturation processes, the extended family and community, gender roles, generational differences, and adolescent and youth issues. The text section "Cultural Influences on Communication" discusses the subtle aspects of nonverbal and indirect communications that peace officers (and others in similar public service roles like firefighters, emergency medical technicians, 911 personnel, probation staff) often find troublesome. Several key issues for law enforcement are discussed: underreporting of crimes, differential treatment, increasing Asian/Pacific American community police services, increasing the number of Asian/Pacific peace officers, and the rise in crimes within the Asian/Pacific community.

KEY CONCEPTS

Outline of Key Presentation Points

1. Asian/Pacific American Overview
2. Asian/Pacific Americans Defined
3. 40 Ethnic and Cultural Groups
4. Definition of Refugees

5. Definition of Immigrants

6. Immigration to the United States

7. Anti-Asian Federal, State and Local Laws

8. *People* v. *Hall*: California Supreme Court in 1854

9. Executive Order 9066 in 1942: Japanese American Internment

10. Demographics of Asian/Pacific Americans

11. Key Motivating Perspectives of Asian/Pacific Americans

12. Labels and Terms

13. Myths and Stereotypes

14. Asian/Pacific American Family

15. Children, Adolescents, and Youths

16. Asian/Pacific American Family Violence

17. Asian/Pacific American Verbal and Nonverbal Styles

18. Positive Collaborations with Law Enforcement

19. Increasing Police Services and Community Relationships

PRACTICE QUESTIONS

True or False

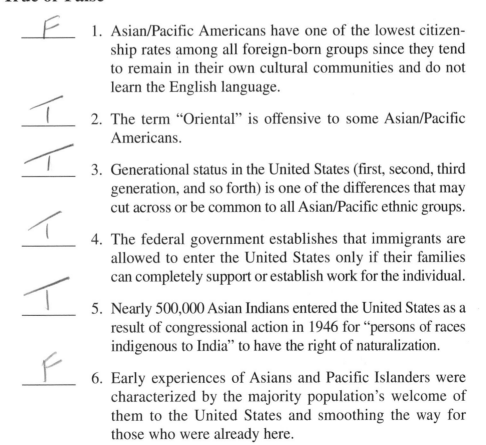

__F__ 1. Asian/Pacific Americans have one of the lowest citizenship rates among all foreign-born groups since they tend to remain in their own cultural communities and do not learn the English language.

__T__ 2. The term "Oriental" is offensive to some Asian/Pacific Americans.

__T__ 3. Generational status in the United States (first, second, third generation, and so forth) is one of the differences that may cut across or be common to all Asian/Pacific ethnic groups.

__T__ 4. The federal government establishes that immigrants are allowed to enter the United States only if their families can completely support or establish work for the individual.

__T__ 5. Nearly 500,000 Asian Indians entered the United States as a result of congressional action in 1946 for "persons of races indigenous to India" to have the right of naturalization.

__F__ 6. Early experiences of Asians and Pacific Islanders were characterized by the majority population's welcome of them to the United States and smoothing the way for those who were already here.

_____ T 7. The Japanese Government did not want a "loss of face" or of international prestige through having its people "banned" from immigrating to the United States and so the "Gentleman's Agreement" was negotiated, which vo luntarily restricted the immigration of Japanese laborers to the United States.

_____ F 8. Congressional resolutions in 1935 reflected clear pro-Pilipino sentiment by providing free, one-way passage for Pilipinos to return to the Philippines to reunite with their families.

_____ T 9. To plan for the changing Asian/Pacific American population base it is critical to recruit and develop officers from the Pilipino, Vietnamese, and Asian Indian communities.

_____ T 10. Song (1996), in his research in Asian/Pacific American communities, found that 70 percent of the battered women indicated that they did not know about community services that could have helped them.

Multiple Choice

1. The population growth of Asian/Pacific Americans can be attributed to:

    a. Higher immigration from the Pacific Rim countries

    b. Greater longevity and higher birth rates

    c. More immigrants admitted for special skills and expertise for work in high-technology industries in the United States

    d. All of the above

2. Which one of the following ethnic and cultural groups is *not* part of the Asian/Pacific American category?

    a. Bhutanese

    b. Hawaiian (or Native Hawaiian)

    c. Sri Lankan (formerly Ceylonese)

    d. Moroccan

3. Although many ethnic groups have come in under the sponsorship of the federal government with refugee or émigré status, the largest numbers have come from:

    a. Afghanistan, as a result of the efforts to rid the country of al Qaida

    b. Southeast Asia, as a result of the past upheaval brought on by the Vietnam War refugees

    c. North Korea, as a result of the political prisoners escaping from Communism

    d. Mainland China, as a result of those persecuted for their religious and political beliefs

4. Being a "good refugee" means:

    a. Participating only in Federal public service and federally subsidized programs

    b. Participating only in the Federal food-stamp and State job-training programs

    c. Avoiding any participation in public service programs

    d. Requesting and participating actively in all local, state, and federal entitlement programs

5. Being a "good immigrant" means:

    a. Participating only in Federal public service and Federal subsidized programs

    b. Participating only in the Federal food-stamp and State job-training programs

    c. Avoiding any participation in public service programs

    d. Requesting and participating actively in all local, state, and federal entitlement programs

6. The Immigration Act of 1917 banned immigration from all countries in the Pacific Rim except for:

    a. The Philippines (a U.S. territory)

    b. India and Pakistan (a source of highly trained and skilled workers needed by the U.S.)

    c. Taiwan (an ally of the U.S.)

    d. Okinawa (a strategic partner and the keystone of the Pacific)

7. According to Prashad (2001), what was the percent of the Asian Indians (between 1966 and 1977) who immigrated to the U.S. under the category of professional and technical workers who were scientists with Ph.D.s and/or engineering degrees?

    a. Less than 10 percent
    b. 33 percent
    c. 69 percent
    d. 83 percent

8. In the case of *People* v. *Hall* heard in the California Supreme Court in 1854, Hall, a white defendant, had been convicted of murdering a Chinese man on the basis of testimony provided by one white and three Chinese witnesses. The California Supreme Court:

    a. Sentenced Hall to life imprisonment at Alcatraz
    b. Gave Hall the death penalty and sent him to the electric chair at San Quentin
    c. Threw out Hall's conviction on the basis that state law prohibited blacks, mulattos, or Indians from testifying in favor of or against whites in court
    d. None of the above

9. Which state in the U.S. and which U.S. city have the largest Hmong populations in the country?

    a. Texas and New York City, NY
    b. California and New Orleans, LA
    c. Minnesota and Fresno, CA
    d. Florida and Tucson, AZ

10. Which one of the following cases or situations are positive examples of collaborative and cooperative efforts among the law enforcement, criminal justice, and community advocacy systems and the Asian and Pacific American communities?

    a. Mark Anthony Lewis rape case in Chicago, IL
    b. Asian/Pacific American bilingual community service officers (CSOs), nonsworn officers with badges and uniforms who serve the Southeast Asian communities in San Diego, CA
    c. Storefront outreach community-policing locations in Boston, MA
    d. All of the above

Fill-in-the-Blanks

1. For the past four decades, the Asian/Pacific American population has experienced the largest proportional increases of any ethnic minority population in the United States (over 100 percent growth for the decades from 1960 to 1990 and _76 percent_ growth for the decade from 1990 to 2000).

2. The term Asian/Pacific Americans is actually a contraction of two terms, Asian Americans and _Pacific Island_ peoples.

3. Whether one is from the Central Asian nation of Uzbekistan, the Southeast Asian nation of Vietnam, or the Pacific Island nation of Micronesia, the demographic variable of ethnicity, if one were _Chinese_, may be a more important identifier than that of "national origin" for some persons or groups.

4. The four largest countries in the world with Muslim populations are in South Asia; they are _____ (Glasse and Smith, 2003).   *Indonesia Pakistan Bangladesh India*

5. The first Asians to arrive in the United States in sizable numbers were the Chinese in the 1840s to work on the plantations in _Hawaii_.

6. The need for engineering and scientific expertise and skills by _high-tech_ companies resulted in many Asian/Pacific immigrants (under special work visas) immigrating to the U.S. in the late 1990s and early 2000s.

7. Since the 1970s, Asian/Pacific American immigration has made up over ___40___ percent of all immigration to the United States (U.S. Bureau of the Census, 2002).

8. Asian/Pacific Americans of the _second generation_ tend to be those we picture when we hear the term "Asian American." This group works very hard at being assimilated into the mainstream, adjusting and changing to be a part of mainstream America.

9. _Latch key_ children within an Asian/Pacific American home are common, especially for families that cannot afford external child care.

10. Asian/Pacific Americans tend to be _high context_ in communication style, which means that the officer needs to provide both i n t e rpersonal and situational contexts for effective communications.

Discussion

1. Discuss how the definition of Asian/Pacific Americans as a group is one of an ever-emerging ethnic mosaic of diverse constituencies in which groups are added and removed based on self-definition and needs for self-choice. What impact does this definition have for law enforcement in Asian/Pacific American communities?

2. Discuss how some of the differences that cut across all Asian/Pacific American groups (e.g., area of residence, degree of acculturation, education, etc.) may affect law enforcement within the Asian/Pacific American communities. What are some of the most prominent differences seen in the Asian/Pacific American communities in your local area?

3. Discuss how understanding some of these key motivating perspectives (Typology of Asian/Pacific Americans, text Exhibit 5.5) might help law enforcement officers to better understand the behaviors exhibited by citizens from these groupings. How would law enforcement agencies utilize the Typology of Asian/Pacific Americans in training their officers for services to those communities?

4. Discuss the impact that stereotypes have had for Asian/Pacific Americans in law enforcement. Provide examples of how stereotypes have affected Asian/Pacific Americans in law enforcement situations, and suggest approaches to help law enforcement officers avoid such stereotypes in their work in Asian/Pacific American communities.

5. Highlight some of the key communication elements that law enforcement officers might encounter when working in Asian/Pacific American communities. Discuss and summarize ways to enhance and enable better communications between Asian/Pacific Americans and law enforcement within these community situations.

TOOLS AND SKILLS IN PRACTICE

1. *Increasing Demographic Understanding of the Asian/Pacific American Communities*—Law enforcement officers need to be able to obtain demographic information and background data on the Asian/Pacific Americans in the communities that they serve. There are several ways to obtain this information:

   a. City, County, Region, and/or State Websites: Go to the websites for the municipalities that are of interest to you and use search terms like "Asian," "Asian Americans," "Pacific Islanders," and any of the specific groups large in number in your community (e.g., "Chinese," "Vietnamese," "Korean," "South Asians," etc.).

   b. Use the U.S. Census Website and Reports: Go to http://www.census.gov and search for information using the search terms provided above for Asian/Pacific Americans.

WHAT ARE YOUR THOUGHTS AND WHAT WOULD YOU DO?

Your department has wisely adjusted to changing times by hiring a bilingual dispatcher to handle the increasing number of Korean-speaking calls for law-enforcement help. Though Koreans comprise approximately 8 percent of the city's population, they comprise 25 percent of the city's crime victims and calls for emergency services. With a significant number of those Korean elderly and immigrant residents unable to speak English, that means many people who need to contact the police also need help to communicate with the police in emergency situations where timely responses can make the difference between life and death. Several of the officers of your station said that this was giving the Korean community "preferential treatment." They said that the 24-hour AT&T translator phone service could have solved the language problem for the Korean community. Besides, they said that the Korean elderly and immigrants should learn English since they have been in the neighborhood for over a decade. What are your thoughts and what would you do?

Critical Thinking Questions

1. What are the facts (observable, verifiable, testable, and confirmable)?

2. What are the assumptions?

3. What are the possible stereotypes?

4. What would be your *personal* reactions to this situation?

5. What would be the possible *Korean elderlys'* reactions to this situation?

6. Would someone from the Korean and Asian/Pacific American community see something different? What would they see differently (if applicable)?

7. What would be your *professional* reactions to this situation?

8. What actions would you take in this situation?

9. If you had to explain your actions to the Korean and Asian/Pacific American community, the AT&T Language Line Representatives, the City's Human Rights Commission, and your superiors in front of the news media, what would you say?

---

c. Use the "Asian Week" Consolidated Report on Asian/Pacific Americans Based on the 2000 Census Data: Go to http://www.AsianWeek.com and search for information using the search terms provided above for Asian/Pacific Americans. Use the publication, *The New Face of Asian Pacific America: Numbers, Diversity and Change in the 21st Century.*

d. Use Search Engines: Use search engines like "Google" or "Yahoo" and enter the search terms "population" and the name of your city, county, region, and/or state.

e. Ask for References from Your Local or College Librarian: The head librarian in your city or college campus would be able to direct you to the sources of demographic data on file or which are in reports on Asian/Pacific Americans.

f. Ask for References from the Branch Public Library Nearest the Asian/Pacific American Community in Your Area: The head librarian in your branch public library (nearest to an Asian/Pacific American community) would be able to direct you to the sources of demographic data on file or in reports on Asian/Pacific Americans.

2. *Identifying Key Ethnic/Cultural Groups and Community Leaders—* Knowing the key Asian/Pacific American groups in one's service area and the community leaders of these groups is critical toward understanding the Asian/Pacific American resources of your area. Four ways to obtain this information are:

a. Use the On-line Information from the Key Newspapers of Your Area: Search the on-line news sources of your local area on Asian/Pacific American groups, issues, and leaders on an ongoing basis. Keep a journal of the groups, issues, and leaders that emerge, as well as the other members and/or representatives named in the news articles.

b. Search "LexisNexis Academic" On-line in Your College Library: Search the "Regional" and the "City" specific news sources for your local area for the prior year using the search terms of the Asian/Pacific American groups and the name of your city or area of interest. Keep a journal of your findings.

c. Use the On-line Information from the Key Asian/Pacific American Newspapers of Your Area (if available): Search the on-line Asian/Pacific American news sources of your local area on Asian/Pacific American groups, issues, and leaders on an ongoing basis. If there are no online services available from the key Asian/Pacific American news sources, ask your local college librarian to obtain a subscription (which may be free in some cases). Keep a journal of the groups, issues, and leaders that emerge, as well as the other members and/or representatives named in the news articles.

d. Use the On-line Information from the College and University Newspapers of Your Area: Search the on-line news sources of the college and university newspapers in your area on Asian/Pacific American groups, issues, and leaders on an ongoing basis. As a result of the interest and community involvement of university and colleges in multicultural topics and concerns, many important issues, events, and people are reported in the local college and university newspapers (that may not be covered in the main-stream news media). Keep a journal of the community groups, issues, and leaders that emerge, as well as the other staff members and/or representatives of the community agencies named in the news articles.

3. *Scanning for Police and Asian/Pacific American Community Issues*—Three approaches are suggested:

   a. For a national and regional perspective, go to the following websites: (1) http://www.aaldef.org—this website provides information about civil rights issues with Asian/Pacific Americans and highlights issues of immigration, family law, government benefits, anti-Asian violence and police misconduct, employment discrimination, labor rights, and workplace issues, and (2) http://www.napalc.org—this website provides a national network of information about legal and civil rights issues affecting Asian/Pacific Americans in terms of litigation, advocacy, public education, and public policy.

   b. For your city or area of interest, go to the on-line reports for the: (a) "Police Commission," (b) "Public Safety Commission," and/or (c) "Emergency Services Commission." Scan the Minutes of the meetings for law enforcement and other public safety issues identified for the Asian/Pacific American community. Note any recurring issues or trends. If on-line services are not available in your area, go the Town Hall or City Hall and read the past Minutes of the above-noted Commissions for the last six months to one year; the Minutes of the Police Commission and other meetings are usually open to the public.

   c. Use the on-line information from the key Asian/Pacific American newspapers of your area (if available): Search the on-line Asian/Pacific American news sources for Police and Asian/Pacific American Community Issues on an ongoing basis. If there are no online services available from the key Asian/Pacific American news sources, ask your local college librarian to obtain a subscription (which may be free in some cases). Keep a journal of the Police and Asian/Pacific American Community Issues that emerge, as well as the people, agencies, leaders, and/or representatives named in the news articles.

4. *Developing Asian/Pacific American Community Partnerships*— Once you begin to get a sense of the different groups in your community and the key leaders of those groups, it would be important to get information on the kinds of services these communities may need by accessing information through the different Asian/Pacific American community resource guides. Go on-line or in person to obtain some of the community resource guides available in your local area. Depending upon the size of the Asian/Pacific American population of your community, some of these resources might focus on the groups as a whole (e.g., Asian Legal Services), children (e.g., Southeast Asian Head Start), elderly (e.g., Korean Community Senior Meals Program), people with disabilities, and so forth.

Review these resource guides to identify the needs of these groups, and make a list of the needs. Brainstorm some ways that the local law enforcement agencies might be able to form community partnerships with these Asian/Pacific American community-based agencies to address the needs that you have identified through the review of the materials and guides.

5. *Improving Law Enforcement Relations in Asian/Pacific American Communities*—Begin building a file in your computer or on 3 × 5 index cards (or in a "blank book" journal). On a daily basis, as you observe in your work, in the news, or in any other sources, note interactions of law enforcement with aspects of the Asian/Pacific American community that are going well and those that could have gone better. For specific law enforcement issues among Asian/Pacific American Officers, log on to the website for the National Asian Peace Officers Association: http://www.napoa.org/—this website provides information to promote the interests of Asian/Pacific American peace officers on community issues, career development and o p p o rtunities, education and workshops, and awareness about the Asian culture. For those interactions that have gone well, identify the key elements and/or aspects that made it go well. For those interactions that could have gone better, brainstorm about ways that the situation could have been improved. What could have been done differently to attain a better outcome? Soon, your file will c o ntain many useful ideas for improving law enforcement services in the Asian/Pacific American communities.

SELF-STUDY ACTIVITIES

Law Enforcement as Not User-Friendly to Asian/Pacific Americans

Using the information that you have gathered using the Tools and Skills #3 in this chapter (Scanning for Police and Asian/Pacifc American Community Issues), did you find any anti-Asian/Pacific American incidents and/or events which may leave Asian/Pacific Americans with the view that law enforcement agencies are not user-friendly? What are the implications of this view for law enforcement? What are ways to improve such possible negative points of view?

Diversity among Asian/Pacific Americans

As noted earlier in this chapter, the Asian/Pacific American category comprises over 40 diverse ethnic and cultural groups. From your findings using the Tools and Skills #1 in this chapter (Increasing Demographic Understanding of the Asian/Pacific American Communities), which groups are you most likely to encounter in crime-fighting and peacekeeping in your community or area of interest? Which groups do you anticipate encountering in your future work?

Asian/Pacific American Group Differences and Law Enforcement

A typology for understanding motives for some of the behaviors of Asian/ Pacific American people (in terms of their generational and immigration status in the United States) is provided in this section. From your findings using the Tools and Skills #1 in this chapter (Increasing Demographic Understanding of the Asian/Pacific American Communities), which groups in your area might be victims of burglaries, house robberies, and gangs?

Effects of Myths and Stereotypes

As noted in the text in this chapter, myths and stereotypes about Asian/Pacific Americans have greatly affected this group. Using the information that you have gathered using the Tools and Skills #3 in this chapter (Scanning for Police and Asian/Pacific American Community Issues), did you find any issues about the effects of Asian/Pacific American stereotypes? What effects would these stereotypes have on Asian/Pacific Americans? What are ways to manage these stereotypes in law enforcement? How might your awareness of Asian/Pacific American stereotypes be helpful in an interview with an Asian/Pacific American about homeland security issues?

Verbal and Nonverbal Variations among Cultures

Using the information that you have gathered using the Tools and Skills #5 in this chapter (Improving Law Enforcement Relations in Asian/Pacific American Communities), did you discover any strategies and approaches about verbal and nonverbal communication styles that could help officers in their approach to Asian/Pacific American citizens? When you can understand the cultural components of the behaviors, does this help you to become more sensitive and objective about your reactions?

Chapter 6

Law Enforcement Contact with African Americans

OVERVIEW

The experience of slavery and racism, as well as cultural differences, have shaped African American culture. Patterns of culture and communication among African Americans differ from those among white Americans and other racial/ethnic groups. In face-to-face communication, officers should not ignore or downplay these differences.

For many African Americans, particularly those in the lower socioeconomic classes, the history of slavery and later discrimination continue to leave psychological scars. Law enforcement officials, in particular, represent a system that has oppressed African Americans. To protect and serve in many African American communities across the nation necessarily means that officers will need to go out of their way to establish trust and win cooperation.

There is tremendous diversity among African Americans, including socioeconomic status, religion, region of the country (rural or urban area), and country of origin. Color and race, however, often determine how the larger society will react to and treat African Americans. Therefore, the racial (as opposed to the cultural) experience of many African Americans is similar.

The changing terms that African Americans have used to refer to themselves reflect stages of racial and cultural growth, as well as empowerment. Officers should respect the terms that African Americans prefer to use. "Negro" and "colored" are no longer used and have been replaced by "African American" in many police communications. Officers can learn to become comfortable asking a citizen which term he or she prefers if there is a need to refer to ethnicity in the conversation. Officers are advised to stop each other when they hear offensive terms being used. Doing so not only contributes to making a department free of overt prejudices but also helps the individual officer to practice control when he or she is faced with volatile citizens.

African Americans react as negatively to stereotypes that they hear about themselves as officers do when they hear such statements as "Police officers are biased against blacks" and "All police officers are capable of brutality." Many of the stereotypes about African Americans stem from ignorance and the impression people receive from the criminal element. Law enforcement officers, in particular, must be sensitive to how their own perceptions of African Americans are formed.

The predominance of households headed by women, particularly in the inner city, coupled with the myth of a black matriarchy has created s i tuations in which officers have dismissed the importance of the father. Despite common myths and stereotypes regarding black women, officers should always approach both parents to get both versions of the story and to consider both opinions in decision-making.

Young African American males, in particular, and their parents (of all socioeconomic levels) feel a sense of outrage and injustice when officers stop them for no apparent reason. Officers will erode any possibility of establishing trust (and later winning cooperation) by stopping youths (and others) because it "looks like they don't belong in a given neighborhood." Every time an instance of racial profiling occurs, police–community and police–youth relations suffer. The use of Ebonics or African American Vernacular English (AAVE) does not represent any deficiency and is not a combination of random errors but rather reflects patterns of grammar from some West African languages. Officers should take care not to convey a lack of acceptance through disapproving facial expressions, a negative tone of voice, or a tendency to interrupt or finish the sentences for the other person. When it comes to "Ebonics," African American Vernacular English (AAVE), or an accent, police should not fake it to be accepted by the group. People will immediately pick up on this lack of sincerity, which in and of itself can create hostility.

People in positions of authority have often misunderstood aspects of black nonverbal communication, including what has been termed the "cool pose." Police officers may interpret certain ways of standing, walking, and dressing as defiant. This can create defensive reactions on the part of the police officer. In many cases, the police officer need not take this behavior personally or feel threatened by it.

Cultural differences in verbal communication can result in complete misinterpretation. Officers should not necessarily equate an African American's expression of rage and verbal threats with a loss of control that leads automatically to violence. Within cultural norms, it can be acceptable to be very expressive and emotional in speech. This is in contrast to an unspoken white mainstream norm, which discourages the open and free expression of emotion, especially anger.

Racial profiling, excessive force, and brutality still exist in policing in the United States. When acts of bias, brutality, and injustice occur, everyone suffers, including officers and entire police departments. Every officer should be on the lookout for unchecked biases within themselves and others that could result in inappropriate language or force with citizens of all backgrounds. They should be aware of their own levels of stress and frustration and have the means and support to release tension before it breaks loose in the streets.

In areas populated by African Americans and other racial and immigrant groups all over the United States, there is a need for increased and more effective police protection. The task of establishing rapport with African Americans at all levels of society is challenging because of what the officer represents in terms of past discrimination. Turning this image around involves a commitment on the part of the officer to break with embedded stereotypes and to have as a goal respect and professionalism in every encounter.

RATIONALE FOR THE FOCUS ON THE KEY CONCEPTS AND TOOLS

Officers and practitioners involved in multicultural law enforcement need to be able to:

1. Summarize the historical background, demographics, and diversity within the African American community in the United States

2. Discuss the implications for law enforcement of communication styles, group identification terms, myths and stereotypes, and family structure of African Americans for law enforcement

3. Understand the impact on law enforcement contact of the extended family and community, gender roles, single-mother families, and adolescent and youth issues

4. Highlight key law enforcement concerns and skills, resources, and practices for addressing some of these concerns

INTRODUCTION

Chapter 6 provides specific cultural and historical information on African Americans which both directly and indirectly affects the relationship between law enforcement officials and citizens. It presents information about demographics and diversity among African Americans as well as issues related to cultural and racial identity. Following the background information is a section on group identification terms and a discussion of myths and stereotypes. Aspects of the family are discussed, including the extended family, the roles of men and women, single-mother families, and adolescents. A section on cultural influences on communication deals with Ebonics (also known as Black English Vernacular), nonverbal and verbal communication, including emotionalism, fighting words, threats, and aggressive behavior. The closing section presents several key concerns for law enforcement, including information on differential treatment, racial profiling, perceptions of and reactions to legal authority, excessive force and brutality, police interaction in poor urban communities, the needs of the inner city, and issues related to women. The summary of the chapter reviews recommendations for improved communication and relationships between law enforcement officials and African Americans.

KEY CONCEPTS

Outline of Key Presentation Points

1. Historical Information
2. Law Enforcement Historical Baggage
3. Demographics of African Americans

4. Diversity among African Americans
5. Religious Background
6. Issues of Identity
7. Group Identification Terms
8. Racial Slurs and Epithets
9. Myths and Stereotypes
10. Viewed in Equal Terms?
11. Perceptions of Police Officers' Actions by Some Blacks
12. The Black Family
13. The Black Single Mother
14. Black Children and Youth
15. "Ebonics" or African American Vernacular English (AAVE)
16. Nonverbal Communication: Style and Stance
17. Black and White Styles in Conflict by Thomas Kochman
18. Threats and Aggressive Behaviors
19. Key Issues in Law Enforcement
20. Homicide Victimization Rates
21. National Urban League's Report: "State of Black America 2003"
22. Addressing the Needs
23. Key to Improved Police–Community Relationships

PRACTICE QUESTIONS

True or False

_____ T 1. Slavery led to a system of inferior housing, schools, health care, and jobs for black people, which persist to this day.

_____ T 2. Cities such as Detroit, Washington, D.C., St. Louis, Chicago, and Cleveland are populated in the majority by African Americans and other black populations.

_____ T 3. In the 1960s and 1970s the Civil Rights and Black Pride movements marked a new direction in black identity.

_____ F 4. African American culture is a matriarchy, with one or more women heading the typical household.

_____ F 5. In order to establish trust and rapport by the police within the African American community, white officers should try to imitate black accents, dialects, and styles of speaking. — pg 172

_____ F   6. Thomas Kochman explains in *Black and White Styles in Conflict* that blacks and whites have great similarities, perspectives, and approaches to many issues, including conversation, public speaking, and power.

_____ T   7. The results of a national survey entitled "Police Attitudes toward Abuse of Authority" showed race to be a divisive issue for American police.

_____ T   8. According to Hills and Trapp (2000), the U.S. Custom Service's own figures show that the "hit rates" for drugs and contraband searches for people of color were lower than for whites.

_____ F   9. In the Huo and Tyler (2000) study, all groups, including African Americans, were equally satisfied with their experiences in the court, and, as a result, there was compliance with court directives.

_____ T   10. According to the Bureau of Justice Statistics (2001), the vast majority of murders for both blacks and whites were intra-racial (i.e., blacks murder other blacks, and whites murder other whites).

Multiple Choice

1. Which of the following factors contribute(s) to the cultural diversity that exists among African Americans today?

    a. Over the last 400 years, black families have come from many different countries (e.g., Jamaica, Trinidad, Belize, Haiti, Puerto Rico, Africa)

    b. "Southern" and "northern" characteristics and differences

    c. Urban and rural characteristics and differences

    d. All of the above

2. One example of African culture that has influenced American black culture or is held in high esteem by many African Americans is (Walker, 1982):

    a. Gaining independence by generating economic resources and property

    b. Partnership with nature and with the spirit world reflected in the approach to ecology and in communication with the spirit world

    c. Focus on individual development and the importance of individual identity over group identity

    d. None of the above

3. Which one of the following statements is not a suggestion offered by Deputy Chief Berry of Reno, NV, for establishing rapport and trust with the single, African American mother?

    a. Proactively engage youth and encourage them to participate in organized social activities

    b. Give your business card to the mothers to show that you are available for further contact

    c. Avoid explaining to the mother her rights, as this might seem condescending to her

    d. Make follow-up visits when there are not problems so that the mother and the children can associate the officer with positive times

4. What is the term developed by Psychologist Richard Majors at the University of Wisconsin to indicate a certain stance and posturing demonstrated by many young black men from the inner city?

    a. "Dude stance"

    b. "Cool pose"

    c. "Ice man"

    d. "Soul stuff"

5. In the Public Policy Institute of California study by Huo and Tyler (2000), these two social scientists asked 1,500 residents of Los Angeles, CA, and Oakland, CA, about their reactions to legal authority. Which of the following is a finding of their study?

    a. Compared to whites, African Americans (and Latinos) report lower levels of satisfaction with their interactions with legal authorities

    b. Much of the difference between minorities and whites in their reactions to legal authorities can be accounted for by differences in their perceptions of how fairly or unfairly they were treated

    c. The perception of fair treatment and positive outcomes was the most important factor in forming reactions to encounters with the police and the courts

    d. All of the above

6. There have been many positive reactions within African American communities that have resulted from the implementation of consent decrees (Davis, 2002). Which of the following statements reflect the perspectives of the African American community on consent decrees?

    a. Consent decrees have given the community greater confidence in the police

    b. Consent decrees gave people an opportunity to feel as though they had a voice

    c. Consent decrees helped white and black officers to work better together

    d. All of the above

7. According to a 2003 ABC/Washington Post poll, what percent of African Americans think that they "receive as equal treatment as whites do from police"? (Sixty-six percent of whites believe that both groups are treated equally.)

    a. Less than 10 percent

    b. 13 percent

    c. 28 percent

    d. 51 percent

8. The National Urban League's report, the "State of Black America 2003," found that African Americans make up nearly half of the people in prison and that the incarceration disparities have been fueled by which of the following conditions?

    a. Drug enforcement policies have had harsher effects on blacks

    b. African Americans were 6 times more likely than whites to be murdered (primarily by another African American)

    c. Both "a" and "b"

    d. None of the above

9. The case of Yvette Bradley at Newark International Airport (April, 1999) is a widely publicized example in the context of searches and U.S. Customs. What happened in this case?

    a. Yvette Bradley was singled out to be strip-searched for no reason immediately apparent to her

    b. Yvette Bradley observed a disproportionately large percentage of black women being singled out for searches

    c. Yvette Bradley was strip searched (by a female officer), and the reason that was given had to do with the designer hat that she was wearing

    d. All of the above

10. Linda Hills, Executive Director, ACLU of San Diego and Imperial Counties, and Randa Trapp, President of the NAACP of San Diego, noted actions that an African American driver and a white driver might both do, but the likelihood of the African American driver being pulled over was far greater than that for the white driver. What were the actions described by Hill and Trapp?

    a. Worn tires slipping on a fresh layer of light rain

    b. Executing a perfect "California rolling stop" at an intersection

    c. Entering the freeway and accelerating to a comfortable 70 mph for the cruise into downtown

    d. All of the above

Fill-in-the-Blanks

1. The majority of African Americans or blacks (the terms will be used interchangeably) in the United States trace their roots to _West Africa_.

2. American police were called on to form _slave patrols_ and to enforce racially biased laws (Williams and Murphy, 1990).

3. _Race_, more so than class, often determines how the larger society reacts to and treats blacks; therefore, the racial (as opposed to cultural) experience of many African Americans in the United States is similar, regardless of an individual's level of prosperity or education.

4. Since there are so many African American homes, especially in the inner city, in which the father is absent, young boys in their middle childhood years between the ages of _7–11_ are at real risk for serious behavior problems and school is often where these behaviors show up.

5. Most language and dialect researchers accept the notion that Ebonics is a dialect with its own rules of grammar and structure (Labov, 1972). Linguists have done years of research on the origins of Ebonics and now believe that it developed from the grammatical structures common to several _West African tribal_ languages.

6. Many African Americans perceive that the mainstream culture is taught _to put down and to control_ their emotions. This is a cultural difference that can be misunderstood by law enforcement.

7. The year 1992, with the case of _Rodney King_, brought public attention to the fact that excessive force and brutality were serious problems in America.

8. Nearly a decade after the Rodney King event, in 1999, Americans and citizens worldwide witnessed another incident of brutality against a black American, _Abner Louima,_ a Haitian immigrant.

9. Authors of the National Urban League's report, the "State of Black America 2003," found that although "blacks make up about 12% of the nation's population, they account for nearly ___half___ of the people in prison."

10. Cross and Renner (1974) explain that the fear of _belittlement_ and fear of _danger_ operate for both the African American citizen and the officer, and these fears cause both sides to misinterpret what might otherwise be non-threatening behavior.

Discussion

1. Discuss whether the African American community's perceptions about law enforcement listed in Exhibit 6.2 in this chapter of the text are still valid today. Which of these perceptions apply to African American police relations in your local community?

2. Provide several examples of the methods inner city male youth may use to "display their manliness" as highlighted by Harvard Medical School psychiatrist, Dr. Alvin Poussaint (2000). Discuss suggestions for what law enforcement officers could do or say to improve rapport and communications with inner city male youth.

3. Discuss the implications of the following statements for law enforcement in the African American community: "When officers go out to make arrests, they'll go immediately into the inner city where they can find the 'lowest hanging fruit.' What I mean is . . . blacks are easy to identify—in the inner city they're standing out on the street and it's natural for officers to be suspicious and try to do their drug arrests there." Do you agree or disagree with the statements made? Do you see such police actions in your local community with African American and/or any other minority populations?

4. Discuss the merits and the problems associated with the use of "consent decrees" to bring about more positive relations between the police and the African American community. Provide an example of the use of "consent decrees" in your local area (or within your state). What were the results, positive and negative, that occurred in your example?

5. The authors noted that there is a perception and (in some cases) it is the reality, that the rape of an African American woman has not always been considered as serious by law enforcement as the rape of a white woman (either legally or psychologically). Discuss the African American interactions with law enforcement that might

> **WHAT ARE YOUR THOUGHTS AND WHAT WOULD YOU DO?**
>
> Your department has received a request for a meeting from community leaders because of the following incident: Around 9 a.m. Thursday, dozens of police officers entered an African American neighborhood grocery store with guns and rifles drawn to execute a search warrant for prescription drugs, such as ampicillin, amoxicillin, and naproxen. Police also took videotapes from the store's surveillance cameras. Employees of the store said they were made to put their hands in the air for 30 minutes while police searched the store with dogs. Employees at the store, including two pregnant women, said that they were made to lie on a concrete floor handcuffed. What are your thoughts and what would you do?
>
> **Critical Thinking Questions**
>
> 1. What are the facts (observable, verifiable, testable, and confirmable)?
> 2. What are the assumptions?
> 3. What are the possible stereotypes?
> 4. What would be your *personal* reactions to this situation?
> 5. What would be the possible *store owners' and store customers'* reactions to this situation?
> 6. Would someone from the African American community see something different? What would they see differently (if applicable)?
> 7. What would be your *professional* reactions to this situation?
> 8. What actions would you take in this situation?
> 9. If you had to explain your actions to the African American community, the store owners, the customers, and your superiors in front of the news media, what would you say?

have led to such perceptions. Brainstorm some ways that law enforcement officers might use to overcome these perceptions, and, in some cases, realities.

TOOLS AND SKILLS IN PRACTICE

1. *Increasing Demographic Understanding of the African American Communities*—Law enforcement officers need to be able to obtain demographic information and background data on the African Americans in the communities that they serve. There are several ways to obtain this information:

   a. City, County, Region, and/or State Websites: Go to the websites for the municipalities that you are interested and use search terms like "Blacks," "African Americans," "Minorities," and any of the specific groups large in number in your community (e.g., "Caribbean Blacks," etc.).

b. Use the U.S. Census Website and Reports: Go to http://www.census.gov and search for information using the search terms provided above for African Americans.

c. Use Search Engines: Use search engines like "Google" or "Yahoo" and enter the search terms "population" and the name of your city, county, region, and/or state.

d. Ask for References from Your Local or College Librarian: The head librarian in your city or on a college campus would be able to direct you to the sources of demographic data on file or within reports on African Americans.

e. Ask for References from the Branch Public Library Nearest the African American Community in Your Area: The head librarian in your branch public library nearest an African American community would be able to direct you to the sources of demographic data on file or within reports on African Americans.

2. *Identify Key Racial/Cultural Groups and Community Leaders—* Knowing the key African American groups in one's service area and the community leaders of these groups is critical to understanding the African American resources of your area. Four ways to obtain this information are:

a. Use the On-line Information from the Key Newspapers of Your Area: Search the on-line news sources of your local area on African American groups, issues, and leaders on an ongoing basis. Keep a journal of the groups, issues, and leaders that emerge, as well as the other community members and/or representatives named in the news articles.

b. Search "LexisNexis Academic" On-line in Your College Library: Search the "Regional" and the "City" specific news sources for your local area for the prior year using the search terms of the African American groups and the name of your city or area of interest. Keep a journal of your findings.

c. Use the On-line Information from the Key African American Newspapers of Your Area (if available): Search the on-line African American news sources of your local area on African American groups, issues, and leaders on an ongoing basis. If there are no online services available from the key African American news sources, ask your local college librarian to obtain a subscription (which may be free in some cases). Keep a journal of the groups, issues, and leaders that emerge, as well as the other community members and/or representatives named in the news articles.

d. Use the On-line Information from the College and University Newspapers of Your Area: Search the on-line news sources of the college and university newspapers in your area on African

American groups, issues, and leaders on an ongoing basis. As a result of the interest and community involvement of universities and colleges with respect to multicultural topics and concerns, many important community issues, and events are reported in the local college and university newspapers (that may not be covered in the mainstream news media). Keep a journal of the groups, issues, and leaders that emerge, as well as the other members and/or representatives named in the news articles.

3. *Scanning for Police and African American Community Issues—*
   Three approaches are suggested:

   a. For a national and regional perspective, go to the following websites: (1) http://www.aclu.org—this website contains multiple locations for information about many issues including racial profiling and (2) http://www.naacp.org and http://www.naacpldf.org—these two related websites contain multiple locations for information about many African American community and law enforcement issues, including racial profiling.

   b. For your city or area of interest, go the on-line reports for the: (a) "Police Commission," (b) "Public Safety Commission," and/or (c) "Emergency Services Commission." Scan the Minutes of the meetings for law enforcement and other public safety issues identified for the African American community. Note any recurring issues or trends. If on-line services are not available in your area, go the Town Hall or City Hall and read the past Minutes of the above-noted Commissions for the last six months to one year; the Minutes of the Police Commission and other meetings are usually open to the public.

   c. Use the on-line information from the key African American newspapers of your area (if available): Search the on-line African American news sources for Police and African American Community Issues on an ongoing basis. If there are no online services available from the key African American news sources, ask your local college librarian to obtain a subscription (which may be free in some cases). Keep a journal of the Police and African American Community Issues that emerge, as well as the people, agencies, leaders, and/or representatives named in the news articles.

4. *Developing African American Community Partnerships—*Once you begin to get a sense of the different groups in your community and the key leaders of those groups, it would be important to get information on the kinds of services these communities may need by accessing information through the different African American community resource guides. Go on-line or in person to obtain some of the community resource guides available in your local area. Depending upon

the size of the African American population of your community, some of these resources might focus on the groups as a whole (e.g., Legal Services), children (e.g., Preschool Program), elderly (e.g., Senior Meals Program), people with disabilities, and so forth. Review these resource guides to identify the needs of these groups, and make a list of the needs. Brainstorm some ways that the local law enforcement agencies might be able to form community partnerships with these African American community-based agencies to address the needs that you have identified through the review of the materials and guides.

5. *Improving Law Enforcement Relations in African American Communities*—Begin building a file in your computer or on 3 × 5 index cards (or in a "blank book" journal). On a daily basis, as you observe in your work, in the news, or in any other sources, note interactions of law enforcement with aspects of the African American community that are going well and those that could have gone better. For the African American law enforcement officers' and criminal justice professionals' perspectives, log on to the two websites:

a. National Organization of Black Law Enforcement (NOBLE): http://www.noblenatl.org—this website provides information on the public-service organization itself and its involvement in issues of interest and concern to law enforcement and the black community. It is the source of information on many subjects including recommended policy and procedures. It provides information on NOBLE activities such as community outreach and professional development. What does NOBLE say about aspects of the African American community that are going well and those that could have gone better in the law enforcement areas?

b. National Association of Black Criminal Justice (NABCJ): http://www.nabcj.org—this website provides information on the organization itself (e.g., member chapters and events) as well as on issues on improving law enforcement. NABCJ seeks to focus attention on relevant legislation, law enforcement, prosecution, and defense-related needs and practices, with emphasis on the courts, corrections, and the prevention of crime. Among its chief concerns is the general welfare and increased influence of African Americans and people of color as it relates to the administration of justice. What does NABCJ say about aspects of the African American community that are going well and those that could have gone better in the criminal justice areas?

For those aspects that have gone well, identify the key elements that made them go well. For those aspects and interactions that could have gone better, brainstorm about ways that the situation could have improved. What could have been done differently to attain a better outcome? Soon, your file will contain many useful ideas for improving law enforcement services in the African American communities.

SELF-STUDY ACTIVITIES

Racism: Effects on Blacks and Whites

Under "Historical Information" in this text chapter, the authors state that the fact of African Americans having been slaves in this country has created great psychological and social problems for blacks and whites for generations to come. From your findings using the Tools and Skills #3 (Scanning for Police and African American Community Issues), did any racism issues emerge from your findings? If so, what are the implications for law enforcement?

"Cool Pose" and the Use of Threats

This chapter of the text provided information about threats, emotional expression (including rage), and the "cool pose" for African American youth. From your findings using the Tools and Skills #5 (Improving Law Enforcement Relations in African American Communities), were there any key findings or suggestions regarding these communication issues with some African American youth? From your findings, describe how an officer would communicate if he or she did not feel threatened by such behavior. Describe how an officer might approach and interact with the citizen if he or she was threatened by the behavior.

When Officers Try to Make a Difference

Many young African American children, especially in housing projects in inner cities, live without a father in the household. This means that they do not have a second authority figure as a role model and are, consequently, deprived of an important source of adult support. No one can take the place of a missing parent, but there are small and large things a police officer can do to at least make an impression in the life of a child. From your findings using the Tools and Skills #5 (Improving Law Enforcement Relations in African American Communities), were there any findings or suggestions regarding actions officers can take to demonstrate their caring of children in these environments? Summarize briefly the kinds of actions, no matter how small.

Racial Profiling

Every criminal justice, policy academy student, and law enforcement representative needs to look closely at instances of racial profiling, study them, and learn from previous officers' mistakes. From your findings using the Tools and Skills #5 (Improving Law Enforcement Relations in African American Communities), were there any key findings or suggestions regarding racial profiling? From your findings, were there perspectives that might be different based upon whether the officer involved were or were not African American? What differences in perspectives did you find?

Chapter 7

Law Enforcement Contact
with Latino/Hispanic Americans

OVERVIEW

The experience of Latino/Hispanic Americans with law enforcement officers in the United States has been complicated (1) by the perceptions of Latino/Hispanic Americans regarding the enforcement of immigration laws against illegal aliens and by the discriminatory treatment received by Latino/Hispanic Americans in the United States and (2) by community conflicts, as well as perceptions of police ineffectiveness and unresponsiveness. Officers should realize that some citizens may still remember this h i story and carry with them stereotypes of police services as something to be feared and avoided. Law enforcement officials need to go out of their way to establish trust, to provide outreach efforts, and to win cooperation in order to effectively accomplish their goals to serve and protect Latino/Hispanic Americans. Building partnerships focused on community collaboration in the fight against crime is important.

The label Latino/Hispanic Americans encompasses over 25 very diverse ethnic, cultural, and regional groups from North, Central, and South America, as well as the Caribbean. Law enforcement officials need to be aware of the differences among the diverse groups (e.g., nationality, native cultural and regional differences and perceptions, and language dialects), as well as the within-group differences that may result from individual life experiences (e.g., sociopolitical turmoil). Since key stereotypes of Latino/Hispanic Americans by mainstream Americans are regarded as more negative than positive, it is important that peace officers make a special effort to extend respect and dignity to this community of very proud people with a culturally rich heritage.

Many Latino/Hispanic Americans are concerned with their ability to communicate clearly and about possible reprisal from the police, as associated with the role of law enforcement in more politically repressive countries. Peace officers need to take the time needed to understand communications and need to be aware that bilingual and non-native English speakers want to communicate effectively with them. Maintaining contact, providing extra time, using translators, and being patient with speakers—these actions all encourage citizens to communicate their concerns. Cultural differences in verbal and nonverbal communication often result in misinterpretation of the message and of behaviors. Officers need to be aware of the nonverbal aspects of some Latino/Hispanic Americans' communication styles, such as eye contact, touch, gestures, and emotionality. Verbal aspects such as accent, mixing English with Spanish, limited vocabulary, and incorrect grammar may give the officer the impression that the individual does not understand what is communicated. As in all cases when English is the second language, it is important to remember that listening and comprehension skills with English are usually better than speaking skills.

Latino/Hispanic Americans, because of their past experiences with law enforcement agencies, along with their own concerns about privacy, self-help, and other factors, are reluctant to report crimes and may not seek police assistance and help. It is important for law enforcement departments and officials to build relationships and working partnerships with Latino/Hispanic American communities. This is helped by outreach efforts such as community offices, bilingual officers, and participation of officers in community activities.

Latino/Hispanic Americans tend to hold a severe, punishment-oriented perception of law enforcement and corrections; that is, citizens have strong authoritarian views and an equally strong sense of "rightness" and of punishing the criminal. Because of this perspective, members from this community may view law enforcement as more severe than it really is. It is important for law enforcement departments and officials to be aware of this and to approach Latino/Hispanic Americans with the knowledge that they may perceive law enforcement as more punitive than it is in actuality.

RATIONALE FOR THE FOCUS
ON THE KEY CONCEPTS AND TOOLS

Officers and practitioners involved in multicultural law enforcement need to be able to:

1. Summarize the historical background, demographics, and diversity within the Latino/Hispanic American community in the United States

2. Discuss the implications for law enforcement of communication styles, group identification terms, myths and stereotypes, and family structure of Latino/ Hispanic Americans

3. Understand the impact on law enforcement contact of the extended family and community, gender roles, generational differences, and adolescent and youth issues

4. Highlight key law enforcement concerns and skills, resources, and practices for addressing some of these concerns

INTRODUCTION

Chapter 7 provides specific ethnic and cultural information on Latino/Hispanic Americans. The label Latino/Hispanic Americans encompasses over 25 different ethnic and cultural groups from Central and South America and the Caribbean. For ease of use, we will use the term Latino/Hispanic Americans to refer to members of these ethnic groupings. We first define this highly diverse group and then provide an historical overview that will contribute to readers' understanding of the relationship between law enforcement personnel and Latino/Hispanic American citizens. We present demographics and elements of diversity among Latino/Hispanic Americans, as well as issues related to ethnic and cultural identity: myths and stereotypes, the extended family and community, gender roles, generational differences, and adolescent and youth issues. The section "Cultural Influences on Communication" introduces the subtle aspects of nonverbal and indirect communications that law enforcement and other related personnel (e.g., 911 dispatchers, emergency medical technicians, criminal justice staff) often find challenging in their interactions with Latino/Hispanic Americans. We present, in the closing section, several key issues for law enforcement: under-reporting of crimes, victimization, differential treatment, racial profiling of Latino/Hispanic Americans, attitudes toward crime and safety, exposure to environmental risks and job hazards, and increasing police services to the Latino/Hispanic American community. Finally, we review recommendations for improved communication and relationships between law enforcement personnel and members of Latino/Hispanic American communities.

KEY CONCEPTS

Outline of Key Presentation Points

1. Over 25 Ethnic and Cultural Groups
2. Hispanic: A Generic Term
3. Federal Standards in 2003
4. Historical Background
5. Demographics
6. Labels and Terms
7. Myths and Stereotypes of Latino/Hispanic Americans
8. Latino/Hispanic American Family
9. Traditional Roles of the Man and the Woman
10. Children, Adolescents, and Youth
11. Cross-National Family Issues
12. Verbal and Nonverbal Styles of Latino/Hispanic Americans
13. Under-Reporting of Crime
14. Crime Victimization Rates
15. Differential Treatment
16. Racial Profiling of Latino/Hispanic Americans
17. Other Law Enforcement Issues and Concerns
18. Increasing Police Services

PRACTICE QUESTIONS

True or False

___T___ 1. "Hispanic" is a generic term referring to all Spanish-surname and Spanish-speaking people who reside in the United States and in Puerto Rico (a Commonwealth).

___F___ 2. "Chicano" refers specifically to Brazilian and Argentinean Americans, and it is used primarily on the West Coast, in the Southwest, and in the Midwest, as well in college communities across the United States that provide an ethnic studies curriculum.

___T___ 3. It makes little sense for many Mexican Americans to be stereotyped as "illegal aliens," especially since more than a million Mexican Americans (some of whom are U.S. citizens and some of whom are not) can trace their ancestry back to families living in the southwestern United States in the mid-1800s.

___T___ 4. The Latino/Hispanic American population numbers about 32.8 million and represents 12.0 percent of the U.S. population (not including the 3.9 million people who live in Puerto Rico).

___F___ 5. The Latino/Hispanic American population tends to be older than the general U.S. population.

___T___ 6. Prior to 1948 many Latino/Hispanic American children were denied access to the educational system available to others and instead were relegated to "Mexican" schools.

___T___ 7. Many Latino/Hispanic Americans have been in the United States for six generations or more, and English is the only language that they speak and write.

___F___ 8. Traditionally, the role of the father in a Latino/Hispanic American family has been that of the disciplinarian, decision-maker, and head of the household.

___T___ 9. The use of children and family members as translators is viewed as professionally and culturally inappropriate.

___T___ 10. As illustrated in the custody case of nine-year-old Elian Gonzalez (Lewis, 2000), today's law enforcement personnel may often have to intervene in Latino/Hispanic American family and domestic disputes involving cross-national political situations in community peacekeeping assignments.

Multiple Choice

1. Growth of Latino/Hispanic populations in all urban and rural areas of the United States has been striking, with half of all Latino/Hispanic Americans living in which two states in the United States?
    a. Arizona and Texas
    b. Texas and California
    c. California and New York
    d. Florida and Texas

2. The population growth of Latino/Hispanic Americans can be attributed to:
    a. Higher birthrates
    b. Higher immigration from Mexico, Central and South America, and the Caribbean
    c. Greater longevity because this is a relatively young population
    d. All of the above

3. Which of the following statements summarizes the objections to the use of the term "Hispanic"?
    a. Hispanic is not derived from any culture or place (i.e., there is no such place as "Hispania")
    b. The term was primarily invented for use by the U.S. Census Bureau
    c. Both "a" and "b"
    d. None of the above

4. The Mexican-American War ended in 1848 with the signing of the Treaty of Guadalupe Hidalgo. What amount was given by the United States to Mexico for the land that is now Texas, New Mexico, Arizona, and California, with more than 100,000 Mexican people living in those areas at the time?
    a. $5 million
    b. $15 million
    c. $50 million
    d. $500 million

5. Which of the following are stereotypes that have affected Latino/Hispanic Americans in law enforcement?
    a. Viewing Latino/Hispanic Americans as "illegal aliens"
    b. Viewing Latino/Hispanic Americans as lazy and as poor workers
    c. Perceiving Latino/Hispanic Americans as uneducated and uninterested in educational pursuits
    d. All of the above

6. Traditional Latino/Hispanic American sex roles can be discussed in the context of the two codes of gender-related behaviors:

    a. *Respecto* and *La familia*

    b. *Compadrazgo* and *Personalismo*

    c. *Machismo* and *Marianismo*

    d. None of the above

7. Which of the following situations were identified in the chapter to cause misunderstanding leading to perceptions of poor community services from police agencies as a result of style differences in c o mmunication between police and Latino/Hispanic Americans?

    a. Lack of the use of "I" statements and/or self-reference

    b. Lack of eye contact

    c. Speaking Spanish to others in the presence of a law enforcement officer

    d. All of the above

8. In law enforcement situations, Latino/Hispanic Americans may exhibit behaviors that appear to be evasive, such as claiming not to have any identification or by saying that they do not speak English. Which one of the following events might help explain this behavior?

    a. The person prefers to provide the information at the Police Station when he/she has more time to do it

    b. The person fears that the police and law enforcement agencies are aligned with a politically repressive government

    c. The person hopes that the law enforcement officer will provide an interpreter

    d. None of the above

9. Which one of the following statements is *not* a finding from the Bureau of Justice Statistics published report, "Criminal Victimization in the United States, 1997," about Latino/Hispanic Americans?

    a. Latino/Hispanic Americans experienced higher rates of v i ctimization from violent crime than all other populations

    b. Latino/Hispanic Americans suffered a higher rate of household crimes (e.g., burglary, household larceny, motor vehicle theft) than all other populations

    c. Latino/Hispanic American victims of violent crime were more likely to be accosted by a stranger than were African American victims or Caucasian (white) victims

    d. All of the above

10. Which of the following factors explains why law enforcement officials have often found it difficult to get cooperation from Latino/Hispanic American crime victims?

    a. Lack of familiarity with and trust in police services

    b. Stereotypes and images of law enforcement agencies as d i scriminatory

    c. Perceived lack of effectiveness of the law enforcement agencies

    d. All of the above

Fill-in-the-Blanks

1. Between the 1990 and 2000 censuses, the Latino/Hispanic American population increased by more than ___50___ percent.

2. _La Raza_ is a term used, primarily on the West Coast and in the Southwest, to refer to all peoples of the Western Hemisphere who share a cultural, historical, political, and social legacy of Spanish and Portuguese colonists and Native Indian and African people; it has its origins within the political struggles of this region and the mixing of the races, *el mestizaje.*

3. In 1976, Congress passed Public Law 94-311, called the ___Roybal___, which required the inclusion of a self-identification question on Spanish origin or descent in government surveys and censuses.

4. The majority of the Latino/Hispanic American groups migrated into the United States after ___1910___ because of the economic and political changes that occurred as a result of the Mexican Revolution.

5. ___The Jones Act___ made Puerto Ricans citizens of the United States.

6. The third wave of immigrants leaving Cuba from Mariel occurred from the summer of 1980 to early 1982, and within this group of *Marielito* were many ___criminals___ released by Fidel Castro and included in the boatlift.

7. Stereotypic views of Latino/Hispanic Americans reduce individuals within this group to ___simplistic___ and have led many Americans to lump members of these diverse groups into one stereotypic group, "Mexicans."

8. Latino/Hispanic cultures are group oriented, and people from young to old tend to congregate as groups rather than as individuals or c o uples, and _hanging out_ as a group tends to be the preferred mode of socialization.

9. _La familia_ is perhaps one of the most significant considerations in working and communicating with Latino/Hispanic Americans.

10. With central values like _respecto_ and _machismo_ in the Latino/Hispanic American culture, it is critical for the father and other family members to demonstrate control in family situations.

Discussion

1. Discuss how the definition of Latino/Hispanic may be considered by many to be a "megalabel," associated with stereotypical perceptions that do not represent well all members within this group. What are ways that a law enforcement officer can show sensitivity to the use of the term "Latino/Hispanic" to those within this community?

2. Discuss the implications to law enforcement of the key demographic variables of age, size of household, urban household, and language spoken in the Latino/Hispanic American population. Suggest ways that a law enforcement officer might better understand the impact of these key demographic variables in his/her law enforcement work within the Latino/Hispanic American community.

3. Discuss how the seven-part Typology of Latino/Hispanic Americans may be useful in understanding and in summarizing some of the differences between individuals within the Latino/Hispanic American groups. Which Latino/Hispanic American groups within the Typology would be most likely to be served within your local community?

4. Discuss the impact of Latino/Hispanic American cultural influences on communication. Summarize several examples of both verbal and nonverbal styles of Latino/Hispanic American communication styles, and illustrate how these styles might result in conflict and misunderstanding in interactions with a law enforcement officer.

5. Discuss some of the key differences found for Latino/Hispanic Americans in the National Opinion Survey on Crime and Justice conducted in 1996 (Hornor, 1999) on attitudes toward crime and safety by Latino/Hispanic American respondents when compared to all other respondents. Summarize your recommendations as to ways that law enforcement officers can better serve the Latino/Hispanic American community in several of the areas highlighted by the National Opinion Survey on Crime and Justice.

WHAT ARE YOUR THOUGHTS AND WHAT WOULD YOU DO?

Hispanic day laborers in your patrol area have become victims of armed robberies. Over a nine-month period last year, there were 34 robberies of Latino/Hispanic American victims in one apartment complex alone. Local police statistics indicate that the majority of person-to-person robberies and home invasion r o bberies in the last three years has involved Latino/Hispanic victims. Your department has assigned you to reach out to the Latino/Hispanic American community to do some crime prevention and education work. Several of the officers of your station said that this was going to be a waste of time and that the Latino/Hispanic American community do not trust the police anyway. What are your thoughts and what would you do?

Critical Thinking Questions

1. What are the facts (observable, verifiable, testable, and confirmable)?

2. What are the assumptions?

3. What are the possible stereotypes?

4. What would be your *personal* reactions to this situation?

5. What would be the possible *robbery victims'* and *community residents'* reactions to this situation?

6. Would someone from the Latino/Hispanic American community see something different? What would they see differently (if applicable)?

7. What would be your *professional* reactions to this situation?

8. What actions would you take in this situation?

9. If you had to explain your actions to the Latino/Hispanic American community, the robbery victims, officers who made the comments, and your superiors in front of the news media, what would you say?

TOOLS AND SKILLS IN PRACTICE

1. *Increasing Demographic Understanding of the Latino/Hispanic American Communities*—Law enforcement officers need to be able to obtain demographic information and background data on the Latino/Hispanic Americans in the communities that they serve. There are several ways to obtain this information:

    a. City, County, Region, and/or State Websites: Go to the websites for the municipalities in which you are interested and use search terms like "Hispanic," "Hispanic Americans," "Latino," and any of the specific groups large in number in your community (e.g., "Mexican American," "Cuban," "Colombian," "Puerto Rican," etc.).

    b. Use the U.S. Census Website and Reports: Go to http://www.census.gov and search for information using the search terms provided above for Latino/Hispanic Americans.

c. Use the LULAC Website for the Demographic Data on Latino/Hispanic Americans: Go to the website for the League of United Latin American Citizens (LULAC): http://www.lulac.org—this website provides information on education, training, scholarships, and services to underprivileged and unrepresented Latino/Hispanic Americans. LULAC is the largest and oldest Latino/Hispanic organization in the U.S., with over 115,000 members.

d. Use Search Engines: Use search engines like "Google" or "Yahoo" and enter the search terms "population" and the name of your city, county, region, and/or state.

e. Ask for References from Your Local or College Librarian: The head librarian in your city or on a college campus would be able to direct you to sources of demographic data on file or within reports on Latino/Hispanic Americans.

f. Ask for References from the Branch Public Library Nearest the Latino/Hispanic American Community in Your Area: The head librarian in your branch public library (nearest to a Latino/Hispanic American community) would be able to direct you to the sources of demographic data on file or within reports on Latino/Hispanic Americans.

2. *Identifying Key Ethnic/Cultural Groups and Community Leaders*—Knowing the key Latino/Hispanic American groups in one's service area and the community leaders of these groups is critical to understanding the Latino/Hispanic American resources of your area. Four ways to obtain this information are:

a. Use the On-line Information from the Key Newspapers of Your Area: Search the on-line news sources of your local area on Latino/Hispanic American groups, issues, and leaders on an ongoing basis. Keep a journal of the groups, issues, and leaders that emerge, as well as the other community members and/or representatives named in the news articles.

b. Search "LexisNexis Academic" On-line in Your College Library: Search the "Regional" and the "City" specific news sources for your local area for the prior year using the search terms of the Latino/Hispanic American groups and the name of your city or area of interest. Keep a journal of your findings.

c. Use the On-line Information from the Key Latino/Hispanic American Newspapers of Your Area (if available): Search on an ongoing basis the on-line Latino/Hispanic American news sources of your local area on Latino/Hispanic American groups, issues, and leaders. If there are no online services available from the key Latino/Hispanic American news sources, ask your local college librarian to obtain a subscription (which may be free in some cases). Keep a journal of the groups, issues, and leaders that emerge, as well as other community members and/or representatives named in the news articles.

d. Use the On-line Information from the College and University Newspapers of Your Area: Search on an ongoing basis the on-line news sources of the college and university newspapers in your area on Latino/Hispanic American groups, issues, and leaders. As a result of the interest and community involvement of university and colleges with respect to multicultural topics and concerns, many important issues, events, and people are reported on in the local college and university newspapers (that may not be covered in the mainstream news media). Keep a journal of the groups, issues, and leaders that emerge, as well as other community members and/or representatives named in the news articles.

3. *Scanning for Police and Latino/Hispanic American Community Issues*—Three approaches are suggested:

a. For a National and Regional Perspective, Go to the Following Websites: (1) http://www.latino.sscnet.ucla.edu/community/nclr.html— this website provides information about capacity-building assistance to support and strengthen Hispanic community-based programs and information regarding applied research, policy analysis, and advocacy for Latino/Hispanic Americans, and (2) http://www.lulac.org—this website provides information on education, training, scholarships, and services to underprivileged and unrepresented Latino/Hispanic Americans.

b. For Your City or Area of Interest, Go to the On-line Reports for the Following: (a) "Police Commission," (b) "Public Safety Commission," and/or (c) "Emergency Services Commission." Scan the Minutes of the meetings for law enforcement and other public safety issues identified for the Latino/Hispanic American community. Note any recurring issues or trends. If on-line services are not available in your area, go the Town Hall or City Hall and read the past Minutes of the above-noted Commissions for the last six months to one year; the Minutes of the Police Commission and other meetings are usually open to the public.

c. Use the On-line Information from the Key Latino/Hispanic American Newspapers of Your Area (if available): Search the on-line Latino/Hispanic American news sources for Police and Latino/Hispanic American Community Issues on an ongoing basis. If there are no online services available from the key Latino/Hispanic American news sources, ask your local college librarian to obtain a subscription (which may be free in some cases). Keep a journal of the Police and Latino/Hispanic American Community Issues that emerge, as well as the people, agencies, leaders, and/or representatives named in the news articles.

4. *Developing Latino/Hispanic American Community Partnerships*— Once you begin to get a sense of the different Latino/Hispanic American groups in your community and the key leaders of those groups, is important to get information on the kinds of services these communities may need by accessing information through the different Latino/Hispanic American community resource guides. Go on-line or in person to obtain some of the community resource guides available in your local area. Depending upon the size of the Latino/Hispanic American population of your community, some of these resources might focus on the groups as a whole (e.g., Latino Immigration Services), children (e.g., Hispanic Bilingual Preschool), elderly (e.g., Hispanic Community Senior Healthcare Services), people with disabilities, and so forth. Review these resource guides to identify the needs of these groups and make a list of the needs. Brainstorm some ways that the local law enforcement agencies might be able to form community partnerships with these Latino/Hispanic American community-based agencies to address the needs that you have identified through the review of the materials and guides.

5. *Improving Law Enforcement Relations in Latino/Hispanic American Communities*—Begin building a file in your computer or on 3×5 index cards (or in a "blank book" journal). On a daily basis, as you observe in your work, in the news, or in any other sources, note interactions of law enforcement with aspects of the Latino/Hispanic American community that are going well and those that could have gone better. For the Latino/Hispanic American law enforcement officers' and criminal justice professionals' perspectives, log on to the two websites:

   a. Hispanic American Police Command Officers Association (HAPCOA): http://www.hapcoa.com/—this website provides information to promote the interests of Hispanic American peace officers for recruitment, career development, promotion, and retention of qualified Hispanic police command officers. What does HAPCOA say about aspects of the Latino/Hispanic American community that are going well and those that could have gone better in the law enforcement areas?

   b. Latin American Law Enforcement Association (LALEY): http://www.laley.org/—this website provides law enforcement links important to the Latino/Hispanic American community in the areas of advocacy, education, and leadership, and identification of key organizations. What does LALEY say about aspects of the Latino/Hispanic American community that are going well and those that could have gone better in the criminal justice areas?

For those aspects that have gone well, identify the key elements that made them go well. For those aspects that could have gone better, brainstorm about ways that the situation could have improved. What could have been done differently to attain a better outcome? Soon, your file will contain many useful ideas for improving law enforcement services in the Latino/Hispanic American communities.

SELF-STUDY ACTIVITIES

Latino/Hispanic Americans Viewing Law Enforcement as Not Sensitive

Using the information that you have gathered using the Tools and Skills #3 in this chapter (Scanning for Police and Latino/Hispanic American Community Issues), did you find any immigration, law enforcement, and/or events that may leave Latino/Hispanic Americans with the view that law enforcement agencies are not "sensitive, effective, or responsive"? What are ways to improve such possible negative points of view?

Diversity among Latino/Hispanic Americans

Latino/Hispanic Americans consist of over 25 diverse regional, national, ethnic, and cultural groups. From your findings using the Tools and Skills #1 in this chapter (Increasing Demographic Understanding of the Latino/Hispanic American Communities), which groups are you most likely to encounter in crime-fighting and peacekeeping in your community or area of interest? Which groups do you anticipate encountering in your future work?

Effects of Myths and Stereotypes

Myths and stereotypes about Latino/Hispanic Americans have affected this group greatly. Using the information that you have gathered using the Tools and Skills #3 in this chapter (Scanning for Police and Latino/Hispanic American Community Issues), did you find any issues about the effects of Latino/Hispanic American stereotypes? What are some of the Latino/Hispanic American stereotypes that you have heard of or have encountered? What effects might these stereotypes have on Latino/Hispanic Americans? What are ways to manage these stereotypes in law enforcement? In what ways can you help an officer who uses stereotypes about Latino/Hispanic Americans to become aware of the effects of these stereotypes?

Verbal and Nonverbal Variations among Cultures

Using the information that you have gathered using the Tools and Skills #5 in this chapter (Improving Law Enforcement Relations in Latino/Hispanic American Communities), did you discover any strategies and approaches about verbal and nonverbal communication styles that can help officers in their approach to Latino/Hispanic American citizens? When you can understand the cultural components of behaviors, does this help you to become more sensitive and objective about your reactions? In what ways might you use your understanding about Latino/Hispanic American family dynamics in law enforcement?

Chapter 8

Law Enforcement Contact with Arab Americans and Other Middle Eastern Groups

OVERVIEW

Officers should keep in mind several basic Arabic and Other Middle Eastern cultural values when interacting with Arab American and Other Middle Eastern citizens:

1. A person's honor, dignity, and reputation are of paramount importance, and no effort should be spared to protect them, especially the person's honor.

2. Loyalty to the person's family takes precedence over any other need; thus an individual is completely intertwined with his or her family.

3. Communication should be courteous and hospitable; honor and face-saving govern interpersonal interactions and relationships at all times.

Arab Americans and other Middle Eastern Americans have been wrongly characterized and stereotyped by the media; as with all stereotypes, this has affected people's thinking about Arab Americans and other Middle Eastern group members. Officers should be aware of stereotypes that may influence their judgments. Common stereotypes of Arabs include that they are illiterate and backward, that the women are passive and uneducated, and that they are thieves and terrorists.

Officers can demonstrate to Muslim Arabs a respect for their culture and religion by (1) respecting the times when people pray (five times a day); (2) maintaining courteous behavior in mosques, such as not stepping on prayer mats, not walking in front of people praying, and speaking softly; and (3) working out solutions with community members regarding religious celebrations (e.g., parking problems, noise).

The basic unit for Arab Americans and other Middle Eastern groups, especially recent arrivals and traditional families, is not the individual but the family (including the extended family). If a family member is involved in a police incident, officers should expect that other family members will become actively involved. Officers should not automatically assume that this involvement is an attempt to interfere with police affairs. The traditional Arabic family is used to working out conflicts themselves; this is further reason for all members to become involved.

Traditionally and outwardly, the father is the head of the household, and much of the conversation should be directed toward him. Officers should, however, keep in mind that many Arab women are outspoken and vocal. Officers should not dismiss their input simply because men may appear to be, at least publicly, the ones with the power. Traditional Arab women who do not freely communicate with men, however, may have difficulty expressing themselves to a male police officer. Nevertheless, in their own families, they are often the real decision-makers. Officers may consider various ways of getting information (e.g., the use of a female translator, female police officer, as well as indirect and open-ended questions).

Officers should consider a number of specific cultural practices and taboos when communicating with Arab Americans who have preserved a traditional lifestyle. Officers should avoid even casually touching women and should be respectful of the need some Arab women have to be modest. They should never point the soles of their shoes or feet at a person. Officers can expect Arab Americans and other Middle Eastern Americans to extend hospitality by offering coffee or food (which should not be considered as a bribe, but rather a cultural practice). Arab Americans may stand closer to each other than other Americans do when talking. This is not meant to be threatening; it is largely unconscious and reflects a cultural preference for closer interpersonal interaction.

There are cultural differences in communication style that can affect the officers' judgments and reactions. Becoming highly emotional (verbally and nonverbally) and speaking loudly is not looked down on in the Arab world. Officers who may have a different manner of communication should not express irritation at this culturally different style. Nor should they necessarily determine that the people involved are being disrespectful. Developing patience with culturally different styles of communication is a key cross-cultural skill. When a person speaks with an accent, it does not necessarily mean that he or she is not fluent in English or is illiterate. Many highly educated Arab Americans speak English fluently but with an accent and would be insulted if they were treated as if they were not educated.

In areas with Arab American merchants and store owners, as well as many poor residents, there is great potential for conflict. Arab American merchants, such as grocers and liquor store owners, need to be able to depend on local police services. Many do not feel that they have the protection they need. Police officers may be in positions to explain to other residents why Arab American store owners do not usually hire people from the community. Explanations will not resolve the conflicts, but at least officers can attempt to make some people understand the economic realities of life for these refugees and immigrants.

With post-9/11 and the focus on homeland security, Arab Americans and other Middle Eastern Americans have become targets of prejudice, racism, hate crimes, and hate incidents. Police departments need to monitor communities and keep informed of world events so that Arab American and other Middle Eastern Group communities have greater protection during times when they may be more vulnerable to hate crimes.

RATIONALE FOR THE FOCUS ON THE KEY CONCEPTS AND TOOLS

Officers and practitioners involved in multicultural law enforcement need to be able to:

1. Summarize the historical background, demographics, and diversity within the Arab American and other Middle Eastern communities in the United States

2. Discuss the implications for law enforcement of communication styles, group identification terms, myths and stereotypes, and family structure of Arab Americans and other Middle Eastern groups

3. Understand the impact on law enforcement of the extended family and community, cultural practices, gender roles, generational differences, adolescent and youth issues

4. Highlight key law enforcement concerns and skills, resources, and practices for addressing some of these concerns

INTRODUCTION

Chapter 8 provides specific cultural information on the largest group of Middle Easterners to settle in the United States—Arab Americans. An explanation of the scope of the term Middle Easterner as it is used in this chapter begins the chapter and provides information briefly on non-Arab Middle Eastern groups. This is followed by a summary of the two major waves of Arab immigration to the United States. The chapter presents demographics and the diversity among Arab Americans as well as information on basic Arab values and beliefs. The background information leads into a discussion of commonly held stereotypes of Arabs as well as how these stereotypes contributed to anti-Arab incidents or backlash after September 11, 2001. A brief presentation of some aspects of the Islamic religion is included in the chapter, as well as a summary of the commonalities between Islam, Christianity, and Judaism. Elements of family life are presented, including a discussion of the role of the head of the h o u s ehold and issues related to children and "Americanization." The next section presents various cultural practices and characteristics, including greetings, approach, touching, hospitality, verbal and nonverbal communication, gestures, emotional expressiveness, and general points about English language usage. The final section describes several key concerns for law enforcement, with information on perceptions of police, women and modesty, Arab store owners in urban areas, and hate crimes against Arab Americans, especially those that occurred after the September 11 terrorist attacks. In the chapter summary, readers will find recommendations for improved communication and relationships between law enforcement p e rsonnel and Arab American communities.

KEY CONCEPTS

Outline of Key Presentation Points

1. Should I Say "Arab," "Arabic," or Arabian"?

2. Middle Eastern Countries

3. Not All Middle Easterners are Arabs

4. Other Arab Countries Outside of the Middle East

5. Iran: Non-Arab Country

6. Turkey: Non-Arab Country

7. Israel: Non-Arab Country

8. Arab Immigration to the United States

9. Demographics in the United States

10. Differences and Similarities

11. Arab Clothing Differences

12. Basic Arab Values

13. Negative Stereotypes

14. "Terrorist" Stereotype and Post-9/11 Backlash

15. Islamic Religion

16. The Qur'an (Koran) and the Pillars of Islam

17. Taboos in the Mosque

18. Ramadan: The Holy Month

19. Knowledge of Religious Practices

20. Arab Family Structure

21. Head of the Household

22. Children and "Americanization"

23. Cultural Practices: Greetings, Approach, Touching, and Hospitality

24. Verbal and Nonverbal Communication

25. Perception of and Relationships with the Police

26. Women and Modesty

27. Hate Crimes against Arab Americans

28. Sensitivity to New Legislations

PRACTICE QUESTIONS
True or False

_____ 1. The largest Muslim population is in Asia, and not the Middle East.

_____ 2. Libya is an Arab country that is not in the Middle East.

_____ 3. Israel is the only country in the Middle East in which the majority of the population is not Muslim.

_____ 4. American Jews are Sephardim, having come originally from Spain, other Mediterranean countries, and the Arabic countries of the Middle East.

_____ 5. The second wave of Arabic immigrants to the United States, beginning after World War II, came in large part as students and professionals because of economic instability and political unrest within their countries.

_____ 6. The Saudi Arabian government places restrictions on women by mandating that they do not mix with men, that a woman must always be veiled, and that she not travel alone or drive a car.

_____ 7. Traditional Arab society upholds honor; the degree to which an Arab can lose face and be shamed publicly is foreign to the average Westerner.

_____ 8. The original lyrics of the opening song of Disney's *Aladdin*, "Arabian Nights," are sung by a character in the film who has been portrayed as an Arab stereotype: "Oh I come from a land, from a faraway place/ Where the caravan camels roam/ Where they cut off your ear if they don't like your face/ It's barbaric, but hey, it's home."

_____ 9. Extended Arab American family members are often as close as the "nuclear family" (mother, father, children) and are not seen as secondary family members.

_____ 10. Arab Americans, especially if they are new to the country, tend to have a conversational distance that is farther apart from each other than do other Americans. In Arab culture, it is considered offensive to "feel a person's breath," so there is greater distance between people when talking.

Multiple Choice

1. Which one of the following countries is *not* part of the Middle East and is *not* an Arab country?

   a. Bahrain

   b. Afghanistan

   c. Syria

   d. Yemen

2. What percent of Iranians and Turks are Muslim, with Islam being the most common religion among people in many other Middle Eastern countries?

   a. Less than 50 percent

   b. 51 to 75 percent

   c. 76 to 95 percent

   d. More than 99.8 percent

3. What three cities in the United States have the largest Jewish Iranian populations? (Many of the Jewish Iranians now in the United States had left Iran after the fall of the Shah.)

   a. Chicago, Philadelphia, and Washington, DC

   b. St. Louis, Detroit, and Boston

   c. San Francisco, Los Angeles, and New York City

   d. None of the above

4. Arab American populations are largest in the area(s) of:

   a. Los Angeles/Orange County

   b. The greater New York area

   c. Detroit

   d. All of the above

5. Arab American police Corporal Mohamed Berro of the Dearborn, Michigan, Police Department makes a distinction between immigrants (who have "few problems adjusting to the United States") and refugees. He explains that refugees, having been forced to leave their country of origin, believe that:

   a. Since they were forced to leave, they had better plan on settling in and staying in the U.S.

   b. They are here temporarily because they are waiting for a conflict to end

   c. They would find it impossible to return having lived in the U.S. even briefly

   d. None of the above

6. Which one of the following statements is a stereotype often related to hearing the word "Arab"?
   a. Wealthy sheik
   b. Violent terrorist
   c. Sensuous harem owner; man with many wives
   d. All of the above

7. Which one of the following actions is *not* part of the five "Pillars of Islam" or central guidelines that form the framework of the religion?
   a. Profession of faith in Allah (God)
   b. Alms giving (concern for the needy)
   c. Conducting a holy war against those who oppose Islam
   d. Fasting during the month of Ramadan (sunrise to sunset)

8. Which of the following behaviors would help law enforcement officers to show respect for Islamic customs and beliefs?
   a. Never step on a prayer mat or rug with your shoes on
   b. Avoid walking in front of people who are praying
   c. Invite people out of a prayer area to talk to them
   d. All of the above

9. Which one of the following gestures is *not* included by Devine and Braganti (1991) in their section entitled "Customs and Manners in the Arab World"?
   a. "What does it mean?" or "What are you saying?" Hold up the right hand and twist it as if you were screwing in a light bulb one turn
   b. "Stop!" Hold up both hands with fingers extended and palm facing oneself
   c. "Go away." Hold the right hand out with the palm down, and move it as if pushing something away from you
   d. "Wait a minute." Hold all fingers and thumb touching with the palm up

10. Which one of the following describes some of the reactions police officers have to Arab American communication style?
    a. Police see Arab emotionalism as a threat. Arabs, as with other Mediterranean groups such as Israelis or Greeks, tend to shout when they are excited or angry and are very animated in their communication.
    b. Police are uncomfortable with Arabs repeating themselves with phrases such as "I swear by God."
    c. Police are unfamiliar with the shouting, yelling, and animated speech of Arabs.
    d. All of the above

Fill-in-the-Blanks

1. Arabian is an adjective that refers to _____, or the Arabian Peninsula.

2. Iranians use the Arabic script in their writing, but for the most part speak mainly _____, not Arabic.

3. Eighty percent of the Israeli population is Jewish (*Central Intelligence World Fact Book*, 2003), with the Jewish population divided into two main groups: _____ and _____.

4. The first wave of Arab Immigrants came to the United States between 1880 and World War I and was largely from Syria (the part of Syria that became the country of Lebanon; at the time these areas were part of the Turkish Ottoman Empire). Of the Arab immigrants who settled in the United States during this wave, approximately _____ were Christian.

5. The Detroit–Dearborn area has the largest Arab community in the United States, with Arab Americans constituting about one-fourth of the population in Dearborn. A large percentage of the Detroit area's Middle Eastern population is _____.

6. From a traditional Arab view, it may not be appropriate for a person to give totally honest responses if they result in _____, especially for self or family members (this may not apply to many established Arab Americans).

7. Similar to the Jewish and Chinese calendars, the Islamic calendar is based on the _____, and dates for the celebration of Ramadan vary from year to year.

8. Newer Arab American refugees or immigrants may be reluctant to accept police assistance. Because families are tightly knit, they can also be _____, whereby members prefer to keep private matters or conflicts to themselves.

9. Most Arab women do not change their names after they are married or divorced. They therefore may not understand the distinction between a _____ name and a _____ name.

10. Hospitality in the Arab culture is not an option; it is more an obligation or duty. In some parts of the Arab world, if you thank someone for their hospitality, they may answer with a common expression meaning, "_____."

Discussion

1. Discuss the importance of law enforcement knowledge about p u blic events such as Israeli Independence Day celebrations and Israeli or Palestinian political rallies. Identify why these events h ave the potential for confrontation, although the majority of these events have been peaceful. Summarize the kinds of issues faced by police presence at such events (e.g., excessive police presence can escalate hostilities).

2. Highlight the diversity among Arab American groups. Briefly explain why understanding this diversity will assist officers in not categorizing Arabs as one homogeneous group and will encourage people to move away from stereotypical thinking. What do you c o nsider to be the top three differences among Arab American groups most important for law enforcement officers to know in order to distinguish between groups?

3. Briefly describe the impact of distorted information with respect to ethnic groups and how stereotypes interfere with a true understanding of a people, especially when it comes to law enforcement. Explain what is meant by the statement of Laurence Michalak, cultural anthropologist and former director of the Center for Middle Eastern Studies at the University of California, Berkeley, that the Arab stereotype, while it teaches us very little about the Arabs, "teaches us a good deal about ourselves and about mechanisms of prejudice."

4. Discuss how different groups of Arab Americans may have very d i screpant perceptions of the police as a result of how the institution of policing and the manner in which citizens are required to behave with police differs in various parts of the Arab world of the Middle East. Provide several examples about police events in the Middle East that might contribute to these differing perceptions of the police in America.

5. Discuss some of the racial and ethnic tensions that exist between Arab grocers and liquor storeowners in low-income areas (such as Detroit and Cleveland) and members of other minority groups. Suggest some ways that the police could be helpful in easing the tensions and helping to build more positive communities involving Arab small business owners and other minority groups.

TOOLS AND SKILLS IN PRACTICE

1. *Increasing Demographic Understanding of the Arab Americans and Other Middle Eastern Communities*—Law enforcement officers need to be able to obtain demographic information and background data on the Arab Americans and other Middle Eastern groups in the communities that they serve. There are several ways to obtain this information:

WHAT ARE YOUR THOUGHTS AND WHAT WOULD YOU DO?

Your department has received a request for a meeting from community leaders to help resolve some community conflicts between Arab American grocery store, liquor shop, and gas station owners and the African American and Latino/Hispanic American patrons of those store. Members of the African American and Latino/Hispanic American have voiced their concerns about o u tsiders coming into their communities, starting businesses, and taking their money out of their communities. Some complained about the disrespect shown by the shopkeepers to the patrons, as well as store owners not hiring people to work from the local African American and Latino/Hispanic American c o mmunities. Most of the small Arab-run grocery stores, liquor stores and gas stations are family-operated businesses where two brothers or a father and two sons, for example, are managing the operation. What are your thoughts and what would you do?

Critical Thinking Questions

1. What are the facts (observable, verifiable, testable, and confirmable)?
2. What are the assumptions?
3. What are the possible stereotypes?
4. What would be your *personal* reactions to this situation?
5. What would be the possible *store owners'* and *store customers'* reactions to this situation?
6. Would someone from the Arab American, African American, and Latino/Hispanic American community see something different? What would they see differently (if applicable)?
7. What would be your *professional* reactions to this situation?
8. What actions would you take in this situation?
9. If you had to explain your actions to the Arab American, African American, and Latino/Hispanic American communities, the store owners, the customers, and your superiors in front of the news media, what would you say?

a. City, County, Region, and/or State Websites: Go to the websites for the municipalities that are of interest to you and use search terms like "Arab," "Arab Americans," "Middle Eastern," and any of the specific large groups in your community (e.g., "Chaldean," "Lebanese," "Palestinian," "Israeli," etc.).

b. Use the U.S. Census Website and Reports: Go to http://www.census.gov and search for information using the search terms provided above for Arab Americans and other Middle Eastern groups.

c. Use the Arab American Institute Foundation (AAI) Website: http://www.aaiusa.org—this website is dedicated to the civic and political empowerment of Americans of Arab descent. AAI provides policy, research, and public affairs services to support a broad range of community activities. In addition, the AAI is also a census information center on demographics of Arab Americans. On the web site, you can access a PDF file entitled "Healing the Nation: The Arab-American Experience after September 11." Go to http://www.aaiusa.org and search for information using the search terms provided above for Arab Americans and other Middle Eastern groups.

d. Use Search Engines: Use search engines like "Google" or "Yahoo" and enter the search terms "population" and the name of your city, county, region, and/or state.

e. Ask for References from Your Local or College Librarian: The head librarian in your city or on a college campus would be able to direct you to the sources of demographic data on file or within reports on Arab Americans and Other Middle Eastern Groups.

f. Ask for References from the Branch Public Library Nearest the Arab Americans and other Middle Eastern Groups in Your Area: The head librarian in your branch public library (nearest an Arab American and other Middle Eastern Community) would be able to direct you to the sources of demographic data on file or within reports on Arab Americans and other Middle Eastern groups.

2. *Identifying Key Ethnic/Cultural Groups and Community Leaders*— Knowing the key Arab Americans and Other Middle Eastern groups in one's service area and the community leaders of these groups is critical to understanding the Arab Americans and other Middle Eastern group resources of your area. Four ways to obtain this information are:

a. Use the On-line Information from the Key Newspapers of Your Area: Search on an ongoing basis the on-line news sources of your local area on Arab Americans and other Middle Eastern groups, issues, and leaders. Keep a journal of the community groups, issues, and leaders that emerge, as well as the other members and/or representatives named in the news articles.

b. Search "LexisNexis Academic" On-line in Your College Library: Search the "Regional" and the "City" specific news sources for your local area for the prior year using the search terms of Arab Americans and other Middle Eastern groups and the name of your city or area of interest. Keep a journal of your findings.

c. Use the On-line Information from the Key Arab American and Other Middle Eastern Group Newspapers of Your Area (if available): Search on an ongoing basis the on-line Arab American and other Middle Eastern group news sources of your local area on Arab Americans and other Middle Eastern groups, issues, and leaders. If there are no online services available from the key Arab American and other Middle Eastern group news sources, ask your local college librarian to obtain a subscription (which may be free in some cases). Keep a journal of the community groups, issues, and leaders that emerge, as well as the other members and/or representatives named in the news articles.

d. Use the On-line Information from the College and University Newspapers of Your Area: Search on an ongoing basis the on-line news sources of the college and university newspapers in your area on Arab Americans and other Middle Eastern groups, issues, and leaders. As a result of the interest and community involvement of university and colleges in multicultural topics and concerns, many important issues, events, and people are reported on in the local college and university newspapers (that may not be covered in the mainstream news media). Keep a journal of the groups, issues, and leaders that emerge, as well as the other community members and/or representatives named in the news articles.

3. *Scanning for Police and Arab Americans and Other Middle Eastern Group Community Issues*—Three approaches are suggested:

a. For a national and regional perspective, go to the following website: http://www.adc.org—this website provides information about the ADC's civil rights efforts and useful summary data about cases and complaints regarding discrimination and hate crimes involving Arab Americans.

b. For your city or area of interest, go the on-line reports for the: (a) "Police Commission," (b) "Public Safety Commission" and/or (c) "Emergency Services Commission." Scan the Minutes of the meetings for law enforcement and other public safety issues identified for the Arab Americans and other Middle Eastern group communities. Note any recurring issues or trends. If on-line services are not available in your area, go the Town Hall or City Hall and read the past Minutes of the above-noted Commissions for the last six months to one year; the Minutes of the Police Commission and other meetings are usually open to the public.

c. Use the On-line Information from the Key Arab American and Other Middle Eastern Group Newspapers of Your Area (if available): Search on an ongoing basis the on-line Arab American and other Middle Eastern group news sources for Police and Arab American and other Middle Eastern group community issues. If there are no online services available from the key Arab American and other Middle Eastern group news sources, ask your local college librarian to obtain a subscription (which may be free in some cases). Keep a journal of the Police and Arab American and other Middle Eastern group community issues that emerge, as well as the people, agencies, leaders, and/or representatives named in the news articles.

4. *Developing Arab American and Other Middle Eastern Group Community Partnerships*—Once you begin to get a sense of the different Arab Americans and other Middle Eastern groups in your community (or nearby area) and the key leaders of those groups, it would be important to get information on the kinds of services, needs, and resources of the identified Arab American and other Middle Eastern group community groups. Go on-line or in person to obtain some of the community resource guides available in your local area. Depending upon the size of the Arab American and other Middle Eastern group populations of your community some of these resources might focus on the groups as a whole (e.g., Job Placement Services), children (e.g., Head Start), immigrants (e.g., Legal Services), people with disabilities, and so forth. Review these resource guides to identify the needs of these groups and make a list of the needs. Brainstorm some ways that the local law enforcement agencies might be able to form community partnerships with these Arab American and other Middle Eastern group community-based agencies to address the needs that you have identified through the review of the materials and guides.

5. *Improving Law Enforcement Relations in Arab American and Other Middle Eastern Group Communities*—Begin building a file in your computer or on 3×5 index cards (or in a "blank book" journal). On a daily basis, as you observe in your work, in the news, or in any other sources, note interactions of law enforcement with aspects of the Arab American and other Middle Eastern group communities that are going well and those that could have gone better. For those interactions that have gone well, identify the key elements and/or aspects that made them go well. For those interactions that could have gone better, brainstorm about ways that the situation could have been improved. What could have been done differently to attain a better outcome? Soon, your file will contain many useful ideas for improving law enforcement services in the Arab American and other Middle Eastern group communities.

SELF-STUDY ACTIVITIES

Police–Ethnic Community Relations

In the section entitled "Islamic Religion," the authors mention an incident which took place at the end of the holy month of "Ramadan" whereby officers ticketed many cars parked across the street from the Mosque. According to community people, the stores adjacent to the parking lots were closed and although parking was technically for customers only, the Arab Americans did not anticipate that there would be a problem utilizing the parking lot after hours. Using the information that you have gathered using the Tools and Skills #3 in this chapter in the text (Scanning for Police and Arab American and Other Middle Eastern Community Issues), did you find any other police relations issues like the mass ticketing? Did you find other examples that would lead community members to say, "They (meaning the police) don't respect us; they don't want to understand us." What is your opinion regarding the way things were handled? Do you have any suggestions as to how this situation could have been prevented? Comment on both what the community and the police could have done to prevent the problem.

Arab American and Other Middle Easterner Communities

From your findings using the Tools and Skills #1 in this chapter (Increasing Demographic Understanding of the Arab American and Other Middle Eastern Communities), which groups are you most likely to encounter in crime-fighting and peacekeeping in your community or area of interest? Which groups do you anticipate encountering in your future work?

Hospitality toward Officers—A Cultural Gesture

Hospitality is a virtue in Arab culture and also functions to help people get to know (and see if they can trust) others with whom they are interacting. Using the information that you have gathered using the Tools and Skills #3 in this chapter (Scanning for Police and Arab American and Other Middle Eastern Community Issues), did you find any issues surrounding this c u ltural emphasis on being hospitable and what an officer should do if offered a cup of coffee and something to eat? If an officer has to decline the hospitality, how should it be done politely? Should department policy regarding the acceptance of hospitality be reexamined in light of this cultural norm? Would your answer be different for departments that have adopted a community-based policing philosophy?

"But It's the Custom in My Country"

In January 1991, the Associated Press reported that a Stockton, California, man originally from Jordan was arrested for investigation of "selling his daughter into slavery" because he allegedly accepted $25,000 for her arranged marriage. After police officers had taken the girl to a shelter, a police lieutenant reported that the father protested that "he was within his rights to arrange his daughter's marriage for a price. The father contacted us and, quite upset, explained it was the custom in his country and is perfectly acceptable. Of course, we explained that you can't do that in this country. It is slavery. . . . The father then went to the shelter [where the daughter was] and was arrested after creating a disturbance." If you were investigating this case, how would you proceed? Use the "Critical Thinking Questions" to map out your response. How might you assess the validity of what the father was saying? If you found out that the act was, indeed, "perfectly acceptable in his country," how would you explain practices such as this in the United States?

Chapter 9

Law Enforcement Contact with Native Americans

OVERVIEW

Those who are entrusted with keeping the peace in rural areas, in cities, or on Indian reservations have a great responsibility to show respect and professionalism when interacting with Native American peoples, who have traditionally been disrespected by governmental authority. It is important to remember that the U.S. government has violated many treaties with American Indians and that their basic rights have not always been protected. Officers need to understand the initial resistance to their efforts to establish rapport and goodwill and not take it personally. They can make an effort to get to know the community in their particular area and make positive contact with American Indian organizations and individuals.

The younger, more environmentally conscious generations of Americans have adopted valuable ideology from the culture of America's original peoples. Officers should convey a respect for Native American values. Native Americans have been victims of forced assimilation whereby their languages, religions, and cultures have been suppressed. These negative effects have stayed with generations of Native Americans. The point of contact between a law enforcement professional and an American Indian can often involve issues related to poor adjustment to urban life. While the law must be upheld, officers must consider the conditions that led some Native Americans toward, for example, alcoholism and unemployment.

Preferred mainstream American ways of communication often run counter to Native American styles of communication. Many American Indians who favor traditional styles of communication will tend toward closed behavior and slow rapport building with strangers (this is a cultural trait for some and does not mean the person is aloof or hostile); silent and highly observant behavior (which does not imply a lack of cooperation); withdrawal if the method of questioning is too aggressive (time, patience, and silence will assist officers in getting the responses they need); and indirect eye contact for members of some but not all tribes (officers' penetrating or intense eye contact may result in intimidating the person and, consequently, in his or her withdrawal).

The extended family is close knit and interdependent among Native American peoples. Officers should keep in mind the following:

- Be respectful and deferential to elders.

- The elders should be asked for their opinion or even advice, where applicable, because they are often major decision makers in the family.

- If there are problems with a child, consider other adults, besides the mother and father, who may also be responsible for child rearing.

- Whenever possible, do not separate children from parents. This can bring back memories of times when children were forcibly taken from their parents and sent to Christian mission schools or government boarding schools far from their homes.

With regard to key issues of law enforcement and contact with American Indians, particularly sensitive areas include use of peyote, allegations of trespassing, violations of sacred sites, fishing, and jurisdiction. All these areas involve matters in which Native Americans feel they have been deprived of their rights: in the case of peyote, the right to religious expression; in the case of trespassing, the right to honor their ancestors (e.g., when visiting burial grounds); and in the case of fishing, the ability to exercise their rights as guaranteed by treaties made with the U.S. government.

Many Native Americans feel that they are abused by a system of government that is neither honest nor respectful of their culture. Many believe that the government degrades the land on which all people depend. To a large extent, Indian rights are still ignored because members of the dominant society do not always uphold the laws made to protect Indians. This background makes relationships and interactions between law enforcement officials and Indians especially difficult. For this reason, law enforcement officials need to go out of their way to demonstrate that they are fair, given the complexities of history and current law. In addition, chief executives and command staff of police departments have a special responsibility to provide an accurate education to officers on American Indian cultural groups (with an emphasis on government–tribal relations) and to address the special needs and concerns of American Indian peoples.

RATIONALE FOR THE FOCUS ON THE KEY CONCEPTS AND TOOLS

Officers and practitioners involved in multicultural law enforcement need to be able to:

1. Summarize the historical background, demographics, and diversity within the Native American community in the United States

2. Discuss the implications of communication styles, group identification terms, myths and stereotypes, and family structure of Native Americans for law enforcement

3. Understand the impact of the family structure and mobility, gender roles, tribal system, reservations, adolescent and youth issues on law enforcement contact

4. Highlight key law enforcement concerns and skills, resources, and practices for addressing some of these concerns

INTRODUCTION

Chapter 9 provides specific cultural information on Native Americans, including aspects of their history which, both directly and indirectly, can affect the relationship with law enforcement officials. It presents information about Native American identity and group identification terms, as well as explains briefly the tribal system, reservations, Native American mobility as well as family structure. Chapter 9 addresses the diversity that exists among Native American groups, and includes a description of cultural differences and similarities found among various Indian groups. We include labels—terms and stereotypical statements that are offensive to Native Americans. The final section outlines several key concerns for law enforcement, including information on perceptions of police, Native American v i ctimization rates, police jurisdiction problems, peyote, medicine bags, trespassing, violation of Indian sacred places, casinos and Indian gaming, and problems related to fishing rights. In the summary of the chapter, we provide a review of recommendations for improved communication and relationships between law enforcement personnel and members of Native American communities.

KEY CONCEPTS

Outline of Key Presentation Points

1. Tribe Names and History
2. Treaties and Treatment
3. Native American Identity
4. The Term "Native American"
5. Native American Populations, Tribes, and Reservations
6. Differences and Similarities among Native Americans
7. Philosophy toward the Earth and the Universe
8. Acculturation to Mainstream Society: Indicators of Problems with Acculturation
9. Research Findings Show
10. National Congress of American Indians
11. Language and Communication
12. Touching and Proxemics
13. Language

14. Offensive Terms, Labels, and Stereotypes

15. Family Related Issues

16. Key Issues in Law Enforcement

PRACTICE QUESTIONS

True or False

_____ 1. The word "Indian" is not a term that Native Americans originally used to designate their tribes or communities.

_____ 2. American Indians continue to fight legal battles over the retention of Indian lands and other rights previously guaranteed by U.S. treaties.

_____ 3. The Native American's strong sense of patriotism and courage emerged once again during the Vietnam era when more than 42,000 Native Americans, more than 90 percent of them volunteers, fought in Vietnam.

_____ 4. Some Native Americans have Spanish first or last names because of intermarriage, and may "look" Hispanic or Latino (e.g., the Hopis).

_____ 5. Many Native Americans, in early encounters, will approach and respond to people with caution—too much openness is to be avoided, as is disclosing personal and family problems.

_____ 6. Pan-Indianism involves the process of synthesizing the collective spiritual reality and traditional wisdom of more than one Native American Nation.

_____ 7. The small-talk that one observes in mainstream society ("Hi. How are you? How was your weekend?" and so on) is traditionally required by Native Americans to establish rapport, relationship, and context.

_____ 8. Avoidance of eye contact by Native Americans with an officer can convey the message that the officer is using an approach that is too forceful and demanding.

_____ 9. According to Rivera (2003), nothing will anger an Indian more than seeing his/her grandmother or grandfather being spoken to belligerently or being ordered around with disrespect.

_____ 10. Many families in urban areas and on reservations have memories of, or have heard stories from elder family members about, the federal government's systematic removal of Indian children from their homes; in many cases, children were placed in boarding schools that were hundreds of miles away.

Multiple Choice

1. Historically, the police officer from outside the reservation has been perceived as a symbol of:
   a. Security and an independent source of safety and protection not influenced by the politics of the reservation
   b. Rigid and authoritarian governmental control that has affected nearly every aspect of an Indian's life, especially on reservations
   c. Sensitivity and knowledegable about Native American culture
   d. None of the above

2. How many American Indians, out of a total Native American population of less than 350,000, served with distinction in the United States military between 1941 and 1945 in both the European and Pacific theaters of World War II?
   a. Less than 10,000
   b. 21,000
   c. 32,500
   d. More than 44,000

3. According to Census 2000, how many people identified themselves as American Indian or Alaska Native?
   a. Approximately 0.5 million (or less than 0.2 percent of the entire U.S. population)
   b. Approximately 1.3 million (or 0.5 percent of the entire U.S. population)
   c. Approximately 2.5 million (or 0.9 percent of the entire U.S. population)
   d. Approximately 5.0 million (or more than 1.5 percent of the entire U.S. population)

4. Which of the three Indian tribes comprise the most populated tribal groupings in North America?
   a. Cherokee, Navajo, and Latin American Indian
   b. Shawnee, Algonquin, and Yakima
   c. Mohegan, Dakota (Sioux), and Pueblo
   d. Choctaw, Osage, and Maricopa

5. According to the Friends Committee on National Legislation (FCNL), the suicide rate for American Indians and Alaska Natives is what percent greater then the rate for all races in the U.S.?

    a. 11 percent greater
    b. 26 percent greater
    c. 54 percent greater
    d. 72 percent greater

6. Which one of the following practices and rituals is identified as a symbol of the growing movement reflecting American Indian pride?

    a. Males wearing long hair (long hair is a sign of a free man, not a slave)
    b. Sacred pipe use (i.e., the pipestone pipe, sometimes referred to as the "peace pipe")
    c. Participation in sweat lodges, purification rituals, and the sacred sun dance for purification
    d. All of the above

7. Which one of the following terms may be considered offensive and/or insensitive to Native Americans?

    a. "Indian giver" to characterize someone who takes back a present or an offer
    b. "Apple" (referring to a highly assimilated Indian, "red" on the outside; "white" on the inside)
    c. "Bottom of the totem pole" meaning lowest ranking
    d. All of the above

8. According to the Bureau of Justice Statistics (BJS) on American Indians and Crime, the rate of violent victimization of Native Americans far exceeds that of other racial or ethnic groups in the United States. Which one of the following rates is true about American Indians of all age groups, geographic locations, economic status levels and both genders?

    a. Native Americans were victims of violent crime at double the rate of blacks, whites, or Asians during 1998
    b. Native American women were victimized by an intimate partner at rates higher than other groups
    c. Both "a" and "b"
    d. None of the above

9. Which one of the following approaches ensures levels of cooperation and positive attitudes toward civil and tribal law enforcement partnerships?

   a. Cross-deputization by the Sac and Fox Nation enables both sets of officers (i.e., from the tribal and civil police) to make arrests in each other's jurisdiction without being sued

   b. Going out of their way by the civil police to work out relationships with local Indian tribes as exemplified by the police department of Albuquerque, New Mexico

   c. Respecting the tribal police, as they are usually the ones who discover the crime, conduct initial interviews, know the personalities and circumstances involved, and provide continued assistance throughout the case

   d. All of the above

10. The Native American Free Exercise of Religion Act of 1993 (Senate Bill 1021, introduced to the 103rd Congress), Title I—Protection of Sacred Sites, gives tribal authority over Native American religious sites on Indian lands. Which one of the following statements is *not* part of the Native American Free Exercise of Religion Act of 1993?

    a. Indian tribes may regulate and protect Native American religious sites located on Indian lands.

    b. Desecration and looting of sacred sites and objects is punishable by law.

    c. Profits from the sale of Native American artifacts will be forfeited and fines will be levied.

    d. Vandalism on Native American archeological sites may result in criminal prosecution.

Fill-in-the-Blanks

1. American military leaders, beginning with George Washington in 1778, recognized American Indians to be _____.

2. Because the determination of tribal membership is a fundamental attribute of tribal sovereignty, the federal government generally _____ to tribes' own determinations when establishing eligibility criteria under special Indian entitlement programs.

3. If law enforcement officers have any doubt, they should inquire as to what tribe the person belongs and then contact the _____ to verify that person's identity.

4. According to Census 2000, for all cities in the United States with a population of 100,000 or more, _____ and _____ had the largest American Indian populations .

5. While acknowledging the character of each Indian tribe or "nation," there is a common set of values and beliefs involving the earth and the universe, resulting in a deep respect for nature and _____.

6. Comparing the suicide rate between white youths and Native American, the most recent statistics from the Pan American Health Organization indicate that, again, for Indian males, ages 15–24 years, it was _____ higher.

7. Many people are now working on revitalizing Native American culture rather than letting it die, and this has resulted in the movement of _____ in which Native Americans across the United States are celebrating their cultural heritage, while organizing politically.

8. According to the Los Angeles Police Department Cross-Cultural Awareness Videotapes, Indians tend not to act impulsively for fear of appearing _____ to themselves or to their family.

9. With regard to their sense of space, most Native Americans are _____ being touched by strangers, whether a pat on the back or the arm around the shoulder.

10. Indians find it _____ when non-Indians make claims which may or may not be true about their Indian ancestry: "I'm part Indian—my great-grandfather was Cherokee . . ." (for example).

Discussion

1. Discuss the reasons why Native Americans may not want to be grouped with Latino/Hispanic Americans even though they may have Spanish surnames and ancestry because of intermarriages among the groups.

2. Discuss some of the differences and similarities among Native American tribes. For example, in Arizona alone, one finds a number of different tribes with varying traditions: there are Hopis in the northeast, Pimas and Papagos in the south, Apache in the North Central region, and Yuman groups in the west. All of these descend from people who came to what is now called Arizona. Identify several differences that might be important to law enforcement officers in their work with Native Americans.

3. Discuss some of the steps taken by the National Congress of American Indians (NCAI) to enhance cultural affiliation, promote the unity of Native Americans, as well as educate the rest of society to become more aware of Native American issues. Briefly describe how NCAI, as the oldest, largest, and most representative Indian organization, is going about promoting and protecting the rights of American Indian and Alaska natives as a whole group. In what ways can law enforcement agencies support the work and efforts of NCAI?

4. Discuss how, for many Native Americans, there are still large networks of relatives who are in close proximity with each other. For example, it is not uncommon for children to be raised by someone other than their father or mother (e.g., grandmother, aunts). What suggestions would you have for law enforcement for cases in which they enter a Native American's home asking to speak to the parents of a child and end up speaking to someone who is not the biological mother or father?

5. Discuss some of the jurisdiction issues encountered in law enforcement efforts with Native Americans. For example, police officers may be put into an unusual situation when it comes to enforcing the law among Indians; they may make an arrest in an area that is c o nsidered to be on "Indian land" (for which tribal police have jurisdiction). Moreover, the land may be adjacent to non-Indian land, sometimes forming "checkerboard" patterns of jurisdiction. What suggestions do you have to ensure cooperation and mutual aid and help in determining jurisdiction in these cases?

WHAT ARE YOUR THOUGHTS AND WHAT WOULD YOU DO?

Your department has received several complaints from merchants in a shopping mall in a predominantly white neighborhood near one of the Native American reservations about "Indian" teenagers and youth "hanging around" and "loitering." The merchants also expressed concerns about the "fund-raising" activities (e.g., asking for donations, selling candy bars, etc.) that some of the Native Americans youths were engaged in at the mall. The merchants wanted the police department to do something about this. You have been assigned to investigate and to talk to the merchants about their concerns and needs. What are your thoughts and what would you do?

Critical Thinking Questions

1. What are the facts (observable, verifiable, testable, and confirmable)?
2. What are the assumptions?
3. What are the possible stereotypes?
4. What would be your *personal* reactions to this situation?
5. What would be the possible *merchants'* and *store customers'* reactions to this situation?
6. Would someone from the Native American community see something d i fferent? What would they see differently (if applicable)?
7. What would be your *professional* reactions to this situation?
8. What actions would you take in this situation?
9. If you had to explain your actions to the Native American community, the merchants, the customers, and your superiors in front of the news media, what would you say?

TOOLS AND SKILLS IN PRACTICE

1. *Increasing Demographic Understanding of the Native American Communities*—Law enforcement officers need to be able to obtain demographic information and background data on the Native Americans in the communities that they serve. There are several ways to obtain this information:

   a. City, County, Region, and/or State Websites: Go to the websites for the municipalities that are of interest to you and use search terms like "American Indians," "Native Americans," "Native," "Indians," and any of the specific groups large in number in your community (e.g., "Navajo," etc.).

   b. Use the U.S. Census Website and Reports: Go to http://www.census.gov and search for information using the search terms provided above for Native Americans. Review the document "The American Indian and Alaska Population: 2000" available online.

   c. Use Search Engines: Use search engines like "Google" or "Yahoo" and enter the search terms "Native American" (and other terms noted in #1 above) and the name of your city, county, region, and/or state.

   d. Ask for References from Your Local or College Librarian: The head librarian in your city or on a college campus would be able to direct you to the sources of demographic data on file or within reports on Native Americans.

   e. Ask for References from the Branch Public Library Nearest the Native American Community in Your Area: The head librarian in your branch public library (nearest an Native American c o mmunity) would be able to direct you to the sources of demographic data on file or within reports on Native Americans.

2. *Identifying Key Racial/Cultural Groups and Community Leaders*— Knowing the key Native American groups in one's service area and the community leaders of these groups is critical to understanding the Native American resources of your area. Four ways to obtain this information are:

   a. Use the On-line Information from the Key Newspapers of Your Area: Search the on-line news sources of your local area on Native American groups, issues, and leaders on an ongoing basis. Keep a journal of the groups, issues, and leaders that emerge, as well as the other community members and/or representatives named in the news articles.

   b. Search "LexisNexis Academic" On-line in Your College Library: Search the "Regional" and the "City" specific news sources for your local area for the prior year using the search terms of the Native American groups and the name of your city or area of interest. Keep a journal of your findings.

c. Use the On-line Information from the Key Native American Newspapers of Your Area (if available): Search on an ongoing basis the on-line Native American news sources of your local area on Native American groups, issues, and leaders. If there are no online services available from the key Native American news sources, ask your local college librarian to obtain a subscription (which may be free in some cases). Search online "The Independent American Indian Review": http://www.world-viewsintl.com/iair/. Keep a journal of the groups, issues, and leaders that emerge, as well as the other community members and/or representatives named in the news articles.

d. Use the On-line Information from the College and University Newspapers of Your Area: Search on an ongoing basis the on-line news sources of the college and university newspapers in your area on Native American groups, issues, and leaders. As a result of the interest and community involvement of universities and colleges with respect to multicultural topics and concerns, many important community issues and events are reported in the local college and university newspapers (that may not be covered in the mainstream news media). Keep a journal of the groups, issues, and leaders that emerge, as well as the other members and/or representatives named in the news articles.

3. *Scanning for Police and Native American Community Issues—* Three approaches are suggested:

a. For a national and regional perspective, go to the following websites: (1) The Office of Tribal Justice (OTJ): http://www.usdoj.gov/otj/—the information contained in this website pertains to the Department of Justice's involvement with Native American tribes and organizations. The office is the single point of contact within the department for meeting responsibilities to the tribes, and (2) National Congress of American Indians (NCAI): http://www.ncai.org—the website for the national organization contains information on issues, events, and other data relevant to the organization and to Native Americans.

b. For your city or area of interest, go the on-line reports for the: (a) "Police Commission," (b) "Public Safety Commission," and/or (c) "Emergency Services Commission." Scan the Minutes of the meetings for law enforcement and other public safety issues identified for the Native American community. Note any recurring issues or trends. If on-line services are not available in your area, go the Town Hall or City Hall and read the past Minutes of the above-noted Commissions for the last six months to one year; the Minutes of the Police Commission and other meetings are usually open to the public.

c. Use on an Ongoing Basis the On-line Information from the Key Native American Newspapers of Your Area (if available): Search the on-line Native American news sources for Police and Native American community issues. If there are no online services available from the key Native American news sources, ask your local college librarian to obtain a subscription (which may be free in some cases). Keep a journal of the Police and Native American community issues that emerge, as well as the people, agencies, leaders, and/or representatives named in the news articles.

4. *Developing Native American Community Partnerships*—Once you begin to get a sense of the different groups in your community and the key leaders of those groups, it would be important to get information on the kinds of services these communities may need by accessing information through the different Native American community resource guides. Go on-line or in person to obtain some of the community resource guides available in your local area. Depending upon the size of the Native American population of your community, some of these resources might focus on the groups as a whole (e.g., Health Services), children (e.g., Preschool Program), elderly (e.g., Senior Meals Program), people with disabilities, and so forth. Review these resource guides to identify the needs of these groups, and make a list of the needs. Brainstorm some ways in which the local law enforcement agencies might be able to form community partnerships with these Native American community-based agencies to address the needs that you have identified through the review of the materials and guides.

5. *Improving Law Enforcement Relations in Native American Communities*—Begin building a file in your computer or on 3×5 index cards (or in a "blank book" journal). On a daily basis, as you observe in your work, in the news, or in any other sources, note interactions of law enforcement with aspects of the Native American community that are going well and those that could have gone better. For those aspects that have gone well, identify the key elements that made them go well. For those aspects and interactions that could have gone better, brainstorm about ways that the situation could have been improved. What could have been done differently to attain a better outcome? Soon, your file will contain many useful ideas for improving law enforcement services in the Native American communities.

SELF-STUDY ACTIVITIES

Popular Stereotypes

Using the information that you have gathered using the Tools and Skills #3 in this chapter (Scanning for Police and Native American Community Issues), did you find any issues about the effects of Native American stereotypes? What are some commonly held stereotypes of Native Americans? What is your personal experience with Native Americans that might counter these stereotypes? How have people in law enforcement been influenced by popular stereotypes of Native Americans?

Recommendations for Effective Contact

Using the information that you have gathered using the Tools and Skills #5 in this chapter (Improving Law Enforcement Relations in Native American Communities), did you discover any strategies and approaches about improving communications and contact with Native Americans? If you have had contact with Native Americans, what recommendations would you give others regarding effective communication, rapport-building, and cultural knowledge that would be beneficial for officers?

The Government's Broken Promises to American Indians

The famous Lakota chief, Sitting Bull, spoke on behalf of many Indians when he said of white Americans: "They made us many promises . . . but they never kept but one: They promised to take our land, and they took it." There was a time when many acres of land in what we now call the United States were sacred to Native American tribes. Therefore, today many of us are living on, building on, and in some cases, destroying the remains of Indian lands where people's roots run deep. From your findings using the Tools and Skills #3 (Scanning for Police and Native American Community Issues), did any "trespassing" issues emerge from your findings? How would you deal with the problem of an Indian "trespassing" on someone's land when he or she claims to be visiting an ancestral burial ground, for example? What could you say or do so as not to totally alienate the Native American and thereby risk losing trust and cooperation?

Jurisdiction

From your findings using the Tools and Skills #3 (Scanning for Police and Native American Community Issues), did any "jurisdictional" issues emerge from your findings? What are law enforcement agents supposed to do in s i tuations whereby the state law is in conflict with a federal law that has been based on treaties with Native Americans signed by the federal government? How can officers who are on the front lines win the respect and cooperation of Native Americans when they are asked to enforce something that goes against the treaty rights of the Indians?

Part 3

MULTICULTURAL LAW ENFORCEMENT ELEMENTS IN TERRORISM AND HOMELAND SECURITY

Part Three provides information on working with multicultural communities in the emerging areas of domestic and international terrorism. Peacekeeping efforts of homeland security within our local, state, regional, national, and global multicultural communities are addressed. All prior research, for example, Howard and Sawyer (2004), indicates that acts of terrorism and efforts toward homeland security start with key elements that are "local" in prevention, response, and implementation. Generally speaking, acts of terrorism in the United States usually involve local law enforcement agencies and other public safety personnel as first responders. Thus, specific strategies and practices regarding the role of law enforcement personnel as first responders are provided as critical background information.

Part 3 highlights law enforcement prevention, response, control, and reporting strategies related to the War on Terrorism and homeland security within multicultural communities. The chapters that follow contain (1) overviews, background, and historical information with respect to law enforcement's emerging roles in the War on Terrorism and in homeland security, (2) self-protection practices and procedures important to law enforcement personnel as first responders to terrorist attacks and incidents, (3) policies, procedures, and practices relevant to multicultural law enforcement in dealing with crimes of terrorism and homeland security, (4) key multicultural law enforcement communication issues in dealing with terrorism and homeland security, and (5) relationships and processes inherent in multi-jurisdictional efforts and responses related to terrorism and homeland security work. Each chapter ends with key concerns relevant to officers, and specific challenges involved in emerging roles and practices in dealing with terrorism and homeland security within multicultural communities.

Chapter 10

Multicultural Law Enforcement and Terrorism: Overview, Response Strategies, and Multijurisdictional Actions

OVERVIEW

Law enforcement agencies today have an emerging and vital role in the War on Terrorism that involves the critical step of building key relationships and networks with multicultural communities, including ethnic and multicultural media sources. Multicultural knowledge and skills of local law enforcement can contribute to uncovering key information, resources, and tools in dealing with the prevention and criminal investigation of terrorism, including intelligence-gathering needs. The chapter covered problems in dealing with terrorism involving multicultural communities and the actions of law enforcement officers' possible bias, prejudice, and stereotyping of certain multicultural groups. The chapter closed with specific recommendations important to the emerging roles of law enforcement officers and other emergency services personnel in dealing with terrorism within multicultural communities.

RATIONALE FOR THE FOCUS ON THE KEY CONCEPTS AND TOOLS

Officers and practitioners involved in multicultural law enforcement need to be able to:

1. Understand the role that law enforcement holds in the war on terrorism within multicultural communities

2. Review the skills needed in diverse communities to prevent and to deal with the aftermath of terrorism

3. Highlight the complexities of solving crimes involving terrorism

4. Provide specific response strategies in terms of collaborative and partnership work within local, state, and federal agencies

5. Delineate recommendations for law enforcement officers and other emergency services personnel in actively responding to terrorism within multicultural communities

INTRODUCTION

Chapter 10 provides specific information on the emerging and vital role that law enforcement holds in the War on Terrorism within multicultural communities. Although crimes involving terrorism affect our nation as a whole (and thus are seen as national in scope), the immediate targets, outcomes, and results are local in effect. Local law enforcement personnel and agencies are called upon to respond, provide assistance, establish order, and protect the immediate and larger community from any additional harm and danger. Multicultural knowledge and the skill that is required in working within diverse communities provide key resources in preventing and dealing with the aftermath of terrorism, investigation of crimes, and required intelligence-gathering. We first provide an overview of the importance of multicultural law enforcement knowledge and skills for handling terrorism. We then define the scope of the problem in dealing with terrorism involving multicultural populations and communities. The section on "Local Community Issues/National and Regional Issues" highlights the complexities in responding to and solving crimes involving terrorism. We have provided specific "Response Strategies" and "Key Issues for Law Enforcement" in terms of collaborative and partnership work in the War on Terrorism with the variety of public safety agencies across diverse departmental levels government. Finally, we close the chapter with specific recommendations for law enforcement officers and other emergency services personnel in actively responding to terrorism within multicultural communities.

KEY CONCEPTS

Outline of Key Presentation Points

1. Definitions for the War on Terrorism

2. Historical Background

3. Importance of Multicultural Skills, Knowledge, and Resources

4. Global, National, Regional, or Local?

5. Domestic or International Terrorism?

6. First-Response Challenge for Law Enforcement

7. Forms of Self-Protection for WMD

8. Danger and Harm: TRACEM

9. Evaluation of the Incident Area and Importance of Multicultural Knowledge

10. Public Safety and Protection

11. Critical Incident Stress Debriefing

12. Law Enforcement Response Strategies

13. Law Enforcement Coordination of Efforts

14. Community Assessment

15. Building Community Networks and Resources

16. Other Key Issues in Law Enforcement

PRACTICE QUESTIONS

True or False

_____ 1. In multicultural law enforcement practice, the immediate targets, outcomes, and results of terrorism are national and global in effect.

_____ 2. The primary goal and mission of the terrorist is to create economic chaos in order to destroy the economic power of a country.

_____ 3. Law enforcement is called upon to respond to threats of terrorism, as well as to actual incidents and acts of terrorism.

_____ 4. The targets and tactics of terrorists have changed over time (Hoffman, 1998). In the past, targets of terrorists were always groups or communities (*not* individuals).

_____ 5. Reprisals for U.S. legal actions against domestic and international terrorists increase the likelihood that Americans will be the target of terrorist attacks either in the United States or overseas.

_____ 6. *Time* is used as a protective tool in a terrorist attack.

_____ 7. Asphyxiation harm is defined as injuries resulting from a lack of oxygen in the atmosphere often caused by a heavier than air gas such as argon, carbon dioxide, or chemical vapors in a confined space.

_____ 8. "Agro terrorism," which is harm to our food supply chain, is a subcategory of Weapons of Mass Destruction (WMD).

_____ 9. The goal of "cyber terrorism" is to harm our telecommunication, Internet, and computerized processes and transactions.

_____ 10. Examples of First Priority Level processes and functions would include all essential mission-critical elements such as electrical power, communications, information systems, and command and leadership functions.

Multiple Choice

1. Law enforcement personnel have the role of protecting:
    a. The public from acts of terrorism
    b. Members of multicultural communities who may have no ties to terrorists or criminals but are stereotyped, harassed, or discriminated against because of the biases and prejudices of others
    c. The public from criminal acts not caused by terrorists
    d. All of the above

2. Which of the following is *not* one of the three types of weapons most commonly categorized as "Weapons of Mass Destruction" (WMD)?
    a. Military assault-rifle weapons
    b. Nuclear weapons
    c. Biological weapons
    d. Chemical weapons

3. Prior to modern times, terrorists have granted which of the following categories of people immunity from attack?
    a. Women and children
    b. Elderly and disabled
    c. Doctors and medical personnel
    d. All of the above

4. Clues surrounding a terrorist incident and/or attack will reveal whether domestic or international terrorism was involved and will point toward possible motives and the perpetrators behind the incident. Which of the following might provide a clue to understanding the terrorist's motive?
    a. Types of weapons used
    b. Timing of the event
    c. Extent of destruction encountered
    d. None of the above

5. Which of the following is an example of a symbolic and historical terrorist's target?
    a. African American church
    b. Headquarters of a White supremacist group
    c. Annual men's college volleyball event
    d. Annual women's gymnastic event

6. *Shielding* can be used to address specific types of hazards. Which of the following is an example of shielding?
   a. Self-contained breathing apparatuses
   b. Body armor
   c. Buildings and walls
   d. All of the above

7. Responding to a terrorist event presents unique law enforcement and public safety challenges. One of the first responder's key activities that needs to be simultaneously implemented and coordinated is:
   a. Finalizing the FBI and FEMA coordinated plans
   b. The control of rumors, stereotypes, and attacks on multicultural populations
   c. Perimeter control
   d. Evacuation of religious artifacts

8. In multicultural communities, the decision to evacuate is determined in part by which of the following elements?
   a. Availability of military personnel to escort the community members to safe grounds
   b. Ministers and priests who would be able to lend credibility to the evacuation decision
   c. Degree or severity of public dangers, harms, and threats as estimated by the hazards and risk assessment
   d. None of the above

9. Preparation and planning provide some of the best avenues for successful crisis management and subsequent recovery from a terrorist incident. Which of the following planned steps have been determined to be critical?
   a. Ensure availability of multicultural law enforcement personnel with language expertise
   b. Acquire the necessary protective and communication equipment
   c. Establish a network of multicultural leaders and communities for communication, intelligence, and response implementation
   d. All of the above

10. The involvement of ethnic and multicultural media is critical for releasing information to enable the safety and security of all community residents, and includes serving which of the following functions?
    a. Getting multicultural community leadership to buy-in on plans and procedures
    b. Alleviating any unnecessary fears or concerns
    c. Generating favorable press coverage and media examples
    d. None of the above

Fill-in-the-Blanks

1. Police response to terrorist attacks and the actions that might prevent them are usually accomplished in _____ cities, neighborhoods, and communities.

2. *Terrorism* is defined as, "A violent act or an act dangerous to human life, in violation of the _____ laws of the United States or any segment to intimidate or coerce a government, the civilian p o pulation, or any segment thereof, in furtherance of political or social objectives" (U.S. Department of Justice, 1997).

3. Law enforcement's knowledge, skills, resources, and sensitivity to multicultural community issues and concerns will facilitate the effectiveness of its response in the three stages of a terrorism incident: _____ an act of terrorism.

4. Terrorists in the United States continue a general trend in which fewer attacks are occurring in the United States, but individual attacks are becoming more _____.

5. The more that law enforcement works with a community-policing model to understand the make-up of a multicultural community, the greater the likelihood that officers will have the knowledge to _____ potential terrorist targets within communities.

6. Law enforcement personnel, as first responders to terrorists' crimes, need to know that the forms of self-protection against WMD can be defined in terms of the principals of time, distance, and _____.

7. Knowledge of the multicultural communities, customs, and practices of people affected in an incident would facilitate establishing _____ to enhance public safety, security, and care for the casualties and victims.

8. Following any establishment of perimeters, law enforcement officers may need to communicate to the multicultural community the _____ for their exclusion from the area.

9. The responsibilities for responding to a terrorist incident or attack involving nuclear, biological, and chemical Weapons of Mass Destruction (WMD) materials are outlined in _____.

10. Law enforcement agencies need to understand that, whether in crisis management or in daily peacekeeping, the media has a dual role: to obtain information, stories, and perspectives on the incident for news reporting objectives; and to _____ the community efficiently of impending dangers and threats stemming from the incident.

Discussion

1. Discuss how the FBI's (1996) definitions of the two types of t e r r o rism that occur in the United States, *domestic terrorism,* and *international terrorism* might affect multicultural communities in the U.S. in law enforcement situations.

2. Discuss how multicultural knowledge, skills, and resources are important in multicultural communities for the: (1) preparation of local communities for safety and security with regard to terrorism, (2) prevention of possible terrorists' crimes and incidents, (3) participation in emergency response to terrorism, (4) investigation and information-gathering involving terrorists, and (5) follow-up actions and prosecution of crimes involving and/or resulting from terrorism.

3. Discuss the rationale for terrorists to attack *infrastructure systems* and *services* which may include those structures and operations which are vital for the continued functioning of our country (e.g., communication companies, power grids, water treatment facilities, mass transit, telecommunication towers, and transportation hubs). Provide examples of how different segments of the multicultural community might be more vulnerable and be more harmed by attacks on their infrastructure systems and services.

4. Delineate approaches about the most effective ways to communicate and to rapidly disseminate warnings based upon the multicultural communities involved in a terrorist's attack.

5. On-scene commanders need to be aware of and provide the resources for public safety personnel's critical incident debriefing. Discuss some of the cultural considerations when conducting on-site critical incident debriefings with multicultural personnel.

TOOLS AND SKILLS IN PRACTICE

1. *Understanding the Functions of Police Service in the War on Terrorism*—For your city or town of interest, go to the on-line reports (or the actual Minutes of the meetings on file) for the: (a) "Office of Homeland Security," (b) "Police Commission," (c) "Public Safety Commission" and/or (d) "Emergency Services Commission." Scan the Minutes of the meetings for "war on terrorism" and "homeland security" issues. Note any recurring issues or trends involving different multicultural community groups. If on-line services are not available in your area, go the Town Hall or City Hall and read the past Minutes of the above-noted Office and/or Commissions for the last year; the website and Minutes of the Office of Homeland Security and Police Commission and other meetings are usually open to the public.

WHAT ARE YOUR THOUGHTS AND WHAT WOULD YOU DO?

With the large numbers of Arab Americans and other Middle Eastern groups in your community, your department has been asked by the U.S. Department of Homeland Security (DHS) and by the FBI to help in the identification, location, and interviewing of individuals, their families, and other groups of Arab and/or other Middle Eastern backgrounds for homeland security and the war on terrorism purposes. So far, very little information had been received about this process from DHS or the FBI. However, your department has received a list of names, addresses, telephone numbers, and other identification from DHS. You have been assigned the responsibilities to set this up for your department and to cooperate fully with DHS and the FBI. What are your thoughts and what would you do?

Critical Thinking Questions

1. What are the facts (observable, verifiable, testable, and confirmable)?
2. What are the assumptions?
3. What are the possible stereotypes?
4. What would be your *personal* reactions to this situation?
5. What would be the possible reactions of those *who are to be interviewed* in this situation?
6. Would someone from the Arab American and other Middle Eastern community see something different? What would they see differently (if applicable)?
7. What would be your *professional* reactions to this situation?
8. What actions would you take in this situation?
9. If you had to explain your actions to the Arab American and other Middle Eastern communities, the DHS, the FBI, and your superiors in front of the news media, what would you say?

2. *Identifying Law Enforcement War on Terrorism Issues*—Knowing the key war on terrorism and homeland security issues in one's service area and the programs and services within these functions is critical to understanding the impact of these services upon the multicultural populations of your area. Two ways to obtain this information are:

   a. Use the On-line Information from the Key Newspapers of Your Area: Search, on an ongoing basis, the on-line news sources of your local area for the war on terrorism and homeland security issues that you are interested in researching. Keep a journal of the issues and topics that emerge, as well as the agencies, community members, leaders, and/or representatives named in the news articles and involved in homeland security.

   b. Search "LexisNexis Academic" On-line in Your College Library: Search the news sources for your local area for the prior year using the search terms of "terrorism" and "homeland security" along with the multicultural group(s) and the name of your city or area of interest. Keep a journal of your findings.

3. *Reviewing Law Enforcement Agency Resources and Readiness*—Go to the websites of the Office of Homeland Security and the Police Department for your town or city (or to one that is for the nearest large-size city in your area of interest). Within the two websites, search for and identify as many informational brochures, documents, and/or articles by senior law enforcement leaders and/or executives (e.g., Chief of Police, Deputy Chiefs, etc.) as possible about homeland security and the war on terrorism. Make a list and summary of any content or comments about serving the diverse and multicultural communities of the area with respect to homeland security and the war on terrorism. Review your list and summary of comments to determine the emphasis and importance of senior law enforcement leadership's focus on service to multicultural communities in this regard.

4. *Scanning for Multicultural Group Impact, Concerns, and Assistance*—Once you begin to get a sense of the different groups in your community and the key leaders of those groups, it would be important to get information on the kinds of homeland security issues these communities may have. Go on-line or in person to obtain some of the community resource guides on homeland security available in your local area. Depending upon the diversity of your community, you may find anything from a one-page flyer to a small instructional manual. For example, the neighborhood legal services may have information about civil rights violations and possible hate incidents/crimes related to stereotypes about terrorists. Senior or elderly services might have information about preparing one's home in the case of a terrorist's attack, etc. Review these resource guides to identify the needs of these groups and resources for the groups. Brainstorm some ways that the local law enforcement agencies might be able to form community partnerships with these community-based agencies to address homeland security and terrorism concerns that you have identified through the review of the materials and guides.

5. *Developing Response Scenarios Involving Multi-jurisdictional Actions*—Begin building a file in your computer or on 3 × 5 index cards (or in a "blank book" journal). On a daily basis, as you observe in your work, in the news, or in any other sources, note elements between law enforcement's efforts at homeland security (and the war on terrorism) and aspects of the multicultural community that are going well and those that could have gone better. For those aspects that have gone well, identify the key elements that made them go well. For those aspects that could have gone better, brainstorm about ways that the situation could have been improved. What could have been done differently to attain a more positive outcome? Soon, your file will contain many useful ideas for improving law enforcement homeland security services in multicultural communities.

SELF-STUDY ACTIVITIES

Terrorist Targets in Your Local Community

The chapter provided a four-priority-level approach to implementing a community assessment of possible terrorist targets. Review the possible terrorist targets in your community using the four-priority-level categorization. From your findings using the Tools and Skills #2 (Identifying Law Enforcement War on Terrorism Issues), were there any findings or suggestions regarding actions for protecting possible targets in your community? List the special challenges involved in protecting the top two priority levels of possible terrorist targets in your community. List some of the unique challenges in working with multicultural communities in this regard (either within your community or in a nearby community with multicultural neighborhoods).

Terrorist Issues within Multicultural Communities

Select an area in your city or town that would have the greatest diversity of population (e.g., race, ethnicity, age, income, and other dimensions of diversity) for this next self-study activity. From your findings using the Tools and Skills #4 (Scanning for Multicultural Group Impact, Concerns, and Assistance), were there any findings or suggestions regarding the differential impact to multicultural groups and/or communities? How would you implement and coordinate the four key activities (i.e., Initial Considerations and Assessment, Perimeter Control, Public Protection and Safety Considerations, and Crime Scene Security Considerations) in responding to a possible chemical terrorist incident in the area that you have selected?

Use of Multicultural Media Sources

The authors identified media resources as an effective way to communicate and to disseminate information to community residents. From your findings using the Tools and Skills #4 (Scanning for Multicultural Group Impact, Concerns, and Assistance), were there any key findings or suggestions regarding the use of multicultural media sources? What media resources might you use for communicating a terrorist incident involving B-NICE materials in your city or town? Provide some examples of multicultural media resources that might be used in your area. What approaches might you use to develop positive and effective relationships between these media resources and your local law enforcement agency?

Critical Incident Stress Debriefing (CISD)

CISD has been recognized as an effective tool for use with law enforcement personnel after a traumatic incident. From your findings using the Tools and Skills #5 (Developing Response Scenarios Involving Multi-jurisdictional Actions), were there any findings or suggestions regarding the use of CISD?

Using the suggested list of cultural considerations provided in the chapter, how might you organize and provide CISD to non-sworn, multicultural law enforcement personnel involved in a terrorist attack in your community?

Language and Translation Issues

Select an area in your city or town that would have the greatest diversity of languages spoken. From your findings using the Tools and Skills #5 (Developing Response Scenarios Involving Multi-jurisdictional Actions), were there any findings or suggestions regarding language, communications, and translation issues? How would you plan for and ensure adequate bilingual personnel or other language resources to assist these community residents in the case of a terrorist incident?

Chapter 11

Multicultural Law Enforcement and Homeland Security

OVERVIEW

The experience of law enforcement agencies involved in homeland security and the War on Terrorism within multicultural communities is evolving. Likewise, the emerging roles and functions for law enforcement in homeland security present many challenges for the day-to-day work within the criminal justice system and the Federal Response Plan (FRP) against terrorism. Homeland security challenges for law enforcement agencies include the following: (1) detecting and preventing attacks of terrorism; these can be made more complex within multicultural communities because of the past histories of those communities with law enforcement in the United States, as well as in their native homelands; (2) avoiding stereotypes and possible biased perceptions based on ethnicity, culture, race and religion that may be evoked within multicultural communities, and (3) working with multicultural community leaders regarding their perceptions of police actions and efforts in homeland security. Officers should realize that some citizens may have been victims of terrorism, as well as being harmed by the anti-terrorism efforts within their native homeland (while innocent of any involvement with terrorism). These citizens carry with them stereotypes of police services as something to be feared and avoided. Law enforcement officials need to go out of their way to work with multicultural communities to establish trust, to provide outreach efforts, and to win cooperation in order to effectively accomplish their goals for homeland security efforts. Building partnerships focused on community collaboration in the fight against terrorism is important locally and nationally.

Attitudes and skills that enhance multicultural law enforcement include: (1) respecting cultural behaviors that may be different from one's own, (2) observing and understanding behaviors important to diverse communities, and (3) analyzing and interpreting diverse behaviors for services application within multicultural communities. These same multicultural attitudes and skills form the core elements, when coupled with an intelligence-based approach, in detecting and predicting terrorist actions and activities for homeland security.

Since the establishment of the Department of Homeland Security, law enforcement agencies have been receiving a variety of intelligence information, advisories, warnings, and other pertinent communications regarding the efforts and activities to be implemented within local communities. Local law enforcement agencies and officers, because of their knowledge of the existing multicultural communities and networks, have been called upon to aid in the data-gathering and development of useful intelligence regarding possible terrorists. Such efforts have often produced a mixed reception by law enforcement agencies. When local law enforcement agencies and officers are requested to provide assistance for homeland security information-gathering and the interviewing of possible terrorist suspects, some of the following steps are recommended with the multicultural communities involved:

1. Contact with Community Leaders: Law enforcement officers need to work closely with community leaders to establish a cooperative plan for gathering the needed information. Community leaders could work with the law enforcement agencies' community relations office to develop a communication plan for the effective dissemination of information.

2. Utilize a Communication Plan: It is critical to have a well-developed communication plan to ensure that the proper messages are provided to the multicultural communities involved. This is particularly important when language translations and interpretation services are necessary.

3. Define explicitly and spell out the implications for participation in the data-gathering process: Providing clearly defined procedures and information regarding how the data-gathering and interviews are to be used is most important. Additionally, if there are possible consequences (e.g., with the INS), these elements should be delineated to ensure an ongoing relationship of "trust" with members of the multicultural communities involved.

4. Utilize law enforcement personnel and translators/interpreters from the same or similar multicultural communities: Use of law enforcement personnel who are from the same or similar ethnic or cultural communities would contribute to maintaining relationships, building the trust necessary in such information-gathering processes.

Some multicultural community members, because of their past experiences with law enforcement, may be reluctant to participate in homeland security efforts. It is important for law enforcement departments and officials to build relationships and working partnerships with multicultural communities to ensure effective participation in combating terrorism and implementing homeland security.

Law enforcement agencies need to protect the safety of multicultural communities from harassment and discrimination resulting from the terrorist stereotype. Some victims are harassed and attacked because of the way they look or what they are wearing. Victimization also includes the accusation of terrorism or the identification of an innocent person as a possible terrorist. Multicultural community residents who are unjustly discriminated against or stereotyped as "terrorists" must be able to trust that prosecutors, judges, parole, and probation will utilize their full armamentarium to deter and jail terrorists, as well as those who unjustly terrorize, discriminate, or harass those who are unfairly stereotyped as terrorists.

Although the use of race and ethnicity is allowed under Federal policy and guidelines for the identification of terrorist threats and to stop possible terrorist attacks, law enforcement officers need to be cautious in the use of racial profiling for detecting terrorists and in homeland security matters.

A key challenge for law enforcement efforts in homeland security includes sustaining the community-policing and law enforcement services within multicultural neighborhoods. In times of scarce funding resources, on-the-street, community-policing efforts might take a back seat to homeland security and the fight on terrorism. Moreover, since contact with multicultural communities will increase because of the emerging roles for law enforcement in homeland security, the need for additional bilingual officers and personnel will be paramount for these communities. As part of emergency preparation, the need to provide clear communications and to ensure understanding of emergency instructions will require additional bilingual personnel and translators for these diverse communities.

RATIONALE FOR THE FOCUS
ON THE KEY CONCEPTS AND TOOLS

Officers and practitioners involved in multicultural law enforcement need to be able to:

1. Understand the role that law enforcement has in homeland security within multicultural communities

2. Address the six goals of homeland security in multicultural and diverse communities

3. Highlight the complexities of homeland security involving multi-jurisdictional efforts

4. Provide specific response strategies for homeland security in terms of collaborative work within local, state, and federal agencies

5. Delineate recommendations for law enforcement officers and other emergency services personnel for protecting homeland security within multicultural communities

INTRODUCTION

The President of the United States created the Department of Homeland Security (DHS) as a cabinet-level Department on November 25, 2002 with the main objective of protecting this Nation from terrorism. With the development of the DHS comes many new roles for law enforcement officers and agencies. These include detecting threats of terrorism, coordinating the security efforts against terrorism, developing and analyzing information regarding threats and vulnerabilities, and using information and intelligence provided in coordination with the DHS. The major goals of the Department of Homeland Security focus upon:

1. Preventing attacks of terrorism

2. Reducing vulnerabilities to terrorist attacks

3. Analyzing threats of terrorism and issuing warnings accordingly

4. Providing security for our transportation systems and for the borders of the United States

5. Preparing for emergency readiness and response

6. Minimizing the damage from terrorism and facilitating recovery from terrorist attacks

This chapter focuses on the roles and functions of law enforcement officers and agencies in their work by addressing the six goals of homeland security in multicultural communities. Clearly, criminal justice practices and procedures already define much of the homeland security work and activities within law enforcement agencies. The emphasis in this chapter is on the specific aspects of multicultural law enforcement, which are applicable to homeland security issues in the context of our diverse communities.

KEY CONCEPTS

Outline of Key Presentation Points

1. Major Goals of the Department of Homeland Security (DHS)

2. Definition for Homeland Security

3. Historical Background

4. Policy Focus: Dealing with Enemies and Events Outside of the U.S.

5. Law Enforcement Response Strategies

6. Myths and Stereotypes about Terrorists

7. Key Attitudes and Skills Important in Homeland Security

8. Changing Perceptions of Who the Terrorists Are

9. Developing and Analyzing Information Regarding Vulnerabilities

10. Using Information and Intelligence Provided

11. Working with Multicultural Communities on Prevention and Response

12. Key Issues in Law Enforcement

PRACTICE QUESTIONS

True or False

_____ 1. Prior to September 11, 2001, the United States had very few terrorist incidents and attacks.

_____ 2. Starting around the mid-1990s, involvement of local and regional law enforcement agencies was extensive in the planning, policy development, and implementation of the Federal response to terrorism and homeland security.

_____ 3. Stereotypic views of multicultural groups who might be potential terrorists reduce individuals within this group to simplistic, one-dimensional caricatures and are ineffective for law enforcement.

_____ 4. As noted by Stern (2004), the official profile of a typical terrorist—developed by the Department of Homeland Security to scrutinize visa applicants and resident aliens—applies only to men.

_____ 5. In the case of Timothy McVeigh, the Oklahoma City bomber, law enforcement officials properly interpreted information, and this led to his arrest at a traffic stop.

_____ 6. The work of law enforcement agencies in homeland security and the War on Terrorism will continue to be a "work in progress."

_____ 7. In the area of homeland security, current Federal policy prohibits the use of "racial profiling" except under narrowly defined circumstances to deal with terrorism and terrorist threats.

_____ 8. Behavior-recognition profiles have been ineffective in detecting individuals who might be potential terrorists (Howard and Sawyer, 2004).

_____ 9. The need for bilingual officers and personnel will decrease because of the emerging roles for law enforcement in homeland security.

_____ 10. Foreign terrorist groups include the Popular Front for the Liberation of Palestine (PLO).

MULTIPLE CHOICE

1. One example of the need for greater homeland security efforts in the United States prior to September 11, 2001, included the:

    a. Existence of organized crime in major urban cities

    b. Assassinations of President John F. Kennedy and Rev. Martin Luther King, Jr.

    c. Use of community-oriented policing for peacekeeping in multicultural communities

    d. All of the above

2. To date, most of the training in law enforcement for homeland security has been in the form of:

    a. Short briefings

    b. Readings

    c. Television, by way of the news media

    d. All of the above

3. Some of the current stereotypes that might affect law enforcement officers' perceptions of terrorists include which of the following:

    a. Arab and Middle Eastern Nationality or ethnic/cultural background

    b. Logical and rational, trained assassins

    c. Extremely skilled and trained professionals that cannot be stopped

    d. Members in many diverse groups rallying under the al-Qaida banner

4. According to most terrorism experts, terrorism against America can only be defeated through:

    a. Careful intelligence collection

    b. Resolving the root complaints of the terrorist-supporting population

    c. Cooperative efforts among law enforcement and intelligence agencies

    d. All of the above

5. When local law enforcement agencies and officers are called upon to provide assistance in information-gathering and interviewing possible terrorist suspects within multicultural communities, which of the following is one of the critical steps to include?

   a. Contact community leaders

   b. Conduct information-gathering and interviewing in Federal facilities only

   c. Utilize people from the community as translators and interpreters

   d. Provide monetary rewards for those who step up with information

6. Which of the following are key homeland security issues for law enforcement in multicultural communities?

   a. Reluctance to report and participate in Homeland Security efforts

   b. Victimization where harassment and discrimination resulted from being stereotyped as terrorist

   c. Differential treatment because of law enforcement officers' perceptions of them as threats to homeland security or as possible terrorists

   d. All of the above

7. Which of the following is a reason for the significant under-representation of multicultural and bilingual personnel in federal, state, and local law enforcement and criminal justice positions?

   a. Positive recruitment of minority and under-represented groups in law enforcement

   b. Concern with and fear of background checks, physical requirements, and the application process

   c. Promotion of multicultural and bilingual personnel to higher management positions

   d. None of the above

8. According to Homeland Security figures, how many immigrants are in the United States illegally?

   a. 250,000

   b. 800,000

   c. 7 million

   d. 23 million

9. According to Malcolm W. Nance, a twenty-year veteran of the U.S. intelligence community's Combating Terrorism Program and author of *The Terrorist Recognition Handbook*, most terrorists are generally:

   a. Insane and behave like automatons
   b. Intelligent and clear thinking
   c. Unmotivated and only follow orders
   d. From wealthy family backgrounds

10. Throughout this text, the authors have emphasized attitudes and skills required of law enforcement officials in a multicultural society such as:

   a. Respecting cultural behaviors that may be different from one's own
   b. Observing and understanding behaviors important to diverse communities
   c. Analyzing and interpreting diverse behaviors within multicultural communities
   d. All of the above

Fill-in-the-Blanks

1. As a result of the perceived advantage of _____ to the United States, many of the efforts and activities for homeland security in the past were located within the functions of the Federal government (e.g., FBI, CIA, military, Department of State), to be implemented outside of the United States.

2. The role of the Department of Homeland Security (DHS) is one of facilitating and developing the avenues of _____ among Federal agencies to ensure viable and effective leadership, policies, and procedures for homeland security in the United States.

3. Terrorist Attack Pre-incident Indicators (TAPIs) is a term used by the _____ to describe actions and behaviors taken by terrorists before they carry out an attack (Nance, 2003).

4. Multicultural skills and knowledge are also elements that can contribute to detecting and predicting terrorist actions and activities for homeland security when coupled with a(n) _____ approach.

5. Prior to the bombing of the Alfred P. Murrah Federal Building in Oklahoma City, one law enforcement and intelligence _____ held that U.S. domestic terrorists were not capable of mass destruction, but were merely a criminal nuisance element of society (Heymann, 2001).

6. Residents in diverse communities representing different races, ethnic backgrounds, religions, and other aspects of diversity, must be able to _____ that they will be treated fairly and protected as part of homeland security.

7. Provisions of Articles IV, V, and VI of the U.S. Constitution, as well as the Bill of Rights, offer powerful protections against law enforcement _____, which, by extension, applies to international terrorists operating on our soil.

8. Law enforcement agencies may also want to include into their _____ Academies' information regarding homeland security and ways that the multicultural communities can participate and provide assistance to the public safety departments.

9. Men from the Sikh religion wear _____, and this is often stereotyped to be indicative of "foreign terrorists."

10. The use of _____ is allowed under Federal policy and guidelines for the identification of terrorist threats and to stop possible terrorist attacks.

Discussion

1. Delineate some of the multicultural examples of Terrorist Attack Pre-incident Indicators (TAPIs) used in law enforcement and others to detect individuals who might be potential criminals or terrorists.

2. Discuss examples of how several of the September 11, 2001, terrorists behaved in ways that threw off any surveillance based upon cultural and religious stereotypes.

3. Discuss how law enforcement officers, without proper intelligence, would find it almost impossible to interpret effectively behaviors that were observed using the examples of the September 11, 2001, terrorists who were involved in traffic stops by the police for speeding on three separate occasions prior to the terrorists' attacks.

4. Discuss and provide examples of how prejudices and stereotypes left unchecked and acted upon can result in not only unfairness, humiliation, and citizen complaints, but also in missed opportunities for building long-term police–community relationships important for homeland security.

5. Discuss how the key challenges in developing and implementing law enforcement efforts in homeland security include sustaining the community-policing and law enforcement services within multicultural neighborhoods.

WHAT ARE YOUR THOUGHTS AND WHAT WOULD YOU DO?

Your department has received several calls from neighborhood "safety watch" groups that there might be a possible al Qaida or other terrorist group cell o p e rating out of a housing project in the neighborhood. These calls to the department indicate that there were very suspicious activities involving several apartments in the housing project. "Arab"- or "Muslim"-looking men (some with head coverings like turbans) seemed to go in and out of those residences at different times of the night and day. The shades for those residences seem to be down all the time (even during daylight hours). People in those residences seem to keep to themselves, and were very unfriendly. They stayed away from the rest of their neighbors. The "safety watch" groups wanted to contact the local police before going to the FBI. You have been assigned to follow up with the safety watch groups and with those who made the report. What are your thoughts and what would you do?

Critical Thinking Questions

1. What are the facts (observable, verifiable, testable, and confirmable)?

2. What are the assumptions?

3. What are the possible stereotypes?

4. What would be your *personal* reactions to this situation?

5. What would be the possible reactions of *the "safety watch" groups* and *those who live in the "suspicious" apartments* to this situation?

6. Would someone from the Arab American and Other Middle Eastern communities (as well as other minority communities) see something different? What would they see differently (if applicable)?

7. What would be your *professional* reactions to this situation?

8. What actions would you take in this situation?

9. If you had to explain your actions to the Arab American and other Middle Eastern communities, the residents of the apartments, the "safety watch" groups, the FBI, and your superiors in front of the news media, what would you say?

TOOLS AND SKILLS IN PRACTICE

1. *Identifying Law Enforcement Roles and Functions in Homeland Security*—Go online as follows: (a) for your city or town of interest, go to the on-line information for the "Office of Homeland Security," (b) for your state go to the Peace Officers Standard and Training (POST) website and search for "homeland security," and (c) for the national perspective, go to http://www.dhs.gov (Department of Homeland Security), and scan the reports and information regarding "law enforcement," "police," "emergency services," "first responders," and "homeland security." Note any recurring issues or trends

involving the roles and functions of the police and of law enforcement. Summarize your findings and keep a list of the roles and f u n ctions identified.

2. *Working with Multicultural Communities on Prevention and Response*—Go to the websites of the Office of Homeland Security and the Police Department for your town or city (or to one that is for the nearest large-size city in your area of interest). Within the two websites, search for and identify as many informational elements about work with multicultural communities in the areas of homeland security. Make a list and summary of any content or comments about serving the diverse and multicultural communities of the area with respect to homeland security and the war on terrorism. Review your list and summary of comments to determine the emphasis and importance of senior law enforcement leadership's focus on service to multicultural communities in this regard.

3. *Developing Response Strategies and Community Intelligence Sources*—Knowing the key homeland security, response strategies, and community information sources in one's service area and the programs and services within these areas is critical toward understanding the impact of these services upon the multicultural populations of your area. Two ways to obtain this information are:

   a. Use the On-line Information from the Key Newspapers of Your Area: Search, on an ongoing basis, the on-line news sources of your local area for the war on terrorism and homeland security issues that you are interested in researching. Keep a journal of the issues and topics that emerge, as well as the agencies, community members, leaders, and/or representatives named in the news articles and involved in homeland security.

   b. Search "LexisNexis Academic" On-line in Your College Library: Search the news sources for your local area for the prior year using the search terms of "terrorism" and "homeland security" along with the multicultural group(s) and the name of your city or area of interest. Keep a journal of your findings.

4. *Preparing for Multicultural Community and Media Reponses*— Begin building a file in your computer or on 3 × 5 index cards (or in a "blank book" journal). On a daily basis, as you observe in your work, in the news, or in any other sources, note elements between law enforcement's efforts at homeland security (and the war on te rrorism) and aspects of communicating and working with the m u lticultural community that are going well and those that could have gone better. Pay particular attention to aspects of media relationship, news releases, and other types of mass communication efforts. For those aspects that have gone well, identify the key elements that made them go well. For those aspects that could have gone better,

brainstorm about ways that the situation could have been improved. What could have been done differently to attain a more positive o u tcome? Soon, your file will contain many useful ideas for improving law enforcement homeland security communications, media efforts, and homeland security informational services in m u lticultural communities.

SELF-STUDY ACTIVITIES

Homeland Security Roles for Law Enforcement in Your Local Community

The chapter provided the six major goals of the Department of Homeland Security (DHS). From your findings using the Tools and Skills #1 (Identifying Law Enforcement Roles and Functions in Homeland Security), were there any critical findings or suggestions regarding actions for the homeland security roles of law enforcement in your community using the six major DHS goals? List the special challenges and opportunities involved in implementing the top two or three DHS goals for law enforcement agencies in your community. What are some of the unique law enforcement challenges related to the implementation of these six goals within multicultural communities?

Stereotyping and Biased Perceptions

Law enforcement officers and agencies must guard themselves from using a stereotype-based or racial profiling approach for detecting terrorism and in providing homeland security. From your findings using the Tools and Skills #2 (Working with Multicultural Communities on Prevention and Response), were there any findings or suggestions regarding what to do about stereotypes and "false reports" in your community? Which groups or individuals in your community might be stereotyped as possible terrorists? What characteristics of these groups and individuals make them susceptible to stereotyping and biased perceptions? What are ways for professional peace officers to guard themselves against such ineffective practices?

Working with Multicultural Groups in Your Community on Homeland Security

The authors recommended some guidelines and approaches for collaborative efforts in information-gathering and in implementing homeland s e c urity efforts within multicultural communities. From your findings using the Tools and Skills #2 (Working with Multicultural Communities on Prevention and Response), were there any findings or suggestions regarding how best to work with multicultural communities on information-gathering? Select one or more multicultural groups that are part of your community (or a part of a nearby community). How would you apply the suggested guidelines and approaches to working with these multicultural groups?

Recruiting and Using Multicultural and Language-Expert Law Enforcement Personnel

The authors noted the importance of having multicultural and language-expert personnel in working with multicultural communities. From your findings using the Tools and Skills #3 (Developing Response Strategies and Community Intelligence Sources), were there any findings or suggestions regarding how one might begin to recruit and develop multicultural and l a nguage-expert personnel? How would you go about recruiting and using such personnel in your local community? Do you see roles for the use of volunteers who have such backgrounds and language-expertise in h o m eland security efforts? What are the advantages and disadvantages of using community volunteers in homeland security activities?

Part 4

RESPONSE STRATEGIES FOR CRIMES MOTIVATED BY HATE/BIAS AND RACIAL PROFILING

Part 4 provides a detailed explanation of strategies for preventing, controlling, reporting, monitoring, and investigating crimes that are based on hate or bias because of the victim's race, ethnicity, national origin, religion, or sexual orientation. Criminal cases of these types have come to be known as bias or hate crimes; non-criminal cases are referred to as incidents. Some agencies refer to these acts as civil rights violations. The chapters that follow contain policies, practices, and procedures for responding to these types of crimes or incidents. We recognize that other groups, such as women, the elderly, the homeless, and the disabled, are sometimes victimized. However, in this book we focus primarily on hate crimes and incidents wherein the motivation was related to the victim's race, ethnicity, national origin, religion, or sexual orientation. The reasons for collecting data on crimes and incidents motivated by hate/bias committed by individuals or organized groups are included in Chapter 13. The end of that chapter provides examples to help students, members of the criminal justice system, and the community to develop sensitive and workable programs for handling these crimes and incidents. The recommended policies, training, practices, and procedures outlined in this text are currently in operation in most law enforcement agencies across the nation and are based on studies and recommendations by the U.S. Department of Justice's Community Relations Service. The Commission on Peace Officer Standards and Training, found in all states of the nation, has been another major source of materials. The final chapter provides information about racial profiling for members of the criminal justice system. The type of policing reviewed in this unit is a civilizing process that will contribute to multicultural coexistence and cooperation. All law enforcement professionals should have a good working knowledge of the guidelines that follow.

Chapter 12

Hate/Bias Crimes: Victims, Laws, Investigations, and Prosecutions

OVERVIEW

Racism and crimes motivated by hate are two of the most challenging issues confronting the United States today. Our nation includes people from around the world who are guaranteed the rights to be free of discrimination, bias, and violence. Yet we continue to witness incidents of hatred manifested in violence toward people perceived as "different." Racism and the resulting hate violence, biased treatment, and discrimination cause divisions between people and deny them their dignity. Racism is a disease that devastates society. Police officers should be at the forefront in the battle to combat such criminal behavior within society. Law enforcement must lead in the protection of human and civil rights of all citizens.

The presence of hate/bias crimes and incidents is often attributed to changing national and international conditions, immigration, and ethnic demographic change translated to a local environment. As immigrants, persons of color, or persons of different religious beliefs or sexual orientation move into previously unintegrated areas, an increased threat of hate/bias crimes can be expected. It is not just a problem for the criminal justice system, but rather must be addressed jointly by the whole community, including families, schools, business, labor, and social services. In taking the lead, law enforcement agencies can motivate other groups to join with them in their efforts to reduce hate violence.

Progress toward tolerance among peoples, mutual respect, and unity has been painfully slow in our country and marked with repeated setbacks. Criminal statutes and civil remedies to curb the problem in various jurisdictions across the nation have also been enacted slowly. Divisive racial attitudes, anti-immigrant sentiment, the increased number of hate/bias incidents, and the deepening despair of minorities and the poor make the need for solutions even more pressing.

RATIONALE FOR THE FOCUS ON THE KEY CONCEPTS AND TOOLS

Officers and practitioners involved in multicultural law enforcement need to be able to:

1. Define as well as differentiate between a hate crime and hate incident

2. Understand the scope of the hate crime problem, including historical perspectives

3. Discuss response strategies to hate crimes and appropriate victim assistance techniques

4. Understand the hate crimes related to anti-Semitism and sexual orientation

5. Explain hate crime laws, investigative procedures, and offender prosecution

INTRODUCTION

Chapter 12 focuses on hate/bias crimes and how they are investigated and prosecuted. The chapter first discusses the scope of the problem, providing historical perspectives and examples. We stress that the law enforcement professional must be aware of discrimination and hate crimes directed toward immigrants and people from different ethnic, national origin, racial, sexual orientation, and religious backgrounds. We present some aspects of urban dynamics as they relate to the economy, hate violence, move-in violence, and hate/bias crimes and incidents. In this chapter, while we devote some attention to crimes against new immigrants, the primary focus is on hate crimes against Jews, gays, and lesbians. We discuss the importance of hate crime investigations and treatment of the victims because of the unique impact on them as well as the community. The chapter highlights the need for law enforcement officials to treat hate violence with the same degree of concern as heinous crimes such as rape and sexual assault. It presents i n f o rmation on special statutes that provide for not only the investigations of hate/bias crimes, but also for increased penalties for the perpetrator.

KEY CONCEPTS

Outline of Key Presentation Points

1. Historical Perspective

2. The Hate/Bias Crime Problem

3. Intergroup Conflict Key Factors

4. U.S. Commission on Civil Rights, Intimidation, and Violence Report (1990)

5. Scope of Hate Crimes Nationally

6. Definition of Hate Crime and Hate Incident
7. Hate Crime Perpetrators
8. Hate Crime Urban Dynamics Theories
9. Mini-Case Discussion: Philadelphia Police Department
10. Jews and Anti-Semitism
11. Lesbian, Gay, Bisexual, or Transgender Victimization
12. War-Related Hate Crimes
13. Hate Crime Laws
14. Hate/Bias Crime and Incident Investigations: General Checklist
15. Models for Investigating Hate/Bias Crimes for Police Departments
16. Models of Effective and Successful Approaches for Police Departments
17. Special Problems in Prosecuting Hate/Bias Crimes
18. Mini-Case Study: Pleasant Hill, CA
19. Law Enforcement and the Victim
20. Officers Involved in the Investigation

PRACTICE QUESTIONS

True or False

_____ 1. Violence motivated by racial, religious, ethnic/national origin, or sexual orientation hatred has existed for generations in the United States and seems to be on the rise.

_____ 2. Victims of hate/bias crimes are particularly sensitive and unsettled because they feel powerless to alter the situation since they cannot change their racial, ethnic, or religious backgrounds.

_____ 3. Hate crimes are the most extreme and dangerous manifestations of racism.

_____ 4. The federal definition of hate crime addresses civil rights violations under Title 18 U.S.C. Section 45.

_____ 5. Federal definitions of hate crime incorporate only violence against individuals or groups, and not crimes against property such as arson or vandalism (e.g., those directed against community centers or houses of worship).

_____ 6. The five states usually reporting the most anti-Semitic incidents are those with the largest Jewish populations and thus the most targets: New York, California, New Jersey, Massachusetts, and Florida.

_____ 7. Hate crimes targeting lesbian, gay, bisexual, or transgender (LGBT) individuals are distinct from other bias crimes because they target a group made up of every other category discussed within this textbook.

_____ 8. Nationally, 2002 was the deadliest year for transgender persons in the United States, with a 30 percent increase in anti-transgender murders over the previous year.

_____ 9. Despite the "Don't Ask, Don't Tell" policy put into place under former President Clinton, the most horrific homophobic hate crimes to date have been committed by military personnel against fellow service members.

_____ 10. Many victims of hate crimes do not report their attacks to police out of fear, and believe that their best defense is to remain quiet.

Multiple Choice

1. In 1994 the International Red Cross estimated that _____ Tutsis of Rwanda were murdered in what many referred to as genocide carried out by Hutu extremists.

   a. 15,000
   b. 250,000
   c. 575,000
   d. 800,000

2. Which are the four key factions identified by Robin Wright as c o ntributing to intergroup conflict?

   a. Ethnocentrism, inhumanity, dollar economy, and slave trade
   b. Stereotyping, abundant resources, politics, and freedom of movement
   c. Migration, power quest, insecurity, and limited resources
   d. None of the above

3. Tracking hate crimes, which are typically underreported, did not begin in earnest until:

   a. 1965
   b. 1984
   c. 1992
   d. 2001

4. The 2002 Bureau of Justice Statistics (BJS) indicated that between 2000 and 2001, hate crimes in the United States:
   a. Decreased by 2.5 percent
   b. Increased by 21 percent
   c. Stayed about the same
   d. Increased only slightly by 0.4 percent

5. Ron Martinelli, a criminologist and former San Jose, CA, police officer, provides a model of urban ecology that explains in simple terms what takes place when new ethnic minorities settle in an ex i s ting core area (inner city) that is often already economically depressed. Martinelli's theory is called the:
   a. Urban Welfare Theory
   b. Core-City Value Theory
   c. Concentric Zone Theory
   d. Old-New Minority Theory

6. Researchers and hate/bias enforcement officials (McDevitt, 1989; Southern Poverty Law Center, 1987) have found that neighborhood integration, competition for jobs and services, and the following key issue create the primary scenario for hate crimes:
   a. Drugs
   b. "Turf" disputes
   c. Religion
   d. Color lines

7. Several different types of groups in the United States have exhibited anti-Semitic attitudes, and some of the most extreme groups have committed hate crimes against Jews. The most glaringly anti-Semitic organizations are white supremacist groups, such as:
   a. Ku Klux Klan (KKK)
   b. Aryan Nation
   c. Posse Comitatus
   d. All of the above

8. The FBI's "Hate Crime Statistics 2001" indicated that bias crimes based on sexual orientation made up what percent of all reported hate crimes, accounting for the fourth-highest category (after race, ethnic/national origin, and religion)?
   a. 5.3 percent
   b. 7.2 percent
   c. 14.3 percent
   d. 28.1 percent

9. Although there are many cases nationwide of individuals attacking LGBT person(s) verbally and/or physically, Grobeson suggests that most gay-bashing suspects fit specific profiles such as:

   a. Being a gang member or member of a white supremacist group
   b. Being from a very poor and economically deprived neighborhood
   c. Having prior relationships with prostitutes and drug dealers
   d. All of the above

10. Many district attorneys' offices in the United States now have attorneys and/or units that specialize in hate crime prosecution. The most effective and successful approaches that build a climate of public safety have been those that have:

    a. Standardized procedures to prosecute hate crime cases, including vertical prosecution of cases
    b. Appointed attorneys to be liaisons with various ethnic, racial, religious, and sexual orientation groups in the community
    c. Provided all attorneys on staff with cultural awareness or sensitivity training
    d. All of the above

Fill-in-the-Blanks

1. History has shown that increasing diversity has led to _____ conflict in countries throughout the world. This fact requires police to seriously consider their role in moderating complex _____ relationships within the communities that they serve.

2. Individuals involved in hate/bias crimes are not the only victims, because often fears of similar crimes can affect _____.

3. A 1993 study by Northeastern University determined that a large number of hate crime perpetrators are _____; sixty percent of offenders committed crimes for the thrill associated with the victimization.

4. The 2002 Bureau of Justice Statistics (BJS) indicated that _____, with 2899 victims of single bias hate crimes in 2001, were by far the largest group of victims (as they have been since the FBI began gathering hate crime statistics).

5. The collection of hate crime information by law enforcement agencies is _____.

6. _____ often results when blue-collar jobs are unavailable, and the distress that accompanies unemployment and rising prices is often directed toward immigrants and minorities manifesting itself in harassment and violence.

7. For the past three decades, _____ have made up one of the fastest-growing immigrant groups in the country. Their numbers have increased seven-fold since 1970 compared to a tripling of the overall immigrant population during that period.

8. The city of Philadelphia tested a way to prevent move-in violence in 1986 by utilizing a newly created and still existing police unit called the _____ Team.

9. The term anti-Semitism means _____, which literally includes Jews and Arabs. Popular use of this term, however, refers to anti-Jewish sentiment.

10. Homophobia is defined as, "an _____ fear, hatred, ignorance, or general discomfort with gay, lesbian, bisexual, or transgender persons topics or issues."

Discussion

1. Discuss the factors identified in the U.S. Commission on Civil Rights, Intimidation, and Violence Report (1990) that contribute to racial intimidation and violence in multicultural and diverse communities in the United States.

2. Provide multicultural examples to illustrate each of the three elements in the Federal definition of "hate crime." Discuss how these elements define hate crimes as different from hate incidents.

3. Discuss and provide examples of how move-in violence can occur when people of one ethnicity or race move into a residence or open a business in a neighborhood composed of people from a different race or ethnicity.

4. Discuss steps that police officers can take to establish rapport and provide protection in Jewish communities (especially around the holiest days of the Jewish year, Rosh Hashanah and Yom Kippur, occurring in the early fall) when there may be heightened anxiety among some community members regarding security and anti-Jewish sentiments.

5. Discuss the reasons postulated for the phenomenon of lesbian, gay, bisexual, and transgender (LGBT) hate crimes being seriously underreported to law enforcement. Provide some examples of how law enforcement agencies might assist the LGBT communities to improve hate-crime reporting.

TOOLS AND SKILLS IN PRACTICE

1. *Scanning for Hate/Bias Crimes in Multicultural Communities*—For your city or area of interest, go to the on-line reports for the: (a) "Police Commission," (b) "Public Safety Commission" and/or

---

WHAT ARE YOUR THOUGHTS AND WHAT WOULD YOU DO?

You are a uniformed police officer and you and your cover officer have been detailed to a bar where a man has been beaten by another patron. The call to the police dispatcher was from the bartender. The other responsible individual involved in the beating has already left the bar. After hearing of the complainant and victim, your cover officer says: "This guy's a 'fag,' and they get beaten up in this bar frequently." He suggests that you don't take a report. The victim also appears reluctant to make a report and makes a statement that he is gay. What are your thoughts and what would you do?

Critical Thinking Questions

1. What are the facts (observable, verifiable, testable, and confirmable)?
2. What are the assumptions?
3. What are the possible stereotypes?
4. What would be your *personal* reactions to this situation?
5. What would be the possible *victim's* reactions to this situation?
6. Would someone from the gay/lesbian community see something different? What would he/she see different (if applicable)?
7. What would be your *professional* reactions to this situation?
8. What actions would you take in this situation? What would you say to your cover officer? What would you say to the victim?
9. If you had to explain your actions to the bartender, the gay/lesbian community, the City's Human Rights Commission, and your superiors in front of the news media, what would you say?

(c) "Emergency Services Commission." Scan the Minutes of the meetings for hate/bias crimes in multicultural communities and other related public safety issues identified (e.g., graffiti, harassment, etc.). Note any recurring hate/bias crime issues or trends involving different multicultural communities. If on-line services are not available in your area, go the Town Hall or City Hall and read the past Minutes of the above-noted commissions for the last six months to one year; the Minutes of the Police Commission and other meetings are usually open to the public.

2. *Identifying Law Enforcement Actions on Hate/Bias Crimes*—For your city or town of interest, go to the on-line reports (or the actual Minutes of the meetings on file) for the: (a) "Police Commission," (b) "Public Safety Commission," (c) "Emergency Services Commission," and/or (d) Board of Supervisors, Selectman, etc. Scan the Minutes of the meetings for law enforcement and other public safety recommendations and/or actions related to hate/bias crimes. If there are specific committees assigned to hate/bias crime issues, go to those Minutes as well. Some towns and cities may have

specific guidelines and policies for hate/bias crime issues. Note any recurring hate/bias crime issues or trends along with the stated actions and recommendations evolving from the town's or city's efforts in dealing with hate/bias crimes involving different multicultural groups. If on-line services are not available in your area, go the Town Hall or City Hall and read the past Minutes of the above-noted Commissions for the last year or two; the Minutes of the Police Commission and other meetings are usually open to the public.

3. *Developing Response Strategies and Community Networks*—From your development of the tools in previous chapters, you would have gathered information about the different ethnic/racial groups in your community and the key leaders of those groups. Review the information you have gathered to determine which of the organizations and groups consider, as part of their service areas, to include dealing with hate/bias crimes and incidents. Depending on the kinds of organizations and agencies, the response strategies and actions by the different organizations may vary greatly. For example, organizations involved in legal services would deal with hate/bias crimes and incidents very differently that those involved in elderly meals programs. Go on-line or in person to obtain some of the community resource guides available in your local area. Depending upon the size of the multicultural populations of your community, some of these resources might focus on the specific ethnic/racial groups as a whole (e.g., Native American Legal Services), specific resources (e.g., Job Counseling Services), specific religious groups (e.g., Anti-Defamation League), people with disabilities, and so forth. Review these resource guides to identify the strategies, approaches, and activities for dealing with hate/bias crimes and incidents and make a list of your findings. Brainstorm some ways that the local law enforcement agencies might be able to form community partnerships with these multicultural community-based agencies to address hate/bias crimes and incidents that you have identified through the review of the materials and guides.

4. *Working with Multicultural Communities on Prevention and Response*—Begin building a file in your computer or on 3 × 5 index cards (or in a "blank book" journal). On a daily basis, as you observe in your work, in the news, or in any other sources, note actions of law enforcement with any element, function, and/or activities related to hate/bias crimes and incidents. For a national perspective on law enforcement prevention and response to hate/bias crimes, log-on to the following websites:

   a. Bureau of Justice Statistics (BJS): http://www.ojp.usdoj.gov.bjs This resource will provide data about hate/bias crimes reported by law enforcement agencies across the nation to the FBI. BJS is also a resource center for justice topics such as hate/bias crimes training, technical assistance, publications and grants.

b. National District Attorneys Association: http://www.ndaa.org
This website is a resource for information on many subjects.
They produced a guide titled "Hate Crime: A Local
Prosecutor's Guide for Responding to Hate Crime," which covers several issues that arise during hate crime prosecutions. By
highlighting model protocols and procedures from offices
around the nation, the resource guide will help prosecutors'
offices develop policies and procedures on handling hate crime
investigations and prosecutions. It also will provide a comprehensive roadmap to individual prosecutors who are handling
hate crime cases. Both prosecutors who are working on their
first hate crime case and more experienced prosecutors of bias
crimes will find the resource guide helpful.

For those law enforcement actions related to hate/bias crimes
and incidents that have gone well, identify the key elements and/or
aspects that made it go well. For those actions that could have
gone better, brainstorm about ways that the situation could
h ave been improved. What could have been done differently to
attain a better outcome? In a short amount of time, your file will
contain many useful ideas for improving hate/bias crimes and
incidents law enforcement services in multicultural communities.

SELF-STUDY ACTIVITIES

Developing Response Strategies and Community Networks for Hate/Bias Crimes and Incidents

Based upon your findings for Tool #3 above, make a list of important elements
in the design of a community-based program to reduce the number of hate/bias
crimes and incidents in your area.

Make a list of criminal statutes in your state, county, and/or city that deal
with and penalize the perpetrator of hate/bias crimes. At the same time,
make a similar list of civil remedies and community responses. The following
issues should be considered: What civil causes of action do state and local
law provide for victims of hate crimes? What bills concerning hate violence
are being considered by the federal government, state legislature, county
board of supervisors, or city council?

Identifying Law Enforcement Actions on Hate/Bias Crimes

As part of your development of Tool #2 above, check with your local human
relations commission for the most recent update on hate crime laws in your
state and community. Also refer to the handbook, "Striking Back at Bigotry"
(a compilation of remedies under state and federal laws for hate violence)
published by the National Institute Against Prejudice and Violence for further
information. (See the textbook appendix for their address.)

Chapter 13

Hate/Bias Crimes: Reporting, Monitoring, and Response Strategies

OVERVIEW

The changing demographics of our communities, coupled with a bleak economic environment, constitute significant factors resulting in an increase in crimes motivated by hate or bias. It is clear that a national, standardized data collection process is essential so that the criminal justice system and respective communities served can grasp the scope of the problem and allocate resources accordingly. Such a system would enhance the prospects for developing an effective response to crimes motivated by hate or bias. Similar monitoring approaches must also be utilized by schools and businesses to ensure that acts of bigotry are tracked and resolved quickly and effectively.

The degree to which the criminal justice system, especially law enforcement agencies, responds to acts of hate and bias intimidation, violence, or vandalism sends a message to victims, communities (especially the groups to which the victims belong), and perpetrators that racism, discrimination, and crimes motivated by hate will not be tolerated. If the criminal justice system reacts swiftly and effectively or is proactive, perpetrators will know that their actions will result in apprehension and prosecution. Those sympathetic to perpetrators may be deterred from similar hate/bias actions. The fears of the victims' groups will be calmed, and trust toward the criminal justice system will be established. Other members of the community who are sensitive to the impact of hate/bias crimes and incidents will also react favorably when state and federal laws are vigorously enforced, leading to long-term benefits for all.

RATIONALE FOR THE FOCUS
ON THE KEY CONCEPTS AND TOOLS

Officers and practitioners involved in multicultural law enforcement need to be able to:

1. Discuss the nationwide reporting system for hate crime data collection
2. Explain the need for standardized and comprehensive statistics for the analysis of trends related to hate crimes and bias
3. Identify extremist hate groups and the organizations that monitor them

4. Develop community response strategies to reduce hate crimes and incidents

5. Understand the scanning methodology and approaches for hate/bias crimes in multicultural communities

INTRODUCTION

Chapter 13 discusses the nationwide reporting system and clearinghouse for hate crimes data collected from state and local police. Criminal justice leaders in every sector of the United States must utilize standardized and comprehensive statistics as one tool to analyze hate crime/bias trends. Using data, they must direct their resources more effectively against crimes of hate or bias and civil rights violations. In the first section of the chapter, we define the problem and establish why data collection is important. The second section continues with a discussion of the various organizations that monitor hate crimes and hate groups. The third section contains information about organized hate groups. In the fourth section, we explore conditions in communities requiring monitoring and subsequent deployment of law enforcement and community resources (community-oriented policing) that will prevent or reduce hate/bias crimes and incidents. The final section presents community response strategies to reduce hate crimes and incidents. The chapter considers the need for the community (religious institutions, schools, public agencies, private organizations, and neighborhood residents) to deal with the problem cooperatively because the challenge of hate crimes is not solely a law enforcement issue.

KEY CONCEPTS

Outline of Key Presentation Points

1. Defining the Problem
2. Purpose of Hate/Bias Data Collection
3. Boston Police Department Example
4. Hate/Bias Crime Prosecution
5. Congressional Directive: Federal Hate Crime Legislation
6. 1990 Hate Crime Statistics Act
7. Uniform Crime Reporting System
8. Importance of Monitoring Hate Groups
9. Organized Hate Groups
10. Number of Hate Groups in the United States
11. Response Alternatives to Organized Hate Groups by the Police
12. Case Study Discussion: Lewiston, Maine
13. The Future of Organized Hate Groups

14. Trend Monitoring in Multicultural Communities

15. Identifying Communities at Risk

16. Neighborhoods and Police Partnership

17. Human Relations Commissions (HRC)

18. Community Relations Services (USDOJ)

19. STEEP Typology

20. Community Resources and Programs to Reduce and Control Hate/Bias Crimes

PRACTICE QUESTIONS

True or False

_____ 1. As part of the Uniform Crime Report (UCR) Program, the FBI publishes statistics in their annual publication, *Hate Crime Statistics*, which covers hate crimes reported in all 50 states.

_____ 2. Police intelligence on hate crimes, held in each of the 50 respective state central repositories, has been very effective in reducing hate crimes.

_____ 3. In response to a growing concern and to understand the scope of the hate crime problem, the U.S. Congress enacted the federal Hate Crimes Statistics Act (HCSA) of 1990 and subsequent acts that amended the directive.

_____ 4. The ideology of Klan members, neo-Nazis, and other white supremacists advocates white supremacy, anti-Semitism, homophobia, and racism.

_____ 5. Black separatist followers such as the House of David and the Nation of Islam share the same agenda as white supremacists of racial separatism and racial supremacy.

_____ 6. Intelligence-gathering holds a minor role in law enforcement's efforts to reduce and prevent hate/bias crimes.

_____ 7. Aggressive, response investigation and prosecution of hate crimes demonstrate that police are genuinely concerned and that they see such crimes as a priority.

_____ 8. One disturbing trend is the age and gender of new members of supremacists groups: They are younger than in the past (including teenagers), and many are young women.

_____   9. The STEEP Typology has been ineffective in monitoring the trends related to hate crimes and hate incidents.

_____   10. The Community Relations Service, an arm of the U.S. Department of Homeland Security (DHS), is a specialized federal conciliation service available to state and local officials to help resolve and prevent racial and ethnic c o nflict, violence, and civil disorder.

Multiple Choice

1. A report of the Southern Poverty Law Center (SPLC) suggests that while published hate crime totals have been running at approximately 8,000 cases a year, the real figure is probably closer to the following number of cases:

   a. 5,000
   b. 10,000
   c. 25,000
   d. 50,000

2. The Simon Wiesenthal Center, based in Los Angeles, is a human rights group named after:

   a. The famous diversity awareness trainer Simon Wiesenthal
   b. The famed Nazi hunter Simon Wiesenthal
   c. The artist-in-residence Simon Wiesenthal
   d. None of the above

3. The followers of the Christian Patriots identity group belong to many different organizations and hold which of the following core beliefs:

   a. White people and people of color are fundamentally two different kinds of citizens, with different rights and responsibilities
   b. The United States is not properly a democracy, but more of a republic in which only people with property should vote
   c. The Federal Reserve banking system is unconstitutional and a tool of the "International Jewish Banking Conspiracy"
   d. All of the above

4. Networking of law enforcement agencies and the sharing of hate group information with other criminal justice agencies include the following:

    a. Formation of a cross-disciplinary coalition against racism

    b. Involvement of state and regional commitments by criminal justice agencies with other public and private entities, including the Internal Revenue Service

    c. Development of multi-tiered intervention strategies targeting enforcement, education, training, victim assistance, media relations, political activism and advocacy, and ongoing self-evaluation

    d. All of the above

5. In the case example of how a community and the police can organize around diversity and counter the actions of hate groups (i.e., by the World Church of the Creator (WCOTC) and the National Alliance) against the Somali immigrant community in Lewiston, Maine, the following approach was taken:

    a. Provide a strong show of force against racism by denying the hate groups' request for a permit to hold a hate rally

    b. Utilize advice from the Southern Poverty Law Center (especially its publication *Ten Ways to Fight Hate: A Community Response Guide*) to plan the community's response to the hate rally

    c. Plan counter-strategies with community activists to disrupt the hate rally with signs, banners, and leaflets

    d. None of the above

6. Experts predict that white supremacists will continue their political activism, which will include:

    a. "White rights" rallies, protests, and demonstrations

    b. Election campaigns by racist candidates

    c. Legislative lobbying

    d. All of the above

7. Academic authorities on hate crimes (e.g., Levin, 1993) identify three types of offenders:

    a. Racist, bigot, and drug user

    b. Thrill seeker, reactive offender, and hard-core offender

    c. Manic-depressive, hate monger, and overt aggressor

    d. None of the above

8. The acronym STEEP stands for:

   a. Social, technological, environmental, economic, and political
   b. Security, transportation, energy, education, and problem
   c. Standard training efforts ensuring progress
   d. Survival, transition, enduring, enabling, and progression

9. Typically, which of the following are social and cultural conditions leading to social unrest?

   a. Poverty and frustration with the system
   b. Perceptions of racism
   c. Unequal treatment
   d. All of the above

10. Some solutions to reduce hate/bias crimes involve going back to basics, involving grassroots institutions such as families, schools, workplaces, and religious organizations. Community resources and programs that are available or can be established include:

    a. Victims' hotline
    b. Conflict resolution panels
    c. Police storefronts
    d. All of the above

Fill-in-the-Blanks

1. The SPLC Report (formerly Klanwatch) and Intelligence Project are two products of the Southern Poverty Law Center (SPLC) located in Montgomery, Alabama. SPLC considers its primary responsibility to be the monitoring of _____ on a national scale and the tracking of hate crimes.

2. The Anti-Defamation League (ADL) was founded in 1913 "to stop the defamation of _____ people and to secure justice and fair treatment to all citizens alike."

3. According to the Center for Democratic Renewal, "The white supremacist movement is composed of dozens of organizations and groups, each working to create a society totally dominated by white Christians, where the human rights of lesbians and gay men and other minorities are denied. Some groups seek to create an all _____ territory; others seek to re-institutionalize Jim Crow segregation."

4. The World Church of the Creator (WCOTC), classified as a neo-Nazi-type group, was founded in 1973 by Ben Klassen, who wrote the organization's manifesto, _____.

5. Despite the differences between black extremist and white supremacist groups and their mutual contempt, these groups are able to join rhetorical forces to demean and slander _____.

6. An example of networking on the West Coast is the _____, which provides training on hate crimes investigations and disseminates information on crimes, hate groups, and individuals active in their respective jurisdictions.

7. Some experts predict that white supremacists will continue to commit traditional crimes (e.g., cross burnings, vandalism) but will also venture into high-tech activities such as _____ infiltration and sabotage.

8. According to Loretta Ross, since the 1980s, women have joined the racist movement in record numbers. This new and dangerous increase accounts for nearly _____ of the membership of some hate groups.

9. _____ involves a demographic analysis of the community with regard to ethnicity/national origin, race, religion, and sexual orientation groups.

10. Many cities and counties nationwide have established a community _____, created as an independent agency, responsible for fostering equal opportunity and eliminating all forms of discrimination.

Discussion

1. Discuss the purpose of hate/bias crime data collection and how establishing a good reporting system within public organizations (e.g., Human Relations Commissions) and the justice system is essential in helping police to better serve multicultural and diverse communities.

2. Delineate the names and numbers of hate groups in the United States and discuss those that might be operating in your local area or state.

3. Discuss some of the response alternatives available to law enforcement departments to fight and control organized hate groups, to track their activities, to establish when they are responsible for crimes, and to assist in their prosecution.

4. Discuss the implications of Loretta Ross' article titled, "White Supremacy in the 1990s," in which she indicated that hate groups since the mid-1990s have been refocusing their energies because "[t]hey are worried that they can never convince the majority of white Americans to join them in their netherworld." What changes in strategies are white supremacy groups using today? What are the implications for law enforcement agencies in your local areas?

WHAT ARE YOUR THOUGHTS AND WHAT WOULD YOU DO?

You are a uniformed police officer and you and your cover officer have been detailed to a neighborhood recreational center where graffiti had been discovered on several external walls about some of the Latino/Hispanic American community children and adults living in the neighborhood. The call to the police dispatcher was from the Recreation Center Director. Written on the walls in bold, permanent felt-tip markers were several Latino/Hispanic American epithets, several swastikas, and the statement, "Mexicans go home or else!" The statement was followed with the "skull and crossbones" symbol. The Recreation Center Director indicated that there had been some recent conflicts and "shouting matches" between some of the Latino/Hispanic American kids and other non-Hispanic kids in the neighborhood at the center. Several of the Latino/Hispanic American parents at the Recreation Center expressed their concerns for the safety of their children who go to the center. Your cover officer suggested that this looked like a hate crime and should be reported accordingly. Furthermore, he thought that this situation needed to be reported to the Human Relations Commission of the town and the Community Relations Services of the U.S. Department of Justice (USDOJ). What are your thoughts and what would you do?

Critical Thinking Questions

1. What are the facts (observable, verifiable, testable, and confirmable)?
2. What are the assumptions?
3. What are the possible stereotypes?
4. What would be your *personal* reactions to this situation?
5. What would be the possible *victims'* reactions to this situation?
6. Would someone from the Latino/Hispanic American community see something different? What would they see different (if applicable)?
7. What would be your *professional* reactions to this situation?
8. What actions would you take in this situation? What would you say to your cover officer? What would you say to the victims?
9. If you had to explain your actions to the Recreation Center Director, the Latino/Hispanic American community, the non-Hispanic community, the City's Human Rights Commission, and your superiors in front of the news media, what would you say?

---

5. Discuss how the STEEP Typology might be used to monitor the trends in your local community. Describe how each of the elements of STEEP might apply to the conditions in your community and the possible effects this may have on multicultural law enforcement.

TOOLS AND SKILLS IN PRACTICE

1. *Monitoring Regional and National Hate/Bias Crimes and Incidents—* Three approaches are suggested to obtain information about regional and national hate/bias crimes and incidents:

a. Go On-line to the Peace Officers Standards and Training (POST) Organization for Your State (or for a nearby state): Go the their "Reports section," and "research sections" (or the POST "library collections of reports"), and use the search terms such as, "hate crimes," "hate incidents," "minorities," "gays," "lesbians," "graffiti," "bias crimes," and "bias incidents." Read the online summary of reports (and actual reports, if available). Make a list of the hate/bias crimes and incidents that are highlighted for your area by the POST reports.

b. Go On-line to the Websites for the Following Group Categories:

- Ethnic/Racial Groups

- Religious Groups

- Gay, Lesbian, and Transgender Groups

Use the search terms such as, "hate crimes," "hate incidents," "minorities," "gays," "lesbians," "graffiti," "bias crimes," and "bias incidents." Read the online summary of reports (and actual reports, if available). Make a list of the hate/bias crimes and incidents that are highlighted based upon the information from a national perspective.

c. Search "LexisNexis Academic" On-line in Your College Library for Your Local and Regional Area for the Prior Year: Using the search terms, such as "hate crimes," "hate incidents," "minorities," "gays," "lesbians," "graffiti," "bias crimes," and "bias incidents," read the online summary of reports (and actual reports, if available). Make a list of the hate/bias crimes and incidents that are highlighted based upon the information from a regional and national perspective.

From the three lists of hate/bias crimes and incidents gathered, write a brief summary report as to what would be your recommended set of top six actions for your local area law enforcement to reduce hate/bias crimes and incidents.

2. *Monitoring Hate/Bias Crime Trends in Multicultural Communities*— Law enforcement officers need to be able to obtain hate/bias crime information and background data on the multicultural communities that they serve. There are several ways to obtain this information:

b. Use Search Engines: Use search engines like "Google" or "Yahoo" and enter the search terms such as "hate crimes," "hate incidents," "minorities," "gays," "lesbians," "graffiti," "bias crimes," and "bias incidents" and the name of your city, county, region, and/or state.

c. Ask for References from Your Local or College Librarian: The head librarian in your city or at a college campus would be able to direct you to the sources of information on file or in reports on hate/bias crimes and incidents.

3. *Using the STEEP Typology for Hate/Bias Crimes Monitoring—* Knowing the relationship of the social, technological, environmental, economic, and political issues that are correlated to police and criminal justice services for the ethnic, racial, and cultural groups in one's service area is critical toward understanding the multicultural challenges of your area. Log on to the on-line information from the key newspapers of your area, as well as any of the "community" news sources in your area. Search these on-line news sources of your local area for the cultural groups and for service issues related to the social, technological, environmental, economic, and political aspects for these cultural groups on an ongoing basis. Keep a j o u rnal of the groups and issues that emerge and their relationship to hate/bias crimes and incidents for these groups. Compile your findings from the lists that you developed about the social, technological, environmental, economic, and political connection to hate/bias crimes and incidents that exist for law enforcement within multicultural communities in your service area.

SELF-STUDY ACTIVITIES

Monitoring Hate/Bias Crime Trends in Multicultural Communities

Using Tool #2 as noted above, determine if your law enforcement agency (where you work or in the community in which you reside) has a system in place for monitoring hate/bias crimes and incidents. If yes, obtain a copy of the statistics for at least the past five years (or as many years as are available) of the hate/bias crimes and determine the following:

1. What trends are noticeable in each category?

2. Do the categories measure essential information that will assist your law enforcement agency in recognizing trends?

3. What would improve the data collection method to make it more useful in measuring trends and making predictions?

4. Has your law enforcement agency actually used the data to track the nature and extent of such crimes and incidents? Did it deploy resources accordingly? Provide the class with examples.

Using the STEEP Typology for Hate/Bias Crimes Monitoring

From the information gathered from Tool #3 (as noted above), make a list of specific community social, economic, and political conditions and events occurring within the law enforcement jurisdiction in which you work or live. Which ones, if any, could potentially be connected to crimes motivated by hate? For each condition listed, make a "comments" column. Suggest what specific factors a peace officer or criminal justice practitioner should look for in the community that would assist the agency in forecasting trends and events.

Monitoring Hate/Bias Crime Trends in Multicultural Communities

Using the Tool #2 as noted above, find out what resources exist in your community to assist victims of hate/bias crimes.

1. Which groups provide victim assistance?

2. Which coalition groups exist, and what types of community outreach programs are offered?

3. What types of pamphlets or other written materials are available?

4. Which groups have speaker bureaus?

5. Which groups are working with local law enforcement agencies with regard to response programs or cultural awareness training?

6. Which groups are working with the district attorney's or prosecutor's office?

Monitoring Hate/Bias Crime Trends in Multicultural Communities

Using Tool #2 as noted above, identify avenues of victim assistance in your area. Research and document the following:

1. Does your state have a crime victims' assistance program? Does it offer victim compensation? What about a victim's bill of rights?

2. What services does the local department of mental staff offer?

3. Do any community groups, rape crisis centers, or crime victim services agencies in the area offer counseling to hate crimes victims?

4. Are any mental health care professionals willing to donate their services to victims of hate crimes?

Chapter 14

Racial Profiling

OVERVIEW

Citizen discontent and lawsuits against law enforcement can originate as a result of racial profiling or use of profiles or profiling which appears to have been based on bias. Law enforcement professionals need to be critical and introspective when analyzing this problem of racism and prejudice in the profession. They need to reflect seriously on the issues involved and respond to both the reality of, and the perceptions on, biased policing. It is imperative that members of the criminal justice community and government officials understand the strong feelings about racial profiling, especially the feelings of those who have been targeted. Racial profiling or racially biased policing must stop, not only because it is illegal, but also because it leads to distrust by the minority community, litigation with expensive settlements, and the results are not worth the negative public opinion. No one of any race should have to fear being stopped or detained by police purely on the basis of skin color, ethnicity or national origin.

One of the first assignments of those involved in addressing the issues would be to agree on a definition of terms. Hopefully, the definitions are uniform standards, adopted statewide. Law enforcement executives should review complaints of racial profiling covering a period of time (five to ten years) to get a handle on the existence and/or perception of the problem and its scope. They should also conduct a series of meetings with community spokespersons and representatives of civil rights groups to elicit and listen to stories and accounts of racial profiling and perceptions of them. If racial profiling is identified as having occurred and appears to have been carried out by a small number of officers, immediate and appropriate action should be taken—an investigation either confirming or refuting claims. The problem should be acknowledged and the public informed that it has been corrected. If a larger problem is identified, then other processes must be set into action to study its scope and how it can be resolved. This is often accomplished through the use of a police–community task force, because racial profiling is not solely a law enforcement problem, but rather one that can be solved only through partnerships that are based on mutual trust and respect. Data collection and its proper interpretation can be one part of a police response to determine if biased policing is taking place and to what degree. The agency executive must work with community leaders to develop a multi-faceted response tailored to the needs of the jurisdiction. Resolution would not only include data collection and analysis, but also training, education, supervision, monitoring, and recruitment within the agency. Every law enforcement agency must adopt a policy that specifies the circumstances in which race or ethnicity can be used as a factor in making enforcement d e c isions. That policy should indicate not only that officers are to patrol in a proactive manner, to investigate aggressively suspicious person(s) and c i rcumstances, and to actively enforce the motor vehicle laws, but also that citizens will only be stopped or detained when there exists reasonable s u spicion to believe they have committed, are committing, or are about to commit an infraction of the law.

RATIONALE FOR THE FOCUS ON THE KEY CONCEPTS AND TOOLS

Officers and practitioners involved in multicultural law enforcement need to be able to:

1. Define "racial profiling" and explain problems associated with using inconsistent definitions

2. Identify seven approaches used in police departments to prevent racial profiling

3. Discuss the rationales for and against collection of racial profiling data

4. Explain the differences between "racial profiling" and the legitimate use of "profiling" in law enforcement

INTRODUCTION

Chapter 14 addresses the topic of racial profiling, a current, central, and controversial area of law enforcement. It provides the core knowledge important to students and professionals within the criminal justice system, including a conceptual definition of "racial profiling," "profiles," and "pro-filing." The chapter also presents historical and background information on the effects of racial profiling on minorities as well as on different ethnic, cultural, and religious groups as a consequence of the current war on terror-ism. The chapter contains a discussion and examples of manifestations of racial profiling and associated elements such as "bias-based policing." There is, additionally, an examination of diverse points of view and perceptions of racial profiling and its impact upon minority communities, citizens, and law enforcement agencies along with statistical data from research on the issues. The chapter includes a section comparing "profiling" as a legitimate tool of law enforcement with "racial profiling" as a bias-based aberration of the tool. These conceptualizations of profiling are defined and presented with field examples and illustrations from several different law enforcement agencies. The chapter includes suggestions for preventing racial profiling in law enforcement.

KEY CONCEPTS
Outline of Key Presentation Points

1. Definitions: Racial Profiling, Profile, Profiling, and Racially Biased Policing
2. Historical Background
3. Profiling Challenges in the War on Terrorism
4. Mini-case #1: Arlington County, Virginia
5. Mini-case #2: I-95, New Jersey
6. Mini-case #3: Orange County, California
7. Use of Profiles and Profiling in Law Enforcement
8. Legitimate Use of Race/Ethnicity
9. Prevention of Racial Profiling in Law Enforcement
10. Arguments in Favor of Data Collection
11. Arguments against Data Collection
12. Data Collection Elements
13. Use of Statistical Benchmarks
14. Community Task Forces for Development and Implementation
15. Mini-case #4: Denver Police Department, Colorado

PRACTICE QUESTIONS
True or False

_____ 1. Racial profiling is a suspect-specific approach to crime fighting, which is legal in most states.

_____ 2. Profiling is any police-initiated action that uses a compilation of the background, physical, behavioral, and/or motivational characteristics about a type of perpetrator.

_____ 3. Prior to September 11, 2001, the use by law enforcement agencies of profiles that included race, ethnicity or national origin, or the act of profiling using the same criteria, had come to be generally frowned upon or even condemned in the United States.

_____ 4. Most of the research on criminal justice has documented that the impact of racial prejudice on criminal justice agents' decision-making has been decreasing in prevalence and importance for at least 30 years.

_____ 5. Proactive policing sometimes involves using legitimate profiling based upon officer experience and training or using profiles provided by their agency.

_____ 6. The Boston Globe (2003) studies, which included a three-part, investigative report series, found that older drivers are less likely to get ticketed, especially if they are white.

_____ 7. The Police Executive Research Forum (PERF) recommends that the following principle be applied: Race/ethnicity should *never* be treated like other demographic descriptors. To avoid charges of racial profiling, police should *not* use race/ethnicity as one factor in the same way that they use age, gender, and other descriptors to establish reasonable suspicion or probable cause.

_____ 8. The Computer Assisted Passenger Prescreening System (CAPPS II), developed in 1998 and first tested in 2003 by the Federal Aviation Administration, is a nationwide p r eflight computer system used to check personal information on every airline passenger.

_____ 9. The Whren decision (*Whren v. United States*) is seen by many civil rights advocates as clearly opening the door for racial profiling because it allows police officers to stop anyone without reasonable suspicion or probable cause, thus providing a mechanism for circumventing the Fourth Amendment requirements of the U.S. Constitution.

_____ 10. An officer who does not have reasonable suspicion may ask for consent to search (except in those states or localities where it is illegal), and the officer may even have the motorist sign a waiver to that effect.

Multiple Choice

1. Racially biased policing occurs when law enforcement:
   a. Inappropriately considers race or ethnicity in deciding with whom and how to intervene in an enforcement capacity
   b. Uses racial profiling as a legal means of identifying criminal activity
   c. Considers behavioral indicators of criminal activities using race only as a descriptor
   d. All of the above

2. Stereotyping involves conscious and unconscious thought processes (to include Senge's "Ladder of Inference" discussed later in the chapter), whereby an individual:

   a. Makes observations and selects data born out of that person's past experiences

   b. Adds cultural and personal meaning to what he or she observes

   c. Makes assumptions based on the meanings that he or she has attributed to an observation

   d. All of the above

3. It is a challenging and complex problem for officers (especially for those strongly committed to non-biased practices who believe in proactive policing) to use profiling or the development of profiles. Which of the following are key issues in developing and using profiling?

   a. Does the person developing and using profiling have some expertise (for example, in behavioral science)?

   b. Is the profile creator objective, unbiased, and non-judgmental in formulating a particular profile?

   c. Who is interpreting the profile?

   d. All of the above

4. According to a 2003 national study by Richard Lundman and Robert Kaufman, professors of sociology at Ohio State, black men are _____ than white men to report being stopped by police for a traffic violation.

   a. 5 percent less likely

   b. 25 percent less likely

   c. 35 percent more likely

   d. 67 percent more likely

5. Most law enforcement officers would maintain that they are not biased, prejudiced, or using racial profiling in their policing methods. Proactive policing sometimes involves:

   a. Using legitimate profiling based upon the officer's experience and training

   b. Using profiles provided by their agency

   c. Both "a" and "b"

   d. None of the above.

6. The provisions of the USA Patriot Act (USAPA), aimed at terrorism, include the following:

    a. Disallow the use of racial profiling

    b. Expand surveillance capabilities (in effect, searches) and allow for nationwide wiretaps under certain circumstances

    c. Allow illegal search and detention for all criminal suspects without reasonable cause

    d. All of the above

7. Under which of the following circumstances may officers stop citizens based solely on their race, sex, religion, national origin, or sexual orientation?

    a. Matching of profiles of drug dealers operating in the neighborhood

    b. Matching of profiles of sex offenders in the community

    c. Matching of profiles of violent and aggressive offenders in a public school area

    d. None of the above

8. To formulate measures to prevent the practice of racial profiling and inappropriate behavior and actions on the part of officers, the authors recommend that the criminal justice system should:

    a. Establish an agency policy to address racial profiling

    b. Perform professional traffic stops

    c. Encourage minority community outreach

    d. All of the above

9. Police managers and supervisors, in order to identify officers who might be biased, should monitor the following key indicator:

    a. Number of citations written for all demographic groups

    b. Number of arrests and successful prosecution

    c. Negative attitude toward training programs that enhance police–community relations

    d. None of the above

10. The San Francisco Police Department created General Order 5.17, 07/17/03 that outlines their policy for policing without racial bias. Which of the following delineate this policy, in which officers can consider race, color, ethnicity, national origin, gender, age, sexual orientation, or gender identity, when making a law enforcement decision?

    a. Investigative detentions, traffic stops, arrests, searches, and property seizures by officers will be based on a standard of reasonable suspicion or probable cause in accordance with the Fourth Amendment of the U.S. Constitution

    b. Officers must be able to articulate specific facts and circumstances that support reasonable suspicion or probable cause

    c. Department personnel may not use, *to any extent or degree*, race, color, ethnicity, national origin, age, sexual orientation or gender identity in conducting stops or detentions, or activities following stops or detentions *except* when engaging in the investigation of appropriate suspect-specific activity to identify a particular person or group

    d. All of the above

Fill-in-the-Blanks

1. Racial profiling is any police-initiated action that relies on the race, ethnicity, or national origin, rather than on the _____ of an individual, or information that leads the police to a particular individual who has been identified as being, or having been, engaged in criminal activity.

2. For reasonable suspicion that a person's behavior is related to c r i minal activity, the officer must have _____ to support his or her actions; a mere suspicion or "hunch" is not sufficient cause to detain a person or to request identification.

3. Profiling in law enforcement is used by officers to look for characteristics that indicate the _____ of criminal acts or factors that tend to correlate with dangerous or threatening behavior.

4. Officers use profiling or written profiles of _____ to identify those they should investigate to determine if they are committing or about to commit a crime.

5. *The New York Times* reported that a 1997 investigation by New Jersey police of their own practices found that "turnpike drivers who agreed to have their cars searched by the state police were overwhelmingly _____."

6. From the findings by Barlow and Barlow (2002) of the 2,100 sworn personnel of the Milwaukee Police Department, they conclude that black men are more likely to be the victims of racial profiling than black women by a ratio of _____ to one.

7. The U.S. Customs Service, the U.S. Border Patrol, and the Drug Enforcement Agency (DEA) have long used profiles as a tool to detain and investigate persons fitting the _____.

8. In the *Travis* opinion, the majority concluded that "_____ may become a legitimate consideration when investigators have information on the subject of a particular suspect."

9. Prominent researcher in racial profiling, John Lamberth (1996), a private consultant in Wilmington, Delaware, found that minorities may be more _____ around police, and officers may misinterpret that as suspicious behavior.

10. Police recruitment messages, verbal and written, must emphasize that those who are _____ (regardless of their race or ethnicity), and cannot distinguish between appropriate and inappropriate behavior and actions, will not be hired.

Discussion

1. Discuss the key issues for law enforcement when there is not a s t a ndard, agreed-upon definition for racial profiling. Identify some of the specific concerns that ethnic and multicultural communities may have with regard to the lack of a clear, agreed-upon definition for racial profiling.

2. Discuss the major challenges faced by criminal justice agencies regarding the issue and impact of the use of profiles and profiling, especially after the September 11, 2001 terrorists attacks on the United States.

3. Discuss how the Police Executive Research Forum (PERF) policy for the legal use of profiling might be applied to the following example. An officer observes the following: (1) The tail light is burned out on a vehicle with a white driver. (2) It is midnight. (3) The car is in a minority neighborhood where drugs are known to be sold. (4) The driver pulls up to the curb and talks briefly to someone standing there. (5) An exchange takes place. (6) The driver drives away. (7) The driver makes furtive movements as if hiding something under the seat when police pull him over.

4. Discuss how Peter Senge's model called the "Ladder of Inference" might explain racial profiling and the use of negative stereotypes by law enforcement officers in ethnic/minority communities.

WHAT ARE YOUR THOUGHTS AND WHAT WOULD YOU DO?

Your Chief of Police has asked you to prepare a response to the community regarding a recent research study reported in the newspapers about racial profiling in your town. The research study was conducted by the Community Justice Institute of a nearby university. In the newspaper article, your police department was noted as having the highest "racial profiling score" of all the municipalities of your state. The research compares the percentage of ethnic/racial minorities living in each town against the percentages of ethnic/racial minorities involved in traffic stops in each town. A high "Racial Profiling Score" would indicate that there were many more ethnic/racial minorities involved in traffic stops in that town than would be expected based upon the percentage of ethnic/racial minorities who are residents in that town. Your Chief wants you to prepare a response to the newspaper article and to suggest possible actions that the department might take to address the high "racial profiling score" received by the department. What are your thoughts and what would you do?

Critical Thinking Questions

1. What are the facts (observable, verifiable, testable, and confirmable)?
2. What are the assumptions?
3. What are the possible stereotypes?
4. What would be your *personal* reactions to this situation?
5. What would be the possible reactions of *drivers who were stopped* to this situation?
6. Would someone from the ethnic/racial minority community see something different? What would they see different (if applicable)?
7. What would be your *professional* reactions to this situation?
8. What actions would you take in this situation? What would say to your Chief? What would you say to the community? To the newspaper and media?
9. If you had to explain your actions to the drivers who were stopped, the e t hnic/racial minority community, the City's Human Rights Commission, and your superiors in front of the news media, what would you say?

---

5. Many states provide racial profiling prevention training, which is typically coordinated, monitored and controlled by the Commission on Peace Officer Standards and Training, an agency that is found in every state. Describe some of the key components of these training programs. Provide your observations as to which of these components are most effective in the prevention of racial profiling in law enforcement practices.

Tools and Skills In Practice

1. *Scanning for Racial Profiling in Multicultural Communities*—Try to find out the impact of racial profiling upon the key cultural groups in your service area and the community leaders who are

c o ncerned about racial profiling issues who are critical toward understanding the multicultural resources of your area. Two ways to obtain this information are:

   a. Use the On-line Information from the Key Newspapers of Your Area: Search on an ongoing basis the on-line news sources of your local area using the search terms "racial profiling" and "biased policing" for the cultural groups that you are interested in researching. Keep a journal of the groups and of the issues that emerge, as well as the members, leaders, and/or representatives named in the news articles.

   b. Search "LexisNexis Academic" On-line in Your College Library: Search the news sources for your local area for the prior five years using the search terms "racial profiling" and "biased policing" for the cultural groups of your city or area of interest. Keep a journal of your findings.

2. *Identifying the Impact of Racial Profiling on Law Enforcement*—For your city or area of interest, go to the on-line reports for the: (a) "Police Commission," (b) "Public Safety Commission," and/or (c) "Emergency Services Commission." Scan the Minutes of the meetings for law enforcement and "racial profiling" issues identified. Search for any guidelines or policies regarding racial profiling. Note any mentioning of racial profiling involving any of the different multicultural communities. If on-line services are not available in your area, go the Town Hall or City Hall and read the past Minutes of the above-noted Commissions for the previous five years or more; the Minutes of the Police Commission and other meetings are usually open to the public. Make a list with a summary of your findings regarding racial profiling and the issues identified for your city or area of interest.

3. *Developing Response Strategies and Community Networks*—Once you begin to get a sense of racial profiling and its impact upon the different groups in your community (along the key leaders of those groups involved in racial profiling or biased policing issues), it would be important to get information on the kinds of approaches and strategies these communities use to address such issues. Go on-line or in person to some of the organizations and agencies in your local area involved or concerned with racial profiling. Depending upon the diversity of your community, some of these resources might focus on ethnic or racial groups, religious groups, sexual o r ientation, and so forth. Obtain any literature and studies from these organizations regarding their work on racial profiling, and rev i ew these documents to identify the approaches and strategies of these groups. Make a list of your findings. Brainstorm some ways that the local law enforcement agencies might be able to form community partnerships with these community-based agencies to address racial profiling that you have identified through the review of the materials and documents.

4. *Working with Multicultural Communities on Prevention and Response*—Begin building a file in your computer or on 3×5 index cards (or in a "blank book" journal). On a daily basis, as you observe in your work, in the news, or in any other sources, note issues of racial profiling and/or biased policing between law enforcement and aspects of the multicultural community. Be sure to note also instances involving multicultural communities and law enforcement that went well (and did not reflect racial profiling and/or biased policing). For those instances that have gone well, identify the key elements and/or aspects that made it go well. For those instances that could have involved racial profiling and/or biased policing, brainstorm about ways that the situation could have been improved. What could have been done differently to attain a more positive outcome? Soon, your file will contain many useful ideas for avoiding racial profiling and for improving law enforcement services in multicultural communities.

SELF-STUDY ACTIVITIES

Identifying the Impact of Racial Profiling on Law Enforcement

Using Tool #2 (as noted above), determine if the police department in your (or nearby) area meets recommended standards regarding policies pertaining to racial profiling:

1. Does the policy clearly define acts constituting racial profiling using the definition provided at the beginning of this chapter?

2. Does the policy strictly prohibit peace officers employed by the agency from engaging in racial profiling?

3. Does the policy provide instructions by which individuals may file a complaint if they believe they were a victim of racial profiling by an employee of the agency?

4. Does the agency provide public education relating to their complaint process?

5. Does the policy require appropriate corrective action to be taken against a peace officer employed by the agency who, after an investigation, is shown to have engaged in racial profiling in violation of the agency's policy? What benchmarks are utilized and who interprets the data?

6. Does the agency require the collection of data relating to traffic stops in which a citation is issued and to arrests resulting from those traffic stops, including information relating to:

- The race or ethnicity of the individual detained
- Whether a search was conducted and, if so, if it was based upon the consent of the person detained

7. Does the agency policy require them to submit a report on the findings and conclusions based upon the data collected to a governing body of the county or state for review and monitoring purposes?

Ban on Racial Profiling by Federal Authorities

In 2003, President Bush issued a ban on racial profiling by federal authorities. Based upon your findings in developing Tool #1 of the text, Scanning for Racial Profiling in Multicultural Communities, note how effective the ban has been and if the exception, which permits the use of race and ethnicity to combat potential terrorist attacks, has been deemed acceptable by the general public. The ban prohibits the use of "generalized stereotypes" based on race or ethnicity by officers but allows them to consider these factors as part of a specific description or tip from a reliable source. How does law enforcement balance the need to reduce crime, especially terrorism, against the potential for accusations of discrimination, race-biased policing, and stereotyping?

Part 5

CULTURAL EFFECTIVENESS FOR PEACE OFFICERS

Part 5 concludes this text by highlighting some of the themes from previous chapters, while discussing broad concepts on the emerging role of peace officers within a twenty-first-century multicultural society.

Chapter 15 analyzes these changes primarily from the perspective of altering the reader's image of law enforcement and understanding the impact of this shift on one's behavior as a public servant. We examine why those who serve the public today are expected to be more tolerant and less ethnocentric in their outlook and dealings with citizens than in the past. The chapter reinforces the meaning of cultural sensitivity and provides a model for understanding cultural differences. It also considers peace officer professionalism and peacekeeping in a diverse society by first defining and presenting the interwoven concepts of leadership, professionalism, and synergy. The analysis focuses on cooperation in statewide and regional law enforcement. One section links professionalism to ethics and interactions with diverse groups, emphasizing the special obligation that peace officers have in upholding respect for human dignity.

Chapter 16 considers all the emerging and changing issues confronting the peace officer in his/her peacekeeping roles and in the use of high technology in multicultural law enforcement. Peace officers need to be competent to deal with their increasing roles in multi-jurisdictional crime-solving efforts (beyond homeland security and terrorism such as the DC sniper, stolen identity, multi-state crime scams). Moreover, the role of peace officers, in assisting and communicating with multicultural communities in disasters, terrorism, controlling rumors resulting from regional events (e.g., anthrax fears), requires additional resources, skills, and the use of new law enforcement tools. Modern law enforcement requires an operating value and culture of improved intra-agency communication, as well as supportive relations with multicultural communities.

Chapter 15

Peace Officer Image
and Cultural Sensitivity

OVERVIEW

For professionals in any facet of the criminal justice system, change begins with leadership modeling the role, and second with the practitioners' image of their role, which is then projected to the public. In the evolving new work culture, adhering to the image of peace officer is appropriate and requires that those in public service become more culturally sensitive in their outlook and approach. Effectively dealing with cultural issues within the field of law enforcement then becomes a means for exercising leadership that demonstrates that sensitive peacekeepers respect cultural uniqueness.

Professional law enforcement leaders must take the initiative to guide their departments to ones that are culturally competent. Also, leaders must capitalize on the diversity of people within the organization and community, establish synergy, and seek to develop human potential for the betterment of both. The challenges for law enforcement, in particular, are to recognize and appreciate diversity within both the community and the workforce, while using such insights advantageously. Human diversity must become a source of renewal rather than tolerable legislated requirements within our agencies, communities, and society. To accomplish this goal within criminal justice systems, multicultural awareness and skills training must become an integral part of the human resource development of peacekeepers (Moran, Harris, and Stripp, 1993; Wederspahn, 2000). The type of peacekeeping advocated in this chapter also requires competent supervision and management with police administration (Holden, 1994; Whisenand and Rush, 1998). It is also important that departments, regionally or statewide, work together to prevent and counter criminality in the community while at the same time promoting the common good and civility. There must be a interagency collaboration, synergy, in regard to not only fighting crime, but also in training, information exchange, and recruitment within a cultural and diversity context.

INTRODUCTION

Chapter 15 considers the changing role and image of peace officers that will result in increased cultural awareness and effectiveness in law enforcement in the twenty-first century. Given the impact of greater diversity on both peacekeeping and law enforcement, we explore how cultural understanding can be translated into more effective community policing. To increase cultural awareness, readers are provided with a simple model for quick analysis of differences in various cultures, ethnic groups, and generations. The content strengthens the case that improved police performance and professionalism are dependent on cross-cultural skills and sensitivity among peace officers.

RATIONALE FOR THE FOCUS ON THE KEY CONCEPTS AND TOOLS

Officers and practitioners involved in multicultural law enforcement need to be able to:

1. Identify the changing role image of law enforcement officers

2. Understand the need for police officers to have a positive self-image and one of being a police *professional*

3. Explain the importance of being culturally aware in outlook and in dealings with citizens, especially in multicultural communities

4. Understand why those who serve the public are held to higher standards than ordinary citizens with respect to the need for tolerance and acceptance of diversity

5. Define and understand the interwoven concepts of leadership, professionalism, and synergy

6. Understand how greater diversity in law enforcement can be translated into more effective community policing

KEY CONCEPTS

Outline of Key Presentation Points

1. Impact of Image on Human Behavior

2. Law Enforcement Role Transitions: Traditional versus Evolving Work Cultures

3. Image Projection

4. Twenty-First-Century Peace Officer Images

5. Creating Positive Police Images

6. Police Culture

7. Police Leadership in Professionalism and Synergy

8. Regional or Statewide Cooperation in Law Enforcement

9. Police Professionalism

10. Organizational Trends in Law Enforcement

PRACTICE QUESTIONS

True or False

_____ T   1. Darrel Stephens, former director of the Police Executive Research Forum (PERF), indicated that citizens are the first line of defense in preventing and fighting crime, not the crime fighter who reacts after the crime is committed.

_____ T   2. According to the research by Longworthy and Travis (1999), police officers project an image to the public based on how they see themselves, and citizens usually respond to that image.

_____ F   3. When Ed Flynn, chief of police for Virginia's Arlington County, reported in 2002 that his department "had also just generated a lot of data showing 'disproportionate' minority arrests," the minority community involved held extensive protests against the police.

_____ F   4. Cultural synergy is a problem-solving technique in which homogeneous or very similar groups of people are brought together to brainstorm solutions and recommendations.

_____ T   5. Probably the greatest area for improvement of synergistic relations is between and among federal, state, and local law enforcement.

_____ T   6. Under Mexican law, based on the Napoleonic law system, the supposed transgressor is considered guilty until proven innocent, the opposite of the U.S. legal system, which is based on English Common Law.

_____ T   7. Unethical behavior is present when officers are deliberately racist, acting with discrimination, prejudice, bigotry, and intolerance toward a fellow officer, citizen, or foreign visitor.

_____ T   8. The police chief should explicitly demonstrate pluralistic leadership and, ideally, be "an ambassador for diversity" with his/her department.

_____ T   9. According to the authors, human diversity must become a source of renewal rather than a tolerable legislated requirement within our agencies.

_____ T   10. For managing or training in a multicultural environment, advanced diversity training that teaches people the skills to communicate and collaborate effectively with each other as colleagues (especially through mixed-gender, mixed-ethnic, and mixed-racial groups) should be conducted.

MULTIPLE CHOICE

1. Comprehending the significance and power of image and its projection becomes critical for law enforcement officers and would-be peacekeepers. According to the authors, law enforcement image is:

   a. A matter of illusion or mere public manipulation of appearances

   b. A vital connection between image and identity, between the way we see ourselves and our actual behavior

   c. A stereotypic cartoon of the "good cop" and the "bad cop"

   d. None of the above

2. The California Code (Section 830) defines a peace officer as including:

   a. Constables

   b. District Attorneys

   c. College Campus Police

   d. All of the above

3. The authors note that leaders need to be both transformational and transcultural. Which of the following is an example of a transformational leader?

   a. Renewing organizations and becoming role models by transmitting intellectual excitement and vision about their work

   b. Helping personnel to manage change by restructuring their mind-sets and values

   c. Transforming work places from the status quo to appropriate environments

   d. All of the above

4. Which of the follow might be a description of the synergistic leader in law enforcement?

   a. Fights effectively for the division's share of the budget over other divisions

   b. Demonstrates skills for gaining political advantage over peers at the department

   c. Promotes participation, empowerment, and negotiation within an organization or community

   d. None of the above

5. Police professionalism, according to Hunter, Mayhill, and Barker (2000), requires:

   a. Intellectual honesty and writing skills

   b. Self-awareness and a positive self-image

   c. Communication skills using tools such as "Verbal Judo"

   d. Pride in the uniform and consistent belief in "police values"

6. Which of the following phrases describes a law enforcement professional?
    a. One who respects the dignity and humanity of everyone contacted in the course of his/her duties by treating all fairly and with equal justice
    b. One who is aware of the impact of agency culture on the professional behavior of officers
    c. One who is a lifetime learner concerned about personal and career development for both self and others
    d. All of the above

7. During the 1960s, the National Commission on the Causes and Prevention of Violence commented on the U.S. police force as being:
    a. Mostly white, stable in economic class, valuing education, and enjoying serving the community
    b. Military background, middle class, family-oriented with strong religious beliefs
    c. Mostly white, upwardly mobile, lower middle class, conservative in ideology, and resistant to change
    d. Mostly male, strong religious values, athletic, flexible, and ethical

8. Elsie Cross Associates recommends which of the following strategies for managing diversity and valuing differences (White, 1992)?
    a. Conduct sensitivity T-group training with police officers and community members
    b. Require that the top command make at least a five-year commitment of resources to redefining the agency culture toward more effective management of diversity
    c. Ease the pain of racism and sexism at the personal and group level in the organization by building on the future and forgetting the past
    d. All of the above

9. In the authors' view, ethical behavior by law officers also encompasses:
    a. Respect for human dignity
    b. Concern for human rights
    c. Value for diversity in the human family
    d. All of the above

10. Which of the following, in the United States, constitute new migrant communities or new groups who have come as refugees fleeing p e rsecution, strife, and distant wars?
    a. North Koreans who have fled from Communism
    b. Congolese and Sierra Leoneans of western Africa
    c. Displaced workers from the Tropical Rain Forest of South America
    d. None of the above

Fill-in-the-Blanks

1. According to Norman Boehm, former director of the California Commission on Peace Officer Standards and Training, police departments must become both _learning_ organizations and enforcement agencies.

2. The best antidote to underachievement or even racism is for a person to have a _healthy self-image_.

3. Criminal justice representatives are now subject to extra scrutiny and _accountability_ when citizens use camcorders to capture their activities for possible review, even on the Internet.

4. Traditional police cultures have transitioned away from the more rigid _military and bureaucratic_ cultures of the past to more flexible, corporate-like, proactive, and high-tech cultures.

5. Culturally sensitive leaders cut across _cultural_ barriers while combating prejudice, bigotry, and/or racism wherever these are found in the organization and community (Simons, Vazquez, and Harris, 1993

6. Since agency representatives come from differing organizational cultures, any interagency collaboration or merger requires the p r a ctice of _cross-cultural communication_ skills.

7. The principal purpose of criminal justice education, whether in universities, colleges, or academies, is to improve _performance_ and to increase professionalism among those in law enforcement.

8. The Florida Criminal Justice Executive Institute's monograph e n t itled "Against Brutality and Corruption" discusses how these twin evils can be countered within law enforcement by officers who demonstrate integrity, wisdom, and _professionalism_.

9. With the influx of a multicultural workforce into the criminal justice fields, _acceptance_ is necessary if the organizational culture is to reflect the needs and concerns of this new generation from a culturally diverse society.

10. When a law enforcement agency has provided the basic training in cultural awareness and inaugurated effective equal employment and affirmative action policies, it is time to adopt another strategic plan that moves the law enforcement agency toward _cultural competence_.

Discussion

1. Discuss some of the emerging roles and implications for law enforcement officers as summarized by Darrel Stephens, former director of the Police Executive Research Forum (PERF), in his comment: "Mechanically bean counting of arrests and putting squad cars on the street is no longer enough."

2. Use the ten benchmarks (see text Exhibit 15.3) to provide a cultural analysis of the police department in your local community. Which of the ten benchmarks seem to emerge strongest in your analysis of your local law enforcement agency?

3. Discuss some of the traits and skills important for a professional in the criminal justice system. Which of these traits and skills do you feel are most important within a multicultural law enforcement context?

4. The chapter provided an example of the actions of an automobile driver who hit someone in a part of rural India and had the expectation that the driver should not stop but instead proceed to the nearest town where the incident would then be reported to the police. Discuss how the example would not be considered a "hit and run" by the driver and might reflect the cultural conditions of rural life within a country.

5. Discuss the importance of the concept of "synergy" which involves the cooperation and the integration of separate parts to function as a whole toward achieving a common goal in community policing. What are some of the elements in community policing that might require law enforcement "synergistic" leadership?

TOOLS AND SKILLS IN PRACTICE

1. *Gathering Information on Peace Officers' Image and Cultural Sensitivity*—Two approaches are suggested to obtain information about peace officers' image and cultural sensitivity for the law enforcement agencies in your area: Go the websites of: (a) the Police Department for your town or city (or to one that is for the nearest large city in your area of interest), and (b) the Personnel or Human Resources Department of your town or city. Within the two websites, search for and identify the information related to cultural sensitivity, cultural competence, and peace officers' image of the law enforcement and criminal justice agencies. Searching terms such as, "cultural sensitivity," "community policing," "minorities," "African American," "cultural competency," "sensitivity training," "police image," "peace officer" etc., will usually bring up the information in the website. If on-line services are not available in your area, go the Town Hall or City Hall and read the past "Annual Reports" for such information. Record in your journal the peace officers' image and cultural sensitivity information that you have obtained.

WHAT ARE YOUR THOUGHTS AND WHAT WOULD YOU DO?

Your department has decided to provide multicultural and diversity training to all its sworn and non-sworn personnel. Your town has had a significant increase in ethnic/racial minority population in the last five years, and your department wanted to increase positive police-community relations through this training. A fellow officer is telling you in the presence of other officers in the break area that he thinks the Department should not be involved in multicultural and diversity training for police officers. He thinks that this kind of training is unnecessary and a waste of taxpayers' money. He said that if people want police services they should learn to speak English like all Americans. He also said that people from ethnic/racial minority communities are the ones that need to change, not the officers in the Police Department. What are your thoughts and what would you do?

Critical Thinking Questions

1. What are the facts (observable, verifiable, testable, and confirmable)?
2. What are the assumptions?
3. What are the possible stereotypes?
4. What would be your *personal* reactions to this situation?
5. What would be the possible *other officers'* reactions to this situation?
6. Would someone from the ethnic/racial minority community see something different? What would they see differently (if applicable)?
7. What would be your *professional* reactions to this situation?
8. What actions would you take in this situation? What would say to your fellow officer? What would you say to the other officers within hearing distance?
9. If you had to explain your actions to the other officers, the ethnic/racial minority community, the City's Human Rights Commission, and your superiors in front of the news media, what would you say?

2. *Obtaining Community Perspectives Affecting Law Enforcement Images*—Complete the form provided in Appendix C in this Study Guide ("Multicultural Community and Law Enforcement Workforce Survey") based upon your impressions of the law enforcement agency in your local area. You may also want to get one other person who is not in your class, but who is a resident of your community, to complete the survey form as well. Score the survey responses for both forms. Based upon the scores in the survey forms, make a list of the workplace and agency cultural issues that are positive and another list of issues that are negative. To corroborate your observations, use the on-line information from the key newspapers of your area; search the on-line news sources of your local area for police image and agency issues on an ongoing basis. Keep a journal of the issues that emerged and match them to the issues identified from your survey observations.

3. *Using Multicultural Community Understanding Methods*—Begin building a file in your computer or on 3 × 5 index cards (or in a "blank book" journal). On a daily basis, as you observe in your work, in the news, or in any other sources, note interactions of law enforcement with aspects of the multicultural communities that are going well (and that are building positive peace officers' images) and those that could have gone better (and that might negatively affect peace officers' image). For specific law enforcement culture and image issues among some of the larger ethnic/racial communities, log on to the websites for the Peace Officers Associations for those communities (e.g., for Asian/Pacific Americans—http://www.napoa.org; for African Americans—http://www.noblenatl.org; for Latino/Hispanic Americans—http://www.hapcoa.com/, etc.). For those interactions that have gone well, identify the key elements and/or aspects that made it go well. For those interactions that could have gone better, brainstorm about ways in which the situation could have been improved. What could have been done differently to attain a better outcome? Soon, your file will contain many useful ideas for improving law enforcement culture, services, and image in the different multicultural communities.

4. *Creating Positive Police Image s*—Using the information and findings from Tool #3 above, focus the use of those findings for the purpose of creating more positive police image. As such, for those interactions that have gone well, identify the key elements and/or aspects that made them go well and how the key element might be used to create positive police images. For those interactions that could have gone better, brainstorm about ways that the situation could have been improved and ways to correct or remediate problems created with negative police images. What could have been done differently to attain a more positive police image? Soon, your file will contain many useful ideas for improving cross-cultural interactions and communications within multicultural communities for creating and improving positive law enforcement images and services.

SELF-STUDY ACTIVITIES

Using Multicultural Community Understanding Methods

Using Tool #3 (as noted above), consider the long-term influence of the institution of slavery on the African American family in general and their male youth in particular. What is the implication of this negative heritage for today's black citizens as a whole and its influence within the subcultures of police officers and criminals? Identify hopeful trends that repair or redress the damage of slavery and discrimination on this valuable segment of the American population.

Using Multicultural Community Understanding Methods

Using Tool #3 (as noted above), consider the dynamics created by the extended families upon providing cultural sensitive law enforcement s e r vices. Many Asian, Near Eastern, and Middle Eastern cultures function with an extended rather than a nuclear family. When such immigrants come to North America, they attempt to carry on this larger family tradition (e.g., food preparation of large meals, working hard in a family-owned business, remodeling and enlarging houses or estates, acquiring several automobiles or a fleet, intermarriage with relatives). Consider how such customs may cause the new arrivals to violate local laws and regulations relative to killing animals, child labor, multiple-family dwellings and occupancy, multiple-car parking on public streets, and so forth. Have you observed anything in this regard about Southeast Asian, Cuban, Haitian, Indian, Pakistan or other immigrants? What can a patrol officer do to help these newcomers from breaking laws of which they are unaware?

Obtaining Community Perspectives Affecting Law Enforcement Images

Using Tool #2 (as noted above), consider how inadequate border management has increased illegal entry and allowed a criminal element from abroad to slip into the United States and to prey on the vast majority of law-abiding immigrants from the "old country," particularly through extortion. Earlier in this century, such thugs and "crime families" were mainly from Europe; today they come in increasing numbers from the former Soviet Union, Latin America, Caribbean Islands, and Asia. Consider how law enforcement nationally can share information and tactics to combat such threats (e.g., from Hong Kong triads, Salvadoran death squads, Russian black marketers, Jamaican Mafia, and Asian gangs). At the same time, how can peace officers gain the confidence of the law-abiding immigrants, many of whom have been culturally conditioned against police in their homelands? What insights can you share on these matters of concern to law enforcement?

Chapter 16

Emerging Strategies, Roles, and Technology for Peace Officers in Multicultural Law Enforcement

OVERVIEW

Law enforcement officers and leaders of the twenty-first century will have to develop criminal justice organizations and services that can effectively recognize, relate to, and operate within the multicultural and global shifts in culture, technological advances, and community/governmental expectations. This chapter has highlighted the emerging issues confronting the peace officer in adapting innovations and advanced technology to changing strategies and roles in multicultural law enforcement. Law enforcement officers in the twenty-first century will need to be more proactive and less reactive. The new generation of peace officers must not only increase their knowledge bases, but must also promote positive law enforcement innovations as noted within this chapter to include: (1) increasing awareness and skills within multicultural communities and special populations like minority and immigrant youths, elderly, and people with mental health problems; (2) embracing and using community-oriented policing practices; (3) curtailing litigation against law enforcement agencies; and (4) utilizing the innovations and advanced technology available to law enforcement agencies. The functional role of peace officers has increased to involve assistance to and communication with multicultural communities in disasters, and terrorist events, as well as controlling possible community confrontations resulting from global or regional events. Training and preparation of future law enforcement personnel for services to multicultural communities will require changes in the curriculum of the police academies, as well as the ongoing and continuing education of law enforcement officers.

In this final unit and chapter, as throughout *Multicultural Law Enforcement*, the authors have shared information and insights about improving public service in diverse communities. Our intention has been to help readers become more proactive with regard to the changing population, while anticipating future developments in both the law enforcement agency and society. The basic premise is that the personal and professional development of modern peace officers requires cultural awareness training that reinforces creative agency policies and practices on this diversity or multicultural issue. Part 1 of this book was devoted to the impact of increasing cultural diversity on the community, peacekeeping, and the law enforcement agency. Part 2 centered on cross-cultural training and communication for peace officers. Part 3 reviewed cultural specifics relevant to officers when they interact with people from Native American, African American, Asian/Pacific Islander, Hispanic/Latino, or Middle Eastern backgrounds. Part 4 examined the matter of culturally and racially motivated hate crimes and response strategies (as well as the issues involved with profiling and racial profiling).

Finally, in Part 5, we have offered an overview of how peace officers can improve their effectiveness in a multicultural workforce and community by practicing greater cultural sensitivity. Numerous concepts, methods, and anecdotes were provided to promote innovative, futuristic professional development of sworn officers and their associates. With the human family in profound transition during the twenty-first century, futurists expect further social disturbances. Thus, our analysis focused on planned changes in the image, operations, services, and skills of law enforcement practitioners within rapidly changing workforces and societies.

Readers are challenged to examine the concepts and techniques presented in these pages, as well as to implement those that are feasible within local agencies and communities. If the strategies proposed here are adopted, the law enforcement field will indeed provide more professional, diverse leadership within the public sector, while presenting positive models in that regard to the private sector. For the professionally minded who will go beyond the content of this book, several appendices and the Instructor's Manual c o mplement the main content of this text.

RATIONALE FOR THE FOCUS ON THE KEY CONCEPTS AND TOOLS

Officers and practitioners involved in multicultural law enforcement need to be able to:

1. Identify the emerging and changing issues in the strategies and roles confronting the peace officer in multicultural law enforcement

2. Understand the need for police officers to adapt to innovations and advanced technology within their increasing roles in local community policing and in multi-jurisdictional crime-solving efforts

3. Explain the role of peace officers to encompass assistance with multicultural communities in disasters, terrorism, and controlling possible community confrontations resulting from global/regional events

4. Understand the emerging roles in working with multicultural special populations such as minority and immigrant youths and people with mental health problems

5. Realize that curtailing litigation against law enforcement agencies is a key challenge for law enforcement leaders and officers requiring changes in police policies

6. Support training and preparation of future law enforcement personnel as requiring changes in the curriculum of the police academies

INTRODUCTION

Chapter 16 will focus upon the emerging and changing issues in the strategies and roles confronting the peace officer in multicultural law enforcement today. Peace officers now need to be able to manage and adapt to innovations and advanced technology within their increasing roles in local community policing and in multi-jurisdictional crime-solving efforts such as homeland security. The role of peace officers has increased in functions to encompass assistance to and communication with multicultural communities in disasters, terrorism, controlling possible community confrontations resulting from global/regional events (e.g., celebration of Israeli Independence Day). The emerging roles for peace officers are highlighted as they pertain to working with multicultural special populations such as minority and immigrant youths and people with mental health problems. Curtailing litigation against law enforcement agencies is a key challenge for law enforcement leaders and officers requiring changes in police policies, training, and practices. Training and preparation of future law enforcement personnel will require changes in the curriculum of the police academies, as well as the ongoing and continuing education of law enforcement officers.

KEY CONCEPTS

Outline of Key Presentation Points

1. Twenty-First Century Challenge
2. The Future of Peacekeeping Strategies in Multicultural Communities
3. Neil Lingle's Research Study
4. Community-Based Policing
5. Critical Success Factors for Community-Based Policing
6. Crime Prevention among Minority and Immigrant Youth
7. Some Anti-Gang and Youth-Oriented Strategies
8. Treatment of People with Mental Disorders within the Justice System
9. Bureau of Justice Study
10. Law Enforcement Strategies in Mental Health
11. Curtailing Litigation against Police Agencies and Officers
12. Scope of the National Problem: Litigation against Police Agencies and Officers

13. Nature of Litigation against the Police

14. Emerging Technology and Multicultural Law Enforcement Innovations

15. Examples of Law Enforcement Innovations in Practice

PRACTICE QUESTIONS

True or False

_____ 1. The President's First Leadership Conference of the International Association of Chiefs of Police (IACP, 1999) recommended that police leaders need to ensure that ethnicities and races are properly represented in the workforce.

_____ 2. Some law enforcement agencies contract with school d i stricts to provide officers on a daily basis for security purposes, as well as to offer role models.

_____ 3. Throughout the United States, the last two decades of the twentieth century witnessed a dramatic increase in individual and class-action suits against law enforcement agencies for mistreatment and killing of citizens by police officers.

_____ 4. Local law enforcement officials seldom need to be informed about current events around the globe, as conflicts outside the United States often have little effect or impact upon local events.

_____ 5. The Researchers, Bartol and Bartol (1999) and Goode (2001), have shown that community-oriented policing not only counters but also actually prevents juvenile delinquency.

_____ 6. The authors recommend that more preventative programs to identify violence-prone youth have to be developed by both police and educators through cooperative efforts.

_____ 7. Improved educational opportunities are an example of an effective approach for the management of gang activities as noted by Britz, Rush, and Barker (2001).

_____ 8. To undercut the white supremacist gangs (sometimes fueled by drugs and alcohol abuse) schools and colleges have begun programs to teach tolerance.

_____ 9. While incarcerated, the mentally ill inmates were more likely than other inmates to be involved in fights and to be charged with breaking prison and jail rules (OJP, 1999).

_____ 10. In 1994, a jury in Los Angeles awarded Rodney King $3.8 million to compensate for police actions.

Multiple Choice

1. The police researcher Neil Lingle (1992), in his futurist study a decade ago on ethnic groups and culture, identified programs that can promote a cooperative and interactive relationship between peace officers and the community that are still applicable today. Which of the following did he recommend?

   a. More cultural awareness and sensitivity training of personnel

   b. More information to officers on external factors affecting their performance (e.g., influence of wealth and economic power, as well as racial or ethnic and political power)

   c. More study of institutional racism, organizational diversity, and the impact of minority employment and promotion on police policies and practices in the future

   d. All of the above

2. The goal of the profiling study by the Northeastern researchers was to:

   a. Determine if police departments stereotype minority drivers

   b. Provide oversight information to the Internal Affairs' departmental investigation of officers involved in racial profiling

   c. Have police departments and communities discuss whether the level of disparity of the findings is explainable

   d. All of the above

3. Mastrofski and Greene (1991) emphasized that if police were to increase a neighborhood's involvement in determining how it is policed, then which of the follow would be included as key issues to be addressed?

   a. To what extent should the community be organized?

   b. Who should be represented?

   c. What should the community do?

   d. All of the above

4. Typically, how many years does it take a law enforcement agency to go from traditional policing to community policing?

    a. One to three years

    b. Five to seven years

    c. Nine to eleven years

    d. None of the above

5. A key, continuing learning process and role function in community-based policing is the ongoing monitoring of important local and global events that might affect multicultural law enforcement. Which of the following public events might be important to monitor?

    a. Anniversary of September 11th World Trade Center terror attack

    b. Anniversary of the Oklahoma Bombing terror attack (April 19th)

    c. Israeli Independence Day

    d. All of the above

6. As noted by Britz, Rush, and Barker (2001), the biggest challenges appear to be in preventing or counteracting rising youth violence. In the nation's inner cities, where unemployed, disadvantaged youths seek identity and support through destructive gang participation, what is the age range of young males involved in violence?

    a. The ages of 6 and 8

    b. The ages of 9 and 11

    c. The ages of 12 and 24

    d. None of the above

7. New York's St. John's University offers students on-the-job, real-world experience in police, corrections, and justice activities through its criminal justice internships. Student interns:

    a. Gain valuable insights into segments of the justice system, from juvenile justice and the district attorney's office to U.S. Marshals or drug enforcement agencies

    b. Jump-start criminal justice careers by gaining three academic credits if the internship is successfully completed

    c. Are helped to determine whether law enforcement is their preferred career field

    d. All of the above

8. In the Bureau of Justice Study (1999), how many mentally ill offenders were estimated to be held in the nation's state and federal prisons and local jails at mid-year 1998?

   a. Less than 10,000
   b. 27,340
   c. 152,950
   d. 283,800

9. Which of the following is *not* a law enforcement strategy to deal with the problems of people with mental health issues within the criminal justice system?

   a. Assistance to local ethnic business organizations that wish to work voluntarily with mental health issues within the community
   b. Development of procedures and policies within the law enforcement agency for dealing with mental health problems
   c. The building of more protected shelters and separated cell-blocks for inmates with mental health issues
   d. Creation of specific police training and educational materials for working with people with mental health problems

10. Between 1997 and 2000, the City of Detroit had to pay $32 million because of lawsuits brought against the police. A city council analysis showed that 78 percent of the money so expended involved cases with only a small number of officers. How many officers were named in more than one suit in Detroit during this period?

    a. Less than 265
    b. 573
    c. 824
    d. More than 850

Fill-in-the-Blanks

1. According to Thibault, Lynch, and McBride (2001), those who would uphold law and order in the twenty-first century will need to be more _____ and less reactive.

2. Law enforcement agencies adopting the community policing strategy have not only become _____ within a community but advocates for public well-being.

3. Critical to the success of any community-based policing program is the resolution of the issue: How willing are police officers to relinquish the social isolation of police cars to become involved with _____ in police-community programs?

4. Community policing also requires obtaining personnel, whether sworn or not, who have the local _____ skills to reach out to new ethnic communities.

5. Chief Eldrin Bell, an African American and the chief of police for Atlanta, Georgia, suggested that government be _____, cleaned up, and made more community directed through use of community councils.

6. Because of greater population diversity in many communities, reduced budgets, increased illegal immigration, social disorder, and domestic terrorism, criminal justice entities were subject to _____.

7. Gangs will increasingly occupy law enforcement time, and agencies must be creative in devising _____ approaches to a c o mmunity's disadvantaged youth, particularly in conjunction with other community organizations.

8. _____ is the largest service event in the world, mobilizing millions of young people, and it is also an opportunity to recruit the next generation of volunteers and educate the public about the role of youth as community leaders.

9. White supremacist groups often become _____ to angry, disaffected young men and women, some of whom are from the underclass and may have parents in jail, as well (1.5 million U.S. parents are in prison).

10. Citizen police academy programs have been successfully used to provide knowledge of the _____ between the community and the law enforcement agency.

Discussion

1. Chief Darrel W. Stephens of Charlotte–Mecklenburg, NC, maintains that community- or problem-oriented policing is the future of law enforcement and is the next stage in the evolution of this profession. Do you agree or disagree with Chief Stephens' observation? Discuss how community- or problem-oriented policing might help elevate the police profession.

2. Discuss how the criminal justice system can improve its handling of troubled youth from the underclass, using the example provided by David Cole, a professor of law at Georgetown University, of an African American youth's reactions to his encounters with law enforcement as a starting point. What kinds of changes might be made to the criminal justice system to better serve troubled youth?

WHAT ARE YOUR THOUGHTS AND WHAT WOULD YOU DO?

With the large numbers of multicultural groups in your community, your Chief of Police wanted to plan ahead for ways to increase police–community relationships, readiness, and effectiveness for collaborative law enforcement efforts. Your chief has asked you to lead a planning group to think through ways to best build police–community relationships and collaborative efforts in areas like homeland security, the war on terrorism, natural disasters, regional crime p r o blems, and multi-jurisdictional law enforcement efforts (e.g., immigration, drug abuse, etc.). You have been assigned the responsibility to set up this p l a nning group as well as to think through some of the key issues involved for the multicultural community, the department, and the local, state, and federal governmental agencies involved. Some of your fellow officers suggest that such efforts should go "high tech," and use the most advanced tools and concepts available. Other officers insist that a good "tried-and-true, old-fashioned" c o mmunity policing approach would best serve the multicultural communities involved. Still other officers insist that members of the multicultural commu-n ities should be asked for their points of view and input before any planning takes place. What are your thoughts and what would you do?

Critical Thinking Questions
1. What are the facts (observable, verifiable, testable, and confirmable)?
2. What are the assumptions?
3. What are the possible stereotypes?
4. What would be your *personal* reactions to this situation?
5. What would be the possible *multicultural communities'* reactions to this situation?
6. Would someone from the multicultural communities see something different? What would he/she see differently (if applicable)?
7. What would be your *professional* reactions to this situation?
8. What actions would you take in this situation?
9. If you had to explain your plans and actions to the multicultural commu-nities, the local, state, and federal governmental agencies involved, and your superiors in front of the news media, what would you say?

---

3. Discuss ways that law enforcement agencies might give assistance to local ethnic business organizations that wish to work with gangs in community ventures and job development. Provide some examples of such assistance provided in your local community.

4. Brainstorm ways that the criminal justice system can help to defuse the stigma of mental illness and promote the well-being of people with mental health problems. Provide examples that illustrate positive support, services, and community connectedness for people with mental health issues in the criminal justice system.

5. Provide examples of three emerging technologies and innovations used by law enforcement to improve its services to multicultural communities. Which of these technologies and innovations are c u rrently used in the local police department of your community?

TOOLS AND SKILLS IN PRACTICE

1. *Identifying Emerging Roles and Technology in Multicultural Law Enforcement*—For your city or town of interest, go to the on-line reports (or the actual Minutes of the meetings on file) for the: (a) "Police Commission," (b) "Public Safety Commission" and/or (c) "Emergency Services Commission." Scan the Minutes of the meetings for law enforcement and other public safety "emerging roles and technology" issues. Use search terms such as, "multicultural," "diversity," "new technology," "new roles," "innovation," "emerging roles," "new skills," "technology training," etc. Note any recurring issues or trends involving different multicultural community groups, as well as emerging roles and new use of technology. If on-line services are not available in your area, go the Town Hall or City Hall and read the past Minutes of the above-noted commissions for the last two years or more; the Minutes of the Police Commission and other meetings are usually open to the public.

2. *Scanning for Multi-Jurisdictional Crimes*—Two approaches are suggested to obtain information about effective multi-jurisdictional activities and efforts:

   a. Go On-line to the Peace Officers Standards and Training (POST) Organization for Your State (or for a nearby state): Go to the "Reports section," and "research sections" (or the POST "library collections of reports"), and use search terms such as, "regional efforts," "joint efforts," "multi-jurisdictional crimes," "collaborative law enforcement," etc. Read the online summary of reports (and actual reports, if available). Make a list of the multi-jurisdictional crimes, activities, and strategies for law enforcement that are highlighted for your area by the POST reports.

   b. Go On-line to Search "LexisNexis Academic" in Your College Library: Search the news sources for your local area for the past five years using search terms such as, "regional crime efforts," "joint law enforcement," "multi-jurisdiction police," "collaborative law enforcement," etc. Keep a journal of your findings. From the two lists of multi-jurisdictional crimes and law enforcement efforts gathered, write a brief summary report as to what would be your recommended set of top six actions for your local area law enforcement collaborative efforts.

3. *Reviewing Emphases on Special Populations*—Go to the website of the police department for your town or city (or to one that is for the

nearest large-size city in your area of interest). Within the police department's website, search for and identify as many documents and/or articles by senior law enforcement leaders and/or executives (e.g., Chief of Police, Deputy Chiefs, etc.) as possible. Make a list and summary of any content or comments about serving "special populations," "mentally ill," "mental health," "youth," "gangs," "elderly," etc., within the multicultural communities of the area. Review your list and summary of comments to determine the emphases, attitudes, and importance of senior law enforcement leadership's focus on service to "special populations" within the multicultural communities.

4. *Preparing for New Technology Use in Law Enforcement*—Go to the website of the Police Department for your town or city (or to one that is for the nearest large city in your area of interest). Within the police department's website, search for and identify as many documents and/or articles by senior law enforcement leaders and/or executives (e.g., Chief of Police, Deputy Chiefs, etc.) as possible. Make a list and summary of any content or comments about using "technology," "innovations in crime solving," "new tools," "planning for the future," etc., within the multicultural communities of the area. Review your list and summary of comments to determine the emphases, attitudes, and importance of senior law enforcement leadership's focus on preparing for the use of new technology in law enforcement within the multicultural communities.

SELF-STUDY ACTIVITIES

Reviewing Emphases on Special Populations

Using Tool #3 (as noted above) would increase your awareness and skills with multicultural communities involving special populations. The chapter emphasized the importance of training and education for skills in working with multicultural communities involving special populations (e.g., minority and immigrant youth, elderly, people with mental health problems). What are the groups or individuals in your multicultural community that might be considered as special populations? What are some of the specific skills and resources for law enforcement needed to address these special populations in your community?

Preparing for New Technology Use in Law Enforcement

Using Tool #4 (as noted above) will highlight for law enforcement officers and their agencies the need to embrace and to utilize the innovations and emerging advanced technologies that are available for effective work in multicultural communities. Using the list of innovations in the textbook as a starting point, brainstorm other innovations and advanced technologies that you think would be important to multicultural law enforcement. In what ways will the items in your brainstormed list have a positive impact upon multicultural communities? Would there be any negative impact upon those communities?

Curtailing Litigation Against Police Agencies and Officers

The authors noted that much innovation is necessary so that a police response will satisfy citizens rather than provoke them to lawsuits against officers and their departments, especially in multicultural communities. Select one or more multicultural groups that are part of your community (or a part of a nearby community) and discuss how nonviolent peacekeeping is particularly critical in ethnic, immigrant, and racially diverse communities. What does it mean to say that police officers should do their duties with honor and integrity?

Appendix A

Self-Assessment of Communication Skills in Law Enforcement

Instructions: For each item, check the box for the response in the column that best describes your approach to the communication process.

	Seldom	Occasionally	Often	Always
1. In communicating, I project a positive image of myself (e.g., voice, approach, tone)	❑	❑	❑	❑
2. When appropriate, I try to show my "receiver" (the person with whom I am communicating—for example, victims, citizens making complaints, suspects, witnesses, and coworkers) that I understand what is being communicated from his or her point of view. I do this by restating this point of view and by showing empathy and concern.	❑	❑	❑	❑
3. I am sensitive to culturally different uses of eye contact, and I establish eye contact where appropriate, but avoid intense eye contact with people for whom less eye contacts more comfortable.	❑	❑	❑	❑
4. I am aware of when my own emotions and how my state of mind affect my communication with others. (For example, I know my own needs, motives, biases, prejudices, and stereotypes.)	❑	❑	❑	❑
5. I refrain from using insensitive and unprofessional language while on the job (including language used in written and computer communications).	❑	❑	❑	❑

	Seldom	Occasionally	Often	Always
6. I try not to let the person with whom I am communicating push my "hot buttons," which would negatively affect my communication (e.g., cause me to go out of control verbally).	❏	❏	❏	❏
7. When speaking with individuals from groups that speak English differently from the way I do, I try not to imitate their manner of speech in order to be "one of them."	❏	❏	❏	❏
8. With nonnative speakers of English, I try not to speak in an excessively loud voice or use incorrect English (e.g., "You no understand me?") in an attempt to make myself clear.	❏	❏	❏	❏
9. I am aware that many immigrants and refugees do not understand police procedures and I make special efforts to explain these procedures (including their rights).	❏	❏	❏	❏
10. I check in a supportive manner to see if people have understood my message and directions and I encourage people to show me that they have understood me.	❏	❏	❏	❏
11. With nonnative speakers of English, I make a special point to simplify my vocabulary, eliminate the use of slang and idioms, and try to use phrases that are not confusing.	❏	❏	❏	❏
12. I make extra efforts to establish rapport (e.g., show increased patience, give more explanations, show professionalism and respect) with individuals from groups that have typically and historically considered the police their enemies.	❏	❏	❏	❏
13. I am sensitive to cultural or gender differences between me and the receiver.	❏	❏	❏	❏

	Seldom	**Occasionally**	**Often**	**Always**
14. I convey respect to all citizens while on duty regardless of their race, color, gender, or other difference from me.	❑	❑	❑	❑
15. When using agency communication channels or media, I communicate professionally, avoiding inappropriate or derogatory remarks.	❑	❑	❑	❑

Appendix B

Impact of Diversity on Law Enforcement Behaviors and Practices Survey

Instructions: There has been a great deal of discussion in recent years about whether the job of police officers have been changing. Some of the discussion revolves around issues related to contact with people from different cultural, racial, or ethnic groups. Please check or enter one answer for each questions.

1. Comparing the job of the officer today with that of the officer a few years ago, I think that today the job is:

   ❑ A lot more difficult
   ❑ Somewhat more difficult
   ❑ About the same in difficulty
   ❑ Somewhat easier
   ❑ A lot easier

2. When I stop a car with occupant(s) of a different racial or ethnic group than myself, I must admit that I am more concerned about my safety than I would be if I stopped a car with the same number of white occupant(s).

   ❑ Strongly agree
   ❑ Agree
   ❑ Neither agree nor disagree
   ❑ Disagree
   ❑ Strongly disagree

3. If an officer notices a group of young people gathering in a public place and the young people aren't known to the officer, they should be watched very closely for possible trouble.

   ❑ Strongly agree
   ❑ Agree
   ❑ Neither agree nor disagree
   ❑ Disagree
   ❑ Strongly disagree

4. If an officer notices a group of young people from another racial or ethnic group gathered in a public place, the officer should plan on watching them very closely for possible trouble.

   ❑ Strongly agree

   ❑ Agree

   ❑ Neither agree nor disagree

   ❑ Disagree

   ❑ Strongly disagree

5. How often do you think it is justifiable to use derogatory labels such as "scumbag" and "dirtbag" when dealing with possible suspects?

   ❑ Very frequently

   ❑ Frequently

   ❑ Occasionally

   ❑ Once or twice in a year

   ❑ Never

6. When I interact on duty with civilians who are of a different race, ethnicity, or culture, my view is that:

   ❑ They should be responded to *very firmly* to make sure that they understand the powers of the police

   ❑ They should be responded to *a little more firmly* to make sure that they understand the powers of the police

   ❑ They should be responded to *the same* as anyone else

   ❑ They should be responded to *somewhat differently*, taking into account their different backgrounds

   ❑ They should be responded to *very differently*, taking into account their different backgrounds

7. When I encounter citizens of a different race, ethnicity, or culture who have committed a violation of the law, my view is that:

   ❑ They should be responded to *very firmly* to make sure that they understand the powers of the police

   ❑ They should be responded to *a little more firmly* to make sure that they understand the powers of the police

   ❑ They should be responded to *the same* as anyone else

   ❑ They should be responded to *somewhat differently*, taking into account their different backgrounds

   ❑ They should be responded to *very differently*, taking into account their different backgrounds

8. When interacting on duty with civilians who have a complaint or a question and who are of a different race, ethnicity, or culture, I try to be very aware of the fact that my usual gestures may frighten or offend them.

   ❑ Strongly agree
   ❑ Agree
   ❑ Neither agree nor disagree
   ❑ Disagree
   ❑ Strongly disagree

9. When interacting on duty with offenders who are of a different race, ethnicity, or culture, I try to be very aware of the fact that my usual behavior may frighten or offend them.

   ❑ Strongly agree
   ❑ Agree
   ❑ Neither agree nor disagree
   ❑ Disagree
   ❑ Strongly disagree

10. How often have you run into difficulty in understanding what a civilian was talking about because of language barriers or accents?

    ❑ Very frequently
    ❑ Frequently
    ❑ Occasionally
    ❑ Once or twice in a year
    ❑ Never

11. How often have you run into difficulty in understanding what an offender was talking about because of language barriers or accents?

    ❑ Very frequently
    ❑ Frequently
    ❑ Occasionally
    ❑ Once or twice in a year
    ❑ Never

12. How often have you run into some difficulty in making yourself clear while talking to a civilian because of language barriers or accents?

   ❑ Very frequently
   ❑ Frequently
   ❑ Occasionally
   ❑ Once or twice in a year
   ❑ Never

13. How often have you run into some difficulty in making yourself clear while talking to an offender because of language barriers or accents?

   ❑ Very frequently
   ❑ Frequently
   ❑ Occasionally
   ❑ Once or twice in a year
   ❑ Never

14. How important is it for the police department to provide training to make its members aware of the differences in culture, religion, race, or ethnicity?

   ❑ Very important
   ❑ Important
   ❑ Neither important nor unimportant
   ❑ Unimportant
   ❑ Very unimportant

15. Personally, I believe that the training I have received on group differences is:

   ❑ Far too much
   ❑ Somewhat too much
   ❑ About the right amount
   ❑ Somewhat too little
   ❑ Far too little

16. The training in the area of group differences has been:

   ❑ Extremely helpful
   ❑ Very helpful
   ❑ Somewhat helpful
   ❑ Not too helpful
   ❑ Not helpful at all

17. My own view is that our department's quality of service could be improved by:

 ❑ Placing greater emphasis on hiring on the basis of the highest score obtained on the entrance examination, making no attempt to diversify by race, ethnicity, or gender

 ❑ Placing greater emphasis on diversity by race, ethnicity, or gender, and somewhat less emphasis on the numerical rank obtained on the entrance examination

 ❑ Giving equal weight to both the score obtained on the entrance examination and diversification by race, ethnicity, or gender

18. What percentage of civilian or internal complaints against employees are adjudicated equitably?

 ❑ Over 80 percent
 ❑ Between 60 and 80 percent
 ❑ Between 40 and 60 percent
 ❑ Between 20 and 40 percent
 ❑ Less than 20 percent

19. Some civilian or internal complaints are adjudicated more favorably toward people from diverse groups rather than toward the majority population.

 ❑ Strongly agree
 ❑ Agree
 ❑ Neither agree nor disagree
 ❑ Disagree
 ❑ Strongly disagree

20. I think that employees of a different race or ethnicity receive preferential treatment on the job.

 ❑ Strongly agree
 ❑ Agree
 ❑ Neither agree nor disagree
 ❑ Disagree
 ❑ Strongly disagree

21. The racial diversity of my coworkers has made it easier for me to see issues and incidents from another perspective.

  ❑ Strongly agree

  ❑ Agree

  ❑ Neither agree nor disagree

  ❑ Disagree

  ❑ Strongly disagree

22. I think that employees of a different race or ethnicity than myself receive preferential treatment on this job. This:

  ❑ Bothers me because I do not think it is justified

  ❑ Does not bother me because I think it is justified

  ❑ Is fair only because it makes up for past discrimination

  ❑ Is not fair, but it makes up for past discrimination

  ❑ Is not an issue; I do not believe minorities get preferential treatment

23. In certain situations, having a partner of a different race or ethnicity than myself is more advantageous than having a partner of my same race or ethnicity.

  ❑ Strongly agree

  ❑ Agree

  ❑ Neither agree nor disagree

  ❑ Disagree

  ❑ Strongly disagree

24. I have received negative feedback from members of the community regarding the conduct of other officers.

  ❑ Strongly agree

  ❑ Agree

  ❑ Neither agree nor disagree

  ❑ Disagree

  ❑ Strongly disagree

25. I have received negative feedback from members of the community regarding the conduct of officers who are of a different race or ethnicity.
    - ❑ Strongly agree
    - ❑ Agree
    - ❑ Neither agree nor disagree
    - ❑ Disagree
    - ❑ Strongly disagree

26. I have received more negative feedback from members of the community regarding the conduct of officers from different races and ethnic backgrounds than about the conduct of white officers.
    - ❑ Strongly agree
    - ❑ Agree
    - ❑ Neither agree nor disagree
    - ❑ Disagree
    - ❑ Strongly disagree

27. In terms of being supervised,
    - ❑ I would much rather be supervised by a man
    - ❑ I would somewhat rather be supervised by a man
    - ❑ I would much rather be supervised by a woman
    - ❑ I would somewhat rather be supervised by a woman
    - ❑ It does not make a difference whether a man or a woman supervises me

28. In terms of being supervised by a man,
    - ❑ I would much rather be supervised by a nonminority
    - ❑ I would somewhat rather be supervised by a nonminority
    - ❑ I would much rather be supervised by a minority
    - ❑ I would somewhat rather be supervised by a minority
    - ❑ It does not make a difference to which group my supervisor belongs

29. In terms of being supervised by a woman,
    - ❑ I would much rather be supervised by a nonminority
    - ❑ I would somewhat rather be supervised by a nonminority
    - ❑ I would much rather be supervised by a minority
    - ❑ I would somewhat rather be supervised by a minority
    - ❑ It does not make a difference to which group my supervisor belongs

If this questionnaire is being used for a training class, please check the one answer in the following questions that best applies to you.

30. What is your sex?

   ❑ Male
   ❑ Female

31. What is your race?

   ❑ White
   ❑ African American or black
   ❑ Latino/Hispanic
   ❑ Native American
   ❑ Asian/Pacific American
   ❑ Other _____

32. How many years have you been employed by the police department?

   ❑ 0 to 5 years
   ❑ 6 to 10 years
   ❑ 11 to 20 years
   ❑ More than 20 years

33. What is your current rank?

   ❑ Officer
   ❑ Sergeant
   ❑ Lieutenant
   ❑ Captain or commander
   ❑ Deputy chief
   ❑ Chief
   ❑ Other _____

34. What is the highest academic degree you hold?

   ❑ High school
   ❑ Associate's degree
   ❑ Bachelor's degree
   ❑ Master's degree
   ❑ Other _____

Appendix C

Multicultural Community and Law Enforcement Workforce Survey

Instructions: For each item, check the box for the response that best describes each group's (African Americans/blacks; Asians; Hispanics; homosexuals, juveniles) perception of the police. Remember, give the response based on how you feel each **group** would answer the statements.

1. In your opinion, how would this group rate the job this police department does?

	Very Good	**Good**	**Fair**	**Poor**	**Very Poor**
Business community	❏	❏	❏	❏	❏
Minority residents	❏	❏	❏	❏	❏
Community leaders	❏	❏	❏	❏	❏
Most residents	❏	❏	❏	❏	❏
Juveniles	❏	❏	❏	❏	❏

2. This group feels that the current relationship between the police and the community is described by which of the following?

	Strongly Agree	**Agree**	**Neither Agree nor Disagree**	**Disagree**	**Strongly Disagree**
Business community	❏	❏	❏	❏	❏
Minority residents	❏	❏	❏	❏	❏
Community leaders	❏	❏	❏	❏	❏
Most residents	❏	❏	❏	❏	❏
Juveniles	❏	❏	❏	❏	❏

3. This group generally cooperates with the police.

	Most of the Time	Sometimes	Rarely	Never
Business community	❑	❑	❑	❑
Minority residents	❑	❑	❑	❑
Community leaders	❑	❑	❑	❑
Most residents	❑	❑	❑	❑
Juveniles	❑	❑	❑	❑

4. Overall, this group thinks that the police department acts to protect the rights of individuals.

	Strongly Agree	Agree	Neither Agree nor Disagree	Disagree	Strongly Disagree
Business community	❑	❑	❑	❑	❑
Minority residents	❑	❑	❑	❑	❑
Community leaders	❑	❑	❑	❑	❑
Most residents	❑	❑	❑	❑	❑
Juveniles	❑	❑	❑	❑	❑

5. Overall, this group feels this department responds to citizen complaints about officers in an objective and fair manner.

	Strongly Agree	Agree	Neither Agree nor Disagree	Disagree	Strongly Disagree
Business community	❑	❑	❑	❑	❑
Minority residents	❑	❑	❑	❑	❑
Community leaders	❑	❑	❑	❑	❑
Most residents	❑	❑	❑	❑	❑
Juveniles	❑	❑	❑	❑	❑

6. This group thinks most contacts with police are negative.

	Strongly Agree	Agree	Neither Agree nor Disagree	Disagree	Strongly Disagree
Business community	❏	❏	❏	❏	❏
Minority residents	❏	❏	❏	❏	❏
Community leaders	❏	❏	❏	❏	❏
Most residents	❏	❏	❏	❏	❏
Juveniles	❏	❏	❏	❏	❏

The next questions ask for your opinions about procedures and practices within the police department.

	Strongly Agree	Agree	Neither Agree nor Disagree	Disagree	Strongly Disagree
7. Overall, police supervisors in this department respond to citizens' complaints about employees in an objective and fair manner.	❏	❏	❏	❏	❏
8a. Most police officers in this department are sensitive to cultural and community differences.	❏	❏	❏	❏	❏
8b. Most civilian employees in this department are sensitive to cultural and community differences.	❏	❏	❏	❏	❏
9a. This department adequately prepares officers to work with members of the community who are of a different race or ethnicity than the majority of the population.	❏	❏	❏	❏	❏
9b. This department adequately prepares civilian employees to work with members of the community who are of a different race or ethnicity than the majority of the population.	❏	❏	❏	❏	❏
10. The police administration is more concerned about police–community relations than it should be.	❏	❏	❏	❏	❏

	Strongly Agree	Agree	Neither Agree nor Disagree	Disagree	Strongly Disagree
11a. Special training should be given to officers who work with community members who are of a different race or ethnicity than the majority population.	❑	❑	❑	❑	❑
11b. Special training should be given to civilian employees who work with community members who are of a different race or ethnicity than the majority population.	❑	❑	❑	❑	❑
12a. Persons of a different race or ethnicity in this city are subject to unfair treatment by some officers in this department.	❑	❑	❑	❑	❑
12b. Persons of a different race or ethnicity in this city are subject to unfair treatment by some civilian employees in this department.	❑	❑	❑	❑	❑
13a. Prejudicial remarks and discriminatory behavior by officers are not tolerated by line supervisors in this department.	❑	❑	❑	❑	❑
13b. Prejudicial remarks and discriminatory behavior by civilian employees are not tolerated by line supervisors in this department.	❑	❑	❑	❑	❑
14. Transfer policies in this department have a negative effect on police–community affairs.	❑	❑	❑	❑	❑
15. Citizen complaint procedures in this department operate in favor of the citizen, not the employee.	❑	❑	❑	❑	❑
16. Internal discipline procedures for employee misconduct are generally appropriate.	❑	❑	❑	❑	❑

	Strongly Agree	Agree	Neither Agree nor Disagree	Disagree	Strongly Disagree
17. With regard to discipline for misconduct, all e m p l oyees in this department are treated the same in similar situations, regardless of race or ethnicity.	❏	❏	❏	❏	❏

18. The procedure for a citizen to use to file a complaint against a department employee should be which of the following?

   ❏ Citizen sends complaint in writing to the department
   ❏ Citizen telephones complaint to the department
   ❏ Citizen comes to the department
   ❏ Any of the above are acceptable means
   ❏ None of the above are acceptable means

Explain. _____

_____

_____

19. How often are racial slurs and negative comments about persons of a different race or ethnicity expressed by personnel in this department?

   ❏ Often
   ❏ Sometimes
   ❏ Rarely
   ❏ Never

20. Special training should be given to assist officers in working with which of the following segments of the community?

	Yes	No
African American/Black (includes Caribbean, Haitian, etc.)	❏	❏
Asian	❏	❏
Hispanic	❏	❏
Homosexual	❏	❏
Juveniles	❏	❏

21. What kind of discipline do you think is appropriate for the first incident of the following types of misconduct? (Assume intentional)

Type of Misconduct	**Verbal Warning**	**Training/ Counseling**	**Oral Reprimand**	**Formal Reprimand**	**Suspension**	**Termination**
Excessive force	❏	❏	❏	❏	❏	❏
False arrest	❏	❏	❏	❏	❏	❏
Discrimination	❏	❏	❏	❏	❏	❏
Use of racial slurs	❏	❏	❏	❏	❏	❏
Criminal conduct	❏	❏	❏	❏	❏	❏
Poor service	❏	❏	❏	❏	❏	❏
Discourtesy to citizen	❏	❏	❏	❏	❏	❏
Improper procedure	❏	❏	❏	❏	❏	❏

This section examines your views about police–community relations training and community participation. Please check the response that best describes your opinion.

22. Do you think training in police–community relations was adequate to prepare you to work with all segments of the community?

    ❏ Yes

    ❏ No

    ❏ Don't know

Explain. If no, please describe why the training was not satisfactory. _____

_____

_____

_____

23. How often do you have opportunities to participate in positive contacts with community groups?

    ❏ Frequently

    ❏ Sometimes

    ❏ Rarely

    ❏ Never

24. Do you think this department has an adequate community relations program?

     ❑   Yes

     ❑   No

     ❑   Don't know

Please explain. _____

_____

_____

_____

25. What subject areas related to community relations would be helpful for in-service training?

_____

_____

_____

26. What do you think is the most important thing that citizens need to understand about the police?

_____

_____

_____

27. How can the police department best educate the public about police policies and practices? Check one only.

     ❑   Through patrol officer contacts with citizens

     ❑   Through public meetings

     ❑   Through the media

     ❑   Selected combinations of the responses above

     ❑   Don't know

     ❑   Other

Explain. _____

_____

_____

Please indicate how important you think each of the following should be to this administration by placing the number that best describes your response next to the appropriate question.

28. Listed are steps that police departments can take to improve police services as they relate to community relations.

1 = Very Important   *2 = Important*   *3 = Not at all important*

_____   Hire more police

_____   Focus on more serious crime

_____   Improve response time

_____   Increase salaries

_____   Provide more training

_____   Raise qualifications for potential applicants

_____   Be more courteous to public

_____   Increase foot patrols

_____   Reduce discrimination

_____   Provide dedicated time for community involvement

Appendix D
Practice Question Answers

CHAPTER 1

True or False

1. F
2. T
3. F
4. T
5. F
6. T
7. T
8. F
9. T
10. T

Multiple Choice

1. d
2. c
3. b
4. d
5. c
6. c
7. d
8. b
9. a
10. c

Fill-in-the-Blanks

1. racial, cultural
2. competence
3. multiracial, multiethnic, multicultural
4. racial
5. fear
6. Culture
7. illegal
8. shorthand
9. democratic
10. respect

CHAPTER 2

True or False

1. T
2. T
3. T
4. T
5. T
6. F
7. T
8. T
9. T
10. T

Multiple Choice

1. b
2. a
3. a
4. b
5. d
6. d
7. d
8. b
9. d
10. a

Fill-in-the-Blanks

1. increasingly
2. civil rights
3. U.S. Army
4. cultural affairs
5. Indianapolis
6. zero-tolerance
7. training
8. white male
9. "flex-management"
10. performance and competency

CHAPTER 3

True or False

1. T
2. T
3. F
4. T
5. T
6. T
7. T
8. T

9. T
10. T

Multiple Choice

1. a
2. d
3. b
4. c
5. a
6. d
7. b
8. c
9. d
10. a

Fill-in-the-Blanks

1. community
2. 14.4 percent were women; 30.5 percent were minorities
3. polygraph
4. Fast tracking
5. community leaders
6. internal
7. Role models and mentoring
8. community-oriented policing
9. strategic marketing plan
10. "glass ceiling"

CHAPTER 4

True or False

1. T
2. T
3. F
4. F

5. T

6. T

7. T

8. F

9. T

10. T

Multiple Choice

1. a

2. c

3. d

4. b

5. c

6. b

7. d

8. d

9. a

10. d

Fill-in-the-Blanks

1. discrimination

2. sender

3. "beating around the bush"

4. rapport

5. "cool," smart, or in-tune

6. prejudice or divisiveness

7. motivators and values

8. tone of voice and body language

9. foot

10. "proxemics"

CHAPTER 5

True or False

1. F

2. T

3. T

4. T

5. T

6. F

7. T

8. F

9. T

10. T

Multiple Choice

1. d

2. d

3. b

4. d

5. c

6. a

7. d

8. c

9. c

10. d

Fill-in-the-Blanks

1. 76 percent

2. Pacific Islander

3. Chinese

4. Indonesia, Pakistan, Bangladesh, and India

5. Hawaii

6. "high-tech" and Internet

7. 40

8. second generation, Type III

9. Latch-key

10. "high context"

CHAPTER 6

True or False

1. T

2. T

3. T

4. F

5. F

6. F

7. T

8. T

9. T

10. T

Multiple Choice

1. d

2. b

3. c

4. b

5. d

6. d

7. c

8. c

9. d

10. d

Fill-in-the-Blanks

1. West Africa

2. "slave patrols"

3. Color

4. 7 to 11

5. West African tribal

6. to shut down and to control

7. Rodney King

8. Abner Louima

9. half

10. belittlement, danger

CHAPTER 7

True or False

1. T

2. F

3. T

4. T

5. F

6. T

7. T

8. T

9. T

10. T

Multiple Choice

1. b

2. d

3. c

4. b

5. d

6. c

7. d

8. b

9. d

10. d

Fill-in-the-Blanks

1. 50

2. La Raza

3. Roybal Resolution

4. 1910

5. The Jones Act of 1917

6. antisocial, criminal, and mentally ill persons

7. simplistic, one-dimensional characters

8. "hanging out"

9. *La familia*—In places where we use the Spanish term, we have done so to indicate the additional cultural meanings encompassed in a term such as *La familia* that is not captured in the English term the "family."

10. *respecto* (respect) and *machismo*

CHAPTER 8

True or False

1. T
2. T
3. T
4. F
5. T
6. T
7. T
8. T
9. T
10. F

Multiple Choice

1. b
2. d
3. c
4. d
5. b
6. d
7. c
8. d
9. b
10. d

Fill-in-the-Blanks

1. Saudi Arabia
2. Farsi or Persian
3. Ashkenazim and Sephardim
4. 90 percent
5. Chaldean, Christian Iraqis who speak the Chaldean language
6. a loss of face
7. lunar cycle, related to the phases of the moon
8. closed "units"
9. "maiden," "married"
10. "Don't thank me. It's my duty."

CHAPTER 9

True or False

1. T
2. T
3. T
4. T
5. T
6. T
7. F
8. T
9. T
10. T

Multiple Choice

1. b
2. d
3. c
4. a
5. d
6. d
7. d
8. c
9. d
10. c

Fill-in-the-Blanks

1. courageous, determined and as having a "fighting spirit"
2. defers
3. tribal headquarters
4. New York and Los Angeles
5. "mother earth"
6. one-third
7. "pan-Indianism"
8. foolish or bringing shame
9. not comfortable
10. offensive

CHAPTER 10

True or False

1. F
2. F
3. T
4. F
5. T
6. T
7. T
8. T
9. T
10. T

Multiple Choice

1. d
2. a
3. d
4. b
5. a
6. d
7. c
8. c
9. d
10. b

Fill-in-the-Blanks

1. local
2. criminal
3. before, during, and after
4. deadly
5. predict
6. shielding
7. control zones
8. reasons
9. Presidential Decision Directive-39 (PDD-39)
10. inform

CHAPTER 11

True or False

1. F
2. F
3. T
4. T
5. T
6. T
7. T
8. F
9. F
10. T

Multiple Choice

1. b
2. d
3. a
4. d
5. a
6. d
7. b
8. c
9. b
10. d

Fill-in-the-Blanks

1. intervening oceans
2. communication
3. intelligence community
4. intelligence-based
5. stereotype
6. trust
7. excess
8. Citizen's Police
9. turbans
10. race and ethnicity

CHAPTER 12

True or False

1. T
2. T
3. T
4. T
5. F
6. T
7. T
8. T
9. T
10. T

Multiple Choice

1. d
2. c
3. c
4. b
5. c
6. b
7. d
8. c
9. a
10. d

Fill-in-the-Blanks

1. intergroup
2. an entire group of citizens, an entire community
3. youthful thrill-seekers
4. African Americans
5. voluntary
6. Scapegoating
7. Middle-Easterners
8. Conflict Prevention and Resolution (CPR)
9. "against Semites"
10. irrational

CHAPTER 13

True or False

1. F
2. F
3. T
4. T
5. T
6. F
7. T
8. T
9. F
10. F

Multiple Choice

1. d
2. b
3. d
4. d
5. b
6. d
7. b
8. a
9. d
10. d

Fill-in-the-Blanks

1. white supremacist groups
2. Jewish
3. "Aryan"
4. The White Man's Bible
5. Jews
6. Bay Area Hate Crimes Investigators Association (BAHCIA)
7. computer system
8. one-third
9. Community profiling
10. Human Relations Commissions (HRCs)

CHAPTER 14

True or False

1. F
2. T
3. T
4. T
5. T
6. T
7. F
8. T
9. T
10. T

Multiple Choice

1. a
2. d
3. d
4. c
5. c
6. b
7. d
8. d
9. c
10. d

Fill-in-the-Blanks

1. behavior
2. specific and articulable facts
3. probability
4. behavioral commonalities or behavioral indicators
5. Black and Latino/Hispanic
6. three
7. "drug courier profile"
8. race or ethnic background
9. nervous, uneasy, or uncomfortable
10. prejudiced

CHAPTER 15

True or False

1. T
2. T
3. F
4. F
5. T
6. T
7. T
8. T
9. T
10. T

Multiple Choice

1. b
2. d
3. d
4. c
5. b
6. d
7. c
8. b
9. d
10. b

Fill-in-the-Blanks

1. learning
2. healthy self-image
3. accountability
4. military and bureaucratic
5. cultural
6. cross-cultural communication
7. performance
8. professionalism
9. system change
10. cultural competence

CHAPTER 16

True or False

1. T
2. T
3. T
4. F
5. T
6. T
7. T
8. T
9. T
10. T

Multiple Choice

1. d
2. c
3. d
4. b
5. d
6. c
7. d
8. d
9. c
10. a

Fill-in-the-Blanks

1. proactive
2. partners
3. neighborhood citizens
4. foreign-language
5. decompartmentalized
6. increased scrutiny and public review
7. nonarrest
8. National Youth Service Day
9. surrogate families
10. Community–police partnership